The Musconetcong Valley
of New Jersey

The Musconetcong Valley

of New Jersey

A Historical Geography

by

Peter O. Wacker

RUTGERS UNIVERSITY PRESS

New Brunswick   **New Jersey**

To my father, Oscar Wacker,
and in memory of my mother,
Linnea Zackariasson Wacker

Preface

This study is an example of one possible approach to the study of historical geography.[1] As such, it is concerned chiefly with an investigation of man's transformation of a particular portion of the earth's surface from its natural state to a cultural (i.e., man-made) landscape. The particular area concerned is the Musconetcong Valley (watershed) of northern New Jersey and the cultural landscapes which are investigated begin with the period of first human occupation (ca. 10,000 years ago) and continue to the end of the period of pioneer occupance by people of northwestern European origin. This is a study in historical geography in the sense of the school of thought emanating from Carl O. Sauer and his students: "Historical geography may be considered as the series of changes which the cultural landscapes have undergone and therefore involves the reconstruction of past cultural landscapes."[2]

A unique opportunity exists in New Jersey, especially in the southern Highlands of the state, to investigate the processes whereby distinct ethnic groups and varied economic interests have transformed the largely forested landscape of aboriginal days to the largely deforested agricultural landscape of today. The Musconetcong Valley was chosen for a chorologic study of these processes in depth for several reasons: (1) Physical geography—The Musconetcong is structurally typical of Highland valleys. It has wide areas of fertile limestone soils, but at the same time is crossed by the Wisconsin terminal moraine. Areas northeast and southwest of the moraine have always shown a contrast in land use. (2) Aboriginal occupance—Fluted projectile points collected in the Musconetcong watershed indicate occupance by Paleo-Indians. The sites occupied by aborigines in the historical period are at least as well known in the Musconetcong Valley as they are elsewhere in the Highlands. Aboriginal impact on the flora and fauna of the region is fairly well known. (3) Occupation by varied ethnic stocks of northwestern

vii

European origin—The Musconetcong Valley lay astride the major routes of penetration into the southern Highlands in the eighteenth century. These routes were used by pioneers of English, New England, Dutch, Scotch-Irish, and German stock, all bringing with them quite varied material culture traits. Acculturation of these groups is quite well illustrated by the changes which ensued in the cultural landscape. This is especially clear in terms of the structures which had been erected in the Valley by the end of the eighteenth century. (4) Economic activities—Pioneer subsistence agriculture, commercial grain farming, the charcoal iron industry, and various local service industries all added their imprint to the cultural landscape in pioneer days. (5) Settlement— The Musconetcong Valley is typical of most parts of the Middle Colonies in that its settlement was for the most part of a dispersed nature. (6) Esthetic considerations—Despite its proximity to the sprawling ugliness of Megalopolis, the Musconetcong Valley is one of the most beautiful major valleys in the Highlands. In the early nineteenth century it could be described as "sublime, and among those prospects to be laid up in memory's store-house, as one of her richest treasures." [3] Much of this character remains in the twentieth century and makes field work all the more pleasant.

Originally, it had been intended that the investigation would include land use during the nineteenth and early twentieth centuries as well. Intensive research, however, has indicated that the major cultural components of the landscape existed by the end of the eighteenth century, and it was decided to end the study chronologically at about that point. We might term this the end of the pioneer period and the end of the "initial occupance" [4] of the area. By the end of the eighteenth century, the more marginal agriculturists, and many of the younger people, were leaving the area to seek better, cheaper land elsewhere. Also, the last major influx of a distinct ethnic group had occurred by the end of the century. Contact with the outside world was improved by the coming of turnpikes in the first two decades of the nineteenth century, and folk building practices were replaced, at least in semi-urban centers, by houses "of all descriptions." [5] Well before the end of the eighteenth century the charcoal iron industry, which had played such a great role in the economy of the region, had declined to unimportance, and service industries continued to function at the water-power sites which had been developed during the middle of the century. Thus, the initial occupance of the region was for the most part completed in the eighteenth century.

P. O. W.

Somerset, New Jersey
August, 1967

Acknowledgments

The writer is greatly indebted to Drs. Fred B. Kniffen, Professor of Geography and Anthropology, Louisiana State University and Daniel Jacobson, Professor of Geography, Michigan State University, as well as to the faculty of the Department of Geography and Anthropology at Louisiana State University for their constant stimulation and guidance. Dr. Jacobson's stimulating teaching and scholarship encouraged the writer to engage in graduate work in culture-historical geography. Dr. Kniffen's advice and skillful guidance led to the successful completion of the doctoral dissertation which was the forerunner of this book.*

Personnel associated with several libraries in the state of New Jersey have rendered great assistance. Among these, Mr. Donald Sinclair and Mr. Anthony Nicolosi, respectively Curator and Assistant Curator of Special Collections, Rutgers University Library, have been especially helpful. Others to whom I am indebted include: Miss May Leonard of the Morristown Public Library, Mrs. Gerald May of the New Jersey Historical Society Library in Newark, Mr. Kenneth Richards and Mrs. Rebecca B. Colesar of the New Jersey State Library in Trenton, Miss Irene K. Lionikis and Mr. Oliver Westling of the Rutgers Library in New Brunswick, Miss Miriam Studley of the Newark Public Library, and Mrs. Ray C. Wilson of the Hunterdon County Historical Society Library in Flemington.

Almost all the cartographic work has been skillfully executed by Mr. Frank Kelland. Several maps are the result of data gathered by the author's students in a Historical Geography of Anglo-America

* Peter O. Wacker, "Forest, Forge, and Farm; An Historical Geography of the Musconetcong Valley, New Jersey," accepted by Louisiana State University and available in the library of that institution or through University Microfilms, Inc., Ann Arbor, Michigan.

course offered in the fall of 1965. The aerial photograph in the illustration section was furnished by Albert C. Jones Associates, Consulting Engineers, Cornwell Heights, Pennsylvania, through the courtesy of Mr. Eugene Engelbrecht.

Several others have rendered help of one kind or another which should not go unacknowledged. These include, in alphabetical order, Mr. and the late Mrs. Fred Alleman of Washington, New Jersey, Dr. Dorothy Cross of the New Jersey Archaeological Survey, Mr. Robert M. Lunny and Mr. Howard W. Wiseman of the New Jersey Historical Society, and Mr. Norman Wittwer of the Hunterdon County Historical Society. Succeeding drafts of the manuscript were typed by Mrs. Joseph Peterson, Mrs. John P. Lichtenstein, and Mrs. Charles I. Welty. Publication has been supported by the Rutgers University Research Council.

Contents

The Musconetcong Valley
of New Jersey

CHAPTER 1

Physical Geography

The Musconetcong River rises at Lake Hopatcong in the northern part of New Jersey, and flows southwest to join the Delaware River at Riegelsville. The total length of the Musconetcong from its source northeast of Lake Hopatcong to its mouth is approximately forty-four miles. The river's drainage system is a long and narrow one, equaling a total of 157.6 square miles.

Weldon Brook, which is held to be the source of the Musconetcong, begins its flow as a modest rivulet approximately 1,260 feet above mean sea level in an area of relatively rugged relief northeast of Lake Hopatcong. Many summits in the immediate vicinity exceed 1,300 feet, and one, Bowling Green Mountain, rises to 1,391 feet. Local relief north of Lake Hopatcong often exceeds 400 feet. The lake, partially man-made, is 2,443 acres in area, lies at 914.57 feet above mean sea level, and nestles among prominences locally termed "mountains," which have summits exceeding 1,100 feet.

Issuing from Lake Hopatcong the stream, now termed "Musconetcong River," flows a little more than a mile southwest to where it has been impounded to create Lake Musconetcong, then reverses itself for almost two miles to flow northwest to meet its major affluent, Lubber's Run. The steep profile of the stream and the relatively rugged terrain through which it flows in this short distance may be ascertained from the fact that the Musconetcong falls approximately fifty-five feet per mile from Lake Hopatcong to the valley of Lubber's Run.

The enlarged river resulting from the junction with Lubber's Run flows more gently, and occupies the southeast side of a rather straight northeast-southwest-trending valley that stretches for approximately thirty-three miles to a junction with the Delaware. Lubber's Run occupies the northern extension of this straight valley. The terrain of

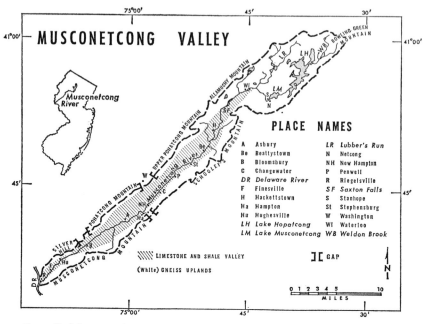

Compiled from various sources.

the valley floor is quite rugged north of Hackettstown and varies from
level to rolling, south of that point. Two miles southwest of Waterloo
the valley floor is approximately one mile wide; it narrows to less than
one-eighth of a mile at Saxton Falls, and expands southwest of Hackettstown, occupying widths of one to two miles, except for a gorge southwest of Bloomsbury. The fall from the mouth of Lubber's Run to
Hackettstown is sixteen feet per mile; from Hackettstown to Bloomsbury, twelve feet per mile; and from Bloomsbury to the mouth of the
river at Riegelsville, sixteen feet per mile.[1]

Flanking the relatively gentle valley floor are several mountains or
hills, which rise four to five hundred feet above the valley and also trend
in a northeast-southwest direction. Southwest of the river are located,
from southwest to northeast, Musconetcong Mountain and Schooley's
Mountain. Northwest of the valley are located, again from southwest to
northeast, Silver Hill, Pohatcong Mountain, Upper Pohatcong Mountain, and Allamuchy Mountain. A gap between Musconetcong Mountain and Schooley's Mountain at Hampton offers easy access to the
Musconetcong Valley from the south; and gaps between Silver Hill and
Pohatcong Mountain near Bloomsbury, and between Pohatcong Mountain and Upper Pohatcong Mountain near Washington allow easy

access to the Pohatcong Valley, which parallels that of the Musconetcong.

The Musconetcong drainage system lies within, and is typical of the
natural region known in New Jersey and southeastern New York as
"the Highlands." The Highlands is so called because of the distinct
break in relief where it meets the lower and geologically distinct Ridge
and Valley physiographic province to the northwest and the Piedmont
physiographic province to the southeast.[2] Characterized by a rugged
plateau-like surface, the Highlands has a northeast-southwest trend and
varies from ten to twenty-five miles in width in New Jersey. Within
New Jersey alone it encompasses approximately nine hundred square
miles, or approximately one-eighth of the area of the state. The
Musconetcong drains approximately one-sixth of the area of the Highlands.

The northeast-southwest trend that characterizes the Highlands also
characterizes the alignment of most of the upland and valley surfaces
within the region. Upland surfaces generally stand several hundred
feet above valley floors and often have summits at or very near the same
altitude.[3] The average height of these summits is one thousand feet
above mean sea level.

Geologically, most of the Highlands consists of very old crystalline
rocks (gneisses), which occur as uplands, and younger sedimentary rocks
(limestones and slaty-shales), which occupy the valley floors. The slaty-
shales, being somewhat more resistant to erosion, often stand as rolling
surfaces a hundred feet or more above the relatively flat limestones.

From the standpoint of landforms, the Musconetcong has been
described as "the type of Highland streams." [4] As do most of the other
rivers in the Highlands, it flows in a southwesterly direction following a
downward-folded belt of limestones and shales. The valley floor itself,
in large part, is the result of a narrow block of the earth's surface having slipped downward, leaving uplands on either side. This rift valley
reaches from at least three miles north of Hackettstown to the low
divide between the Musconetcong and Pohatcong valleys near Washington, New Jersey.

The Musconetcong drainage system, as well as the Highlands in general, has felt the results of glaciation during the ice age (Pleistocene).
Both upland and valley surfaces are replete with effects of the erosional
and depositional activities of the ice sheets. The most recent glacial
advance, termed the Wisconsin, left a distinct mass of transported materials (terminal moraine), which crosses the Musconetcong Valley less
than a mile northeast of Hackettstown. Although the Wisconsin terminal moraine cannot be said to be an especially prominent topographic

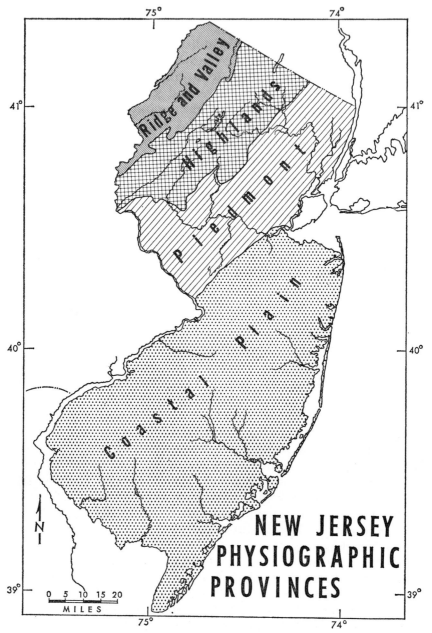

NEW JERSEY
PHYSIOGRAPHIC
PROVINCES

Adapted from Kemble Widmer, *The Geology and Geography of New Jersey* (Princeton: D. Van Nostrand Company, Inc., 1964).

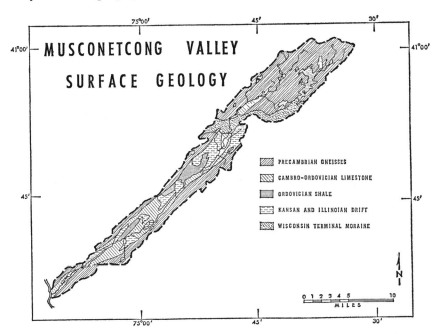

Adapted from J. Volney Lewis, *et al.*, *Geologic Map of New Jersey*, State of New Jersey, Department of Conservation and Economic Development, Division of Planning and Development, Atlas Sheet No. 40, 1950.

feature throughout the Highlands, "the contrast between the flat, level surface of the Musconetcong Valley and the hummocky, tumultuous character of the moraine to the north is striking." [5] South of the terminal moraine, materials deposited by ice advances preceding that of the Wisconsin are found in scattered locations (Kansan and Illinoian drift). Also, stratified gravels that have been washed down from the terminal moraine extend in narrow, interrupted belts all the way to the confluence of the Musconetcong with the Delaware. Deposition from the retreating Wisconsin ice sheet mantles the entire Musconetcong Valley north of the terminal moraine.

In addition to mantling the surface of the landscape that had existed previously with material transported from elsewhere, the Pleistocene epoch accounted for great changes in drainage in the Musconetcong watershed. Lubber's Run was most likely the agent responsible for much of the excavation of the present straight valley; and the Musconetcong northeast of its junction with Lubber's Run is "very likely a postglacial tributary. . . ." [6] Lake Hopatcong occupies a basin that owes its origin largely to excavation by the advancing ice, and was formed because of the blocking of its pre-Pleistocene drainage by glacial deposits. This is not to say, however, that the plethora of ponds and lakes in the portion of the Musconetcong drainage system north of the terminal moraine is entirely of Pleistocene age. Lake Hopatcong itself is partially the result of the artificial impoundment of the Musconetcong at its outlet. Eighteenth- and early nineteenth-century maps reveal the absence of many of today's waterbodies (Appendices I and II). The numerous basins that allowed artificial impoundment were probably at least in part of Pleistocene origin, and in post-Pleistocene times were probably poorly drained, swampy sites, as many of the early surveys indicate. The many poorly drained upland sites still in evidence in the area originated in large part from Pleistocene derangement of the previous system of drainage.[7]

In addition to landforms and hydrography, climate must also be considered as a major component of the physical environment. Although there are no weather stations within the Musconetcong drainage system proper, three exist in locations near enough to give a picture of general climatic conditions in the area. These stations are located at Flemington, Newton, and Phillipsburg, New Jersey. Data collected at these stations over a period of twenty-five years are available (Appendix III). These data indicate that the Musconetcong Valley experiences cold winters, with the three coldest months—December, January, and February—having mean monthly temperatures near or below freezing; and hot summers, with the three warmest months—June, July, and August—having mean monthly temperatures near or above 70°F. Yearly mean temperatures average a little over 50°F. Precipitation is well distributed throughout the year, with a definite warm season maximum of four to five or more inches per month. Total annual precipitation exceeds forty-five inches.

Despite the warm season maximum in monthly precipitation, both nineteenth- and twentieth-century data indicate that the average monthly and daily streamflow reach their minima during the months of May, June, July, August, and September.[8] The discrepancy between streamflow and precipitation can best be explained by the much greater rates of evaporation and transpiration during the summer months.

Another important aspect of man's environment anywhere on earth is the presence or lack of vegetative cover (Appendix IV). The flora of a region exists in large part in response to controls by climate, soils, landforms, and conscious or unconscious interference by man. The Musconetcong drainage system lies within the oak-chestnut region of the plant geographer. This classification is based upon the composition of the forests as they were in the late nineteenth and early twentieth centuries: essentially an association of the sprout hardwoods such as the various species of oaks and American chestnut. Since that time the chestnut has largely vanished because of the introduction of a blight, and has, for the most part, been replaced by oaks.[9]

The composition of the original forests is open to some dispute, but eighteenth-century surveyors' records and other early accounts indicate the presence of deciduous forests composed largely of oak and chestnut.[10] The same species, except for the chestnut, are still found in the area today, although their relative percentages may have changed because of clear-cutting, selective logging, and other human influences.

Surveyors' records and other early accounts also stress the open nature of much of the deciduous woodlands of the state. These open woodlands, and associated meadows, both probably in large part created by the aboriginal population, supported native grasses in abundance.

Forest, meadow, and swamp also contained an abundance of fruits, berries, and tubers, which were widely utilized by the Indians and to some extent by European pioneers. These vegetable resources will be considered in the section of Chapter 2 in which the aboriginal economy of the area is discussed.

The fauna of the Musconetcong Valley was little different from that found elsewhere at the time of first European contact in northeastern North America. Most species still have representatives in the area today, although their total numbers and their percentage of the total fauna have greatly changed because of man's upsetting the ecological equilibrium by forest clearance, elimination of predators, and the like. Species that have been eliminated at least partially through the agency of Europeans include the American gray wolf, panther, beaver, wild turkey, and wild (passenger) pigeon. Several other species may have been eliminated in prehistoric times by the aborigines.

One of the most important of the physical aspects of any environment for a people with a knowledge of agriculture is the quality of the soils available for tillage. The soils of a region exist as a function of the interplay through time of climate, vegetation cover, landforms, and surface geology. In the Musconetcong drainage system the soils have been intensively leached and have developed under a primarily deciduous forest cover. In general, it can be said that most of the region is covered with a mantle of gray-brown forest (podzolic) soils. The general quality of the soils found in the Musconetcong Valley varies quite considerably according to their position north or south of the terminal moraine and also according to whether they are located on uplands or on the valley floor.

Upland surfaces north of the terminal moraine exhibit rough, broken, and mountainous terrain. Most of the area is characterized by stony or gravelly loams on steep slopes. Summits are often bare rock or are mantled with glacially transported boulders. Agriculture is possible only in the limited areas of rolling topography where less stony soils exist. The valley floor north of the terminal moraine is similarly uncongenial to agriculture, since glacial scouring and desposition have altered the original topography and soils to such an extent that there are few areas in which true soils are developed. Valley flats are composed, for the most part, of poorly drained clays; and glacial debris composed of gravels and boulders has hindered post-Pleistocene soil development elsewhere. The terminal moraine itself mantles the valley floor for approximately half a mile. Its texture varies from heavy silts to extremely porous sands and gravels. Some agriculture is possible where topography permits.

The quality of the soils found south of the terminal moraine is generally far better than that of the soils of the most recently glaciated area. Upland gneiss surfaces are often stony, with steep slopes and shallow soil. Slopes are usually well to excessively drained, but many of the relatively level upland areas experience impeded drainage. The land is generally productive where drainage and topography permit.

Slaty-shale uplands rise above the valley floor in two extensive locations south of the terminal moraine. Soils developing on these gently rolling hills are mildly acid brown or shaly silt loams that grade into bedrock at depths of two feet or less. Drainage is good to excessive, except for a few localities, and crops often suffer from a lack of moisture.

The limestone valley floor of the Musconetcong south of the terminal moraine is characterized by gently undulating topography and by soils that, even today, are among the most fertile in the northeastern United States.

Occurring within the limestone valley south of the terminal moraine are limited areas of glacial outwash and floodplain. The glacial outwash occurs chiefly between Hackettstown and Beattystown, and consists of material redeposited downvalley from the terminal moraine. It is characterized by sandy and gravelly materials, which tend to be well drained and form good agricultural soils.

Floodplains occur in extremely narrow, discontinuous pockets immediately adjacent to the river. Seasonal inundation often precludes their use for purposes other than pasture or woodland.[11]

CHAPTER 2

Aboriginal Occupance

Ca. 8,000 B.C.—*Ca.* A.D. 1750

The term applied to the earliest human inhabitants of the western hemisphere is Paleo-Indian. Although no camp or kill sites attributable to these hunters have been found in the Musconetcong drainage system or in the Highlands, the fact of their presence in early days has been established by scattered surface finds of their characteristic fluted javelin or spear points. These projectile points, of Clovis type, have been found in both the environs of the Musconetcong Valley and throughout the drainage basin of the Delaware River.[1]

It is most difficult to date with any precision the time of arrival of these early men. Estimates vary from approximately 10,500 B.C. to 7,000 B.C.[2] In New Jersey the only radiocarbon date in the state which can be applied to the problem of early man's arrival is associated with the remains of a mastodon discovered near Highland Lakes in the very northern portion of the Highlands. The mastodon has been dated as having died 10,890 ± 200 years before present time, indicating that a suitable climate and fauna existed for big-game hunters at that time. Other earlier finds of large Pleistocene mammals in New Jersey indicate the wealth of the fauna found south of the Wisconsin ice at this time.[3]

The origin of the Paleo-Indian cultural tradition lay outside the eastern United States, perhaps on the High Plains east of the Rocky Mountains. With the desiccation of this area during the waning days of the Pleistocene, the big-game animals, and man, may have been encouraged to migrate toward the more salubrious east. The further retreat of the Wisconsin ice encouraged the big-game animals to move farther north, and man followed his food supply. The probable routes of penetration followed the major river valleys, where most of the fluted points in the east have been found to date. Major valleys, such as those of the Ohio and Tennessee Rivers, offered ready access into Virginia, and the Susquehanna and Delaware valleys provided easy routes into the northeastern states. Paleo-Indians also followed tributary streams in search of their quarry. The Musconetcong was one of these.

The Paleo-Indian sites in the eastern part of the United States, and the finds of projectile points attributed to Paleo-Indian occupance, are most often in elevated locations in the valleys of or near major waterways. These sites must have offered vantage points from which to observe the river valleys, which were favorable environments for game such as the mastodon, musk ox, caribou, and other species existing in New Jersey during the waning days of the Pleistocene.

Although little is known of Paleo-Indian and his culture, there is a good possibility that he altered his environment by burning. The game animals of the day were difficult to kill with the simple weapons at hand, and fire may well have been used to drive the game to a strategic point. The Paleo-Indians, composed as they were of small numbers of widely scattered bands, and being extremely mobile, could have altered a very wide area indeed, perhaps in some areas encouraging grasses at the expense of forest vegetation.[4] It is instructive to note that the basal portion of the pollen profile of the Tuckerton tidal marsh, now beneath water, shows evidence of extensive burning on dry land before the rise of the post-Pleistocene seas.[5]

More is known of the prehistoric folk who succeeded the Paleo-Indian bands than is known about the latter. The nearest thoroughly excavated site to the New Jersey Highlands is that of the Abbott Farm, which lies on the Delaware River just south of Trenton, New Jersey, approximately thirty-five miles south of the Musconetcong River. This is one of the best known archaeological sites in the eastern part of North America, and before its recent thorough excavation was long a *cause célèbre* among archaeologists. Unfortunately, it is impossible to state with certainty that the culture history revealed by excavations at the Abbott site is the same or similar to that which obtained in the New Jersey Highlands or in the Musconetcong Valley. But since the latest excavation of the Abbott site is well documented, and since no sites in or near the Highlands have yet yielded as much evidence of the men who succeeded the Paleo-Indians, the culture history revealed at the Abbott site will be assumed for the New Jersey Highlands as well.[6]

The period of time from *ca.* 3,000 B.C. to A.D. 100 has been termed the Archaic Culture Period at the Abbott site. Cultural influences from the west and south found their way into the area at this time. The economy of Archaic man depended on simple hunting, fishing, and gathering. His chief weapon was the spear, which was tipped with variously shaped stone points. Spears were launched both by a spear thrower—an innovation apparently arriving from the west—and by hand. The game sought was of a smaller size than that of the Paleo-Indian period of occupance, since the larger game had either followed the ice farther north, or had become extinct. The black bear, white-tailed deer, gray fox, muskrat, various birds, and the like abounded, however, and furnished a major part of the diet. Fishing was also of some importance. Spearing and netting were practiced, and there is some evidence of the use of lines. Edible nuts, roots, and herbs were plentiful, and were probably utilized much as they were by later peoples. The occurrence of pebble pestles on the site indicates that such foods could have been processed by grinding or pounding.

The ample food supply allowed a relatively sedentary existence. Nevertheless, a certain amount of trading took place. Many tools found at the Abbott site have an origin at least as far north as Lockatong Creek, a little more than ten miles south of the Musconetcong Valley, or in Bucks County, Pennsylvania. Thus, culture contacts could easily have taken place between the Abbott Farm site and Highland sites as yet unknown.

After *ca.* A.D. 100, there was a gradual transition from the Archaic Culture Period to the Early Woodland Culture Period. Physically, the racial stock probably remained the same as it had been in the previous period. Farther west this stock has been described as being of relatively small stature, slight bone structure, and delicate features.

Hunting, fishing, and gathering continued as the major economic activities of the population, with the introduction of the bow and arrow causing the abandonment of the spear thrower.

Another major difference between the Archaic and Early Woodland periods was the use of steatite (soapstone) for ornaments and bowls. This implies that lengthy trips, or trading relationships with peoples located at some distance, took place. The nearest location of steatite was at Phillipsburg, New Jersey, approximately fifty miles by water from the Abbott site and some six or seven miles by water *north* of the Musconetcong. Again, cultural contacts of some kind may well have taken place.

A major change in occupance during the Early Woodland Period occurred toward the end of the period, when the population sporadically or seasonally moved from the bluff where they had been residing down to the floodplain of the Delaware.

During the Middle Woodland Period, which lasted from *ca.* A.D. 350 to *ca.* A.D. 900, several new traits were added to the culture of the inhabitants of the Abbott site. Shellfish, gathered on the Atlantic coast, made an appearance and, more important, toward the end of the period tobacco was probably cultivated. Many cylindrical vessels, large sunken vessels and storage pits, and an abundance of pottery, which had appeared sporadically during the Early Woodland Period, point to a more sedentary population and, indirectly, to the advent of agriculture. The shells regularly procured from the Atlantic coast for tempering pottery indicate extensive contact with the seacoast, and trading relations continued with the north and extended farther in that direction.

One writer [7] suggests that the Indians known in historic times made their way into the area prior to late Middle Woodland times. Quite possibly the Abbott site may have been an early nucleus from which a dispersion of these people took place.

By the advent of the Late Woodland Period, after *ca.* A.D. 900, agriculture came to play a greater role in the economy. Hunting, fishing, and gathering, however, continued as the major foci of the subsistence economy. Shellfish continued to be gathered along the coast, and more contact with Pennsylvania and northern New Jersey took place.

In contrast with the lack of prehistoric data, there is abundant evidence with which to reconstruct the culture of the aborigines dwelling in the Highlands in early historic times. These were the *Lenape,* a term which meant "people" in their Eastern-Central Algonkin tongue. The Lenape were divided into a large number of small, dispersed, and independent groups inhabiting a continuous area extending from Delaware Bay northward through Manhattan Island, and up the west side of the Hudson River to the Catskills in southeastern New York. In the early years of the eighteenth century, under the pressure of European advances to the interior, the Lenape concentrated near the Delaware River and became politically consolidated. The term applied to these Indians collectively, especially by English speakers, was "Delaware," a reflection of their location in the late sixteenth and early seventeenth centuries. [8]

The aborigines inhabiting the portion of New Jersey north of Musconetcong Mountain during the eighteenth century were of the Munsi (or Munsee, Monsey, Minsi, Monthey, Minisink) traditional division of the Delaware. The term Munsi meant "people of the stony country" or, perhaps, "mountaineers," an apt term, since they occupied most of the Highlands. The Munsi formed a distinct cultural group, speaking a dialect that differed considerably from that of the other Delaware. Munsi linguistic affinities were with the Mahicans, Pequots, and other peoples to the northeast. There are some indications that at least a portion of the Indians living in the Highlands, especially in the vicinity of Lake Hopatcong, had come from New England as a result of the wars between the Indians and Europeans in that area.

The Indians of Delaware affinities were never great in total numbers. One estimate places approximately eight thousand Indians in southern New York, eastern Pennsylvania, and all of New Jersey in A.D. 1600. There are no accurate data to enable an estimate of the population of the New Jersey Highlands at that date, but the Indians living on the shores of what is now Lake Hopatcong were said by a nineteenth-century observer to have been two or three hundred in number during the eighteenth century. This is perhaps too high an estimate, although the lake was a favored dwelling place. The population for the entire Musconetcong drainage system was perhaps as high as two or three hundred, but it is difficult to say it with certainty.[9]

The settlement patterns of the historic Munsi were of two main types: semipermanent agricultural villages, and dispersed temporary residences of the fall and winter hunting season. In location, these settlement types had much in common. Both were situated very near a source of potable water—a spring, lake or stream—but were high enough above the source of water to avoid flooding. In addition, if possible, a southern exposure was chosen so that the site would be sunny for most of the day and protected from cold north winds. In the case of the semipermanent village, where hoe gardening was the important activity, the sites were mostly in or near bottoms with easily cultivated, sandy, friable soil.

The semipermanent agricultural villages, except for some exceptions in the very northern part of New Jersey, were not palisaded. Dwellings were known as wigwams, a common Algonkin term, and were placed "two or three rods apart," grouped randomly around a ceremonial structure known as the "Big House."[10] As a rule, each family occupied a separate wigwam. These were of three main types: (1) circular floor plan with a dome-shaped roof, (2) rectangular floor plan with an arched roof, and (3) rectangular floor plan with a gabled roof. The first two were contructed in much the same way. Saplings were placed in the earth two or three feet apart, outlining the floor plan. They were then bent together to form the roof and were tied with bast fiber. This framework was made more secure by saplings tied crosswise over the upright poles. Temporary structures were simply covered with woven mats, but more permanent dwellings were shingled with chestnut, elm, cedar, or other bark. Shingles were tied to the frame and daubed with clay or mud. The gabled house was constructed similarly, except that a rigdepole and side poles set in crotched logs determined the shape of the roof, and the rafters were supported by short, crotched wall posts. A smoke hole was left in the center of the roof and was covered with a piece of skin. One or two doorways, approximately three feet in height, allowed an entrance and an exit. This framework was covered with mats, pieces of bark, or skins.[11]

The wigwams with rectangular floor plans were related to the Iroquois longhouse and were probably used largely by the Munsi, whose culture was most affected by contacts with the north; the dome-roofed type may have been used also by the dispersed Munsi hunters and fishers. In 1698 Thomas wrote of the Delaware Indians that "in *Travel* they lodge in the Woods about a great Fire, with the Mantle of Duffils they wear wrapt about them, and a few Boughs stuck round them." [12]

The gable-roofed structure was described by William Penn in 1683: "Their Houses are Mats, or Barks of Trees, set on Poles, in the fashion of an English Barn, but out of the power of the Winds, for they are hardly higher than a man. . . ." [13] Thomas, in 1698, described Indian dwellings in a similar fashion: "Their Houses are *Matts,* or *Barks* of *Trees* set on Poles, Barn-like, not higher than a Man. . . ." These structures apparently remained as the major form of dwelling for the Munsi well into the eighteenth century, since Smith, in 1765, speaks of them as being "built with poles laid on forked sticks in the ground, with bark, flags, or bushes on the top and sides, with an opening to the south, their fire in the middle. . . ." [14]

The circular house had a diameter of from eight to nine feet, and the longhouse averaged ten by twenty feet in its floor plan. Roofs were from six to eight feet high in both types.

An important structure in every village was the sweathouse, the use of which was considered a panacea by the Indians. The sweathouse consisted of a small oven, large enough to accommodate three or four men, which was built on the side of a running brook. This oven was made of the branches of trees, covered with split bark and earth, and lined with clay. Steam was provided by heating stones in a fire, placing them in the sweathouse, and pouring water on them. After sufficient perspiration had come forth, the participants plunged into the nearby stream.

Dispersed settlement, however, was the rule, especially during the hunting season. This was indicated by Smith's writing of the Indians who remained in the state in 1765: "Their houses . . . were sometimes together in towns but mostly moveable, and occasionally fixed near a spring or other water, according to the conveniencies for hunting, fishing, or other business of that sort. . . ." In addition to the dome-shaped hut most often used by solitary families, rock shelters were also used as dwellings for short periods of time. These consisted of rock overhangs, or caves affording protection from the elements, and had ready access to water and to animal and plant foods.

Sites of aboriginal occupance are not particularly numerous in the Musconetcong Valley. All the sites identified or inferred to date appear to be of the impermanent type, with the exception of two locations.[15] These are the two semipermanent villages sites of Pelouesse and Pechquakock or Araughcun, located respectively on the right bank of the Musconetcong near Hampton, and in the environs of Halsey Island, Lake Hopatcong. The site of Pelouesse, identified as "an old Indian plantation" by John Reading in 1715, has been surveyed by the New Jersey Indian Site Survey. It was found to occupy approximately 650 by 900 feet. Many artifacts and some pottery were surface collected from the sandy gravel soil of the site, which lay ten feet above the level of the river. Pechquakock, as it was known in the seventeenth century, or Araughcun, in the eighteenth century, is largely now beneath the present surface of Lake Hopatcong. The raising of the waters of the lake was done in the latter portion of the eighteenth century and the early portion of the nineteenth century, when successively higher dams were placed at the outlet of the lake. The result was the joining together of the two smaller lakes that had existed previously. The village, or series of villages, which occupied the site of a beach stretching from Prospect Point to Halsey Island and beyond, was apparently the largest concentration of population in the Musconetcong drainage basin. Even in the nineteenth century, low-water periods in the lake revealed the hearths of fifty or more wigwams that had stood there in historic times. This site, unfortunately, has never been systematically surveyed or excavated.[16] John Reading visited Lake "Huppakong" on the first of June, 1716, but mentions only that his party "took up our lodging in an Indian whigwam." Lake Hopatcong in the eighteenth century was an ideal place for Indian habitation since, according to Reading, it was "well stored with fish and a very pleasant place." Also, it offered easy access to a broad area of easily worked fertile soil south of Hurdtown and was surrounded by heavily forested hills, which were inhabited by large numbers of game. Tradition locates an important Indian village west of Waterloo,[17] but neither Reading nor Lawrence mentions such a village in their surveyor's notes and no official survey has ever mapped an Indian site in that area.

In addition to the two definite semipermanent village sites discussed above, almost sixty sites of impermanent occupance have been located by the various official archaeological surveys of the area. None of these has been properly surveyed or excavated and none is in an undisturbed condition. It is of interest to note that of all these sites mapped to date, but six are northeast of the terminal moraine, and but twelve are more than a few feet from the banks of the Musconetcong or a major affluent

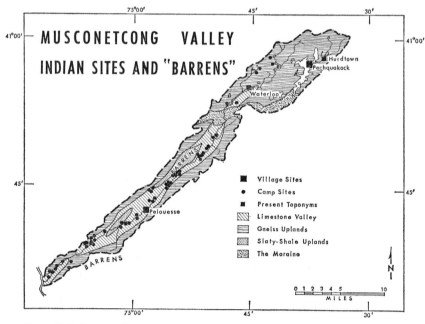

Compiled from various sources.

of the river. Southeast of the terminal moraine most sites are located in the limestone-floored valley. An absence of sites occurs on the slaty-shale uplands, and generally on the gneiss highlands. The clustering of sites along the banks of the stream southwest of Hackettstown; near Beattystown; near Penwell; southwest of Squire's Point; between Hampton and Asbury; and northeast of Bloomsbury suggests that these areas have been favored camp sites through time, perhaps on occasion even sites of semipermanent villages. The distribution of the impermanent sites would seem to indicate that access to water and fertile, easily worked soils would be primary locational factors.

In historical times the New Jersey Indians depended both on an exploitation of the natural products of their environment and on the domestication of certain economically valuable plants. The relative importance of hunting, fishing, gathering, and gardening, however, have long been in dispute. Pehr Kalm, drawing on the information given him by early Swedish settlers, said that the Indians "lived chiefly by hunting"[18] before the coming of Europeans. Samuel Smith, a little more than a decade later, in 1765, stated that "the woods and rivers afforded them the chief of their provisions. . . ." Even in the last decade of the eighteenth century, after the Delawares had moved to Ohio, George

Loskiel, a missionary, indicated that agriculture "is more attended to by the Iroquois than the Delawares, but by both merely to satisfy their most pressing wants. . . . [If] the winter happens to be severe, and the snow prevents them from hunting, a general famine ensues, by which many die." [19] Later writers, however, are by no means unanimous on this point, and a recent study cites numerous data to support the position that among the inland Lenape hoe gardening was of primary importance and was rivaled only seasonally by hunting and fishing. Driver and Massey map the aboriginal subsistence economy of New Jersey as being dominated by the cultivation of maize. (See Appendix IV.)

The garden plots of the Indians were generally located in bottom lands, where the soils were fertile and easily worked with the primitive instruments at hand, which consisted mainly of hoes fashioned from the scapulas (shoulder blades) of deer, or tortoise shells fastened to thick sticks. The gardens, according to Loskiel, were often deliberately kept "at some distance from their dwellings, that they may not be tempted to waste so much [maize], or at least increase the difficulty of getting it." Indian plantations were relatively small. Kalm stated that a typical Indian field encompassed no more ground "than a farmer in our country takes to plant cabbage for his family. At least, a farmer's cabbage and turnip ground, taken together, is always as extensive, if not more so, than all the corn fields and kitchen gardens of an Indian family." In the early nineteenth century, a Moravian missionary estimated that each family grew but two or three acres of maize. [20]

Indian plantations were cleared by means of girdling trees, thus causing them to die and allow the sun's rays to penetrate the forest floor. Brush was removed by hand. Clearance was the responsibility of the men, cultivation of the women. After a number of years of tillage, ten perhaps being a maximum, the old fields were allowed to return to forest or brush, and new plots were cleared. Loskiel's comment was that "when the strength of the soil is exhausted, they remove their plantations for they know nothing of the use of manure and have land enough."

Although several different crops were grown by the Lenape before white contact, maize, or Indian corn, was always the most important food crop. The varieties of maize grown included the most common flint corn, dent corn, popcorn, and a soft white variety known as "squaw corn." The method of cultivation was as follows: "They make heaps like molehills, each about two and a half feet from the others, which they sow or plant in April with maize, in each heap five or six grains; in the middle of May, when the maize is the height of a finger or more, they plant in each heap three or four Turkish beans. . . ." [21] Beans were second in importance among food crops. Many varieties of the common kidney bean were grown, and also the lima bean.

Other food plants grown by the Indians of New Jersey before white contact included the pumpkin, the bottle gourd, the Jerusalem artichoke, and the sunflower. There is also a possibility that the potato-bean was cultivated before white contact, as Loskiel indicates that they were grown by the Delawares on the Muskingum River in Ohio in 1794. Tobacco, a nonfood stimulant and ceremonial plant, which had first appeared in Middle Woodland times, continued to be grown widely.

Storage of food crops took place, according to Loskiel, in "round holes, dug in the earth at some distance from the houses, lined and covered with dry leaves and grass." Kalm described the pits as being less than six feet in depth and lined with bark and grass.

Plant foods were also obtained by gathering. Among the most popular of these was the aforementioned potato-bean, which may also have been cultivated. One of the outstanding students of the Lenape, Charles A. Philhower, indicated the importance of this tuber by stating that "the ground on Indian village sites and the immediate vicinity has been disturbed for a depth of ten to eighteen inches by the natives in digging the tubers of the potato-bean." [22] The Indian name for the plant was *hopniss,* and Pehr Kalm described it as growing in fertile soil, having a root resembling a potato, and being eaten also by the whites, especially as a substitute for potatoes.

Other tubers were also of importance. Kalm mentioned especially *katniss,* now known as the swamp potato, and an aroid, *taw-ho* or *tawhim,* which also grew in swampy areas. *Katniss* grew in low, muddy ground, and was much relished by whites and Indians alike, who boiled or roasted it. *Taw-ho* often grew to the thickness of a man's thigh, but contained an acrid principle when raw, which was eliminated by baking the tubers in an earth oven. The numbers of both *katniss* and *taw-ho* declined rapidly after white contact, because of the fondness of hogs for these tubers. Other wild tubers that were utilized by the Indians include those of the jack-in-the-pulpit, the wild morning glory, American licorice, wild ginger, pepper root, ginseng, sweet flag, cattail flag, and many others. Water plants also elicited the attention of the aborigines. The American lotus was valued for both its submerged stems and its seeds, and the seeds and root of the yellow pond lily were eaten.

Of the trees, especially the nut bearers were valued. Most preferred by the Lenape was the American chestnut, called by them *woapim.* Other valued nut bearers included the black walnut, the butternut, the hickories, certain species of oaks, and the hazelnut. Most villages were surrounded by thickets of hazelnut. Still other trees, such as the hemlock and slippery elm, were valued for their cambium, which yielded a flour when processed; and the spring growth of the sassafras was crushed and cooked with meat. The sugar maple was of importance, and the production of maple sugar was an important winter activity. Women and children also gathered persimmons, grapes, crab apples, plums, cranberries, blackberries, and strawberries from the forests and old fields surrounding their villages.

During the summer months parties often traveled to favored coastal locations and collected shellfish. These were dried, smoked, and carried back to the interior for use as seasoning in cooking. The shells were used for tempering pottery and for making ornaments. Various fresh-water mollusks were gathered for similar use in Highland lakes, ponds, and streams.

Of almost as great importance to the subsistence of the Lenape as agriculture was hunting. Hunting provided not only food but pelts and hides as well, which could be fabricated into clothing. Virtually all local mammals were hunted, but deer, bear, and elk were especially prized. The best preserved and largest number of animal bones that have been associated with a historic Indian site in the Highlands was excavated at the Fairy Hole rock shelter, at the northeastern end of Jenny Jump Mountain, approximately six miles north of the Musconetcong Valley. The bones were largely of the smaller mammals, which may be partially explained by the fact that some of the larger bones had been removed by earlier investigators, and also by the fact that the larger bones may have been thrown down the slope in front of the cave, where small rodents would have a better chance to destroy them. The bones found during the course of the excavation of the shelter and identified at the Academy of Natural Sciences of Philadelphia included: [23]

Procyron lotor	(Raccoon)——many fragments	
Mephitis nigra	(Skunk)——many fragments	
Marmotta monax	(Ground Hog)——few fragments	
Castor canadensis	(Beaver)——teeth	
Sylvilagus floridanus	(Cottontail)——few fragments	
Ondatra zibethica	(Muskrat)——many fragments	
Sciurus carolinensis	(Gray Squirrel)——many fragments	
Eptesicus fuscus	(Brown Rat)——two skulls	
Casteroides	(Giant Beaver, extinct)——tooth	
Erthizon dorsatum	(Porcupine)——few fragments	
Scalops aquaticus	(Mole)——bone	
Blarina brevicauda	(Short-tailed Shrew)——two skulls	
Tamias striarus	(Chipmunk)——few jaws	
Peromyscus	(Mouse)——many fragments	

Microtus	(Meadow Mouse)——many fragments
Neotoma pennsylvanica	(Cave Rat)——many fragments
Lepus	(Hare)——bone
Canis	(Two species) (Wolf and Dog)——jaws
Lynx	(Bobcat)——few fragments
Urocyon	(Gray Fox)——few fragments
Odocoileus	(Deer)——many fragments
Cervus	(Elk)——few fragments

It can be seen, then, that the aboriginal diet was quite varied insofar as mammals were concerned.

The hunting of large game was both a communal and an individual enterprise, the latter form prevailing mainly in the winter. The typical communal hunt for deer in the middle of the seventeenth century has been described as follows: [24]

> When now the sachem wants to arrange his hunt then he commands his people [to position themselves] close together in a circle of ½, 1 or 2 miles, according to the number of people at his command . . . each one roots up the grass about 3 or 4 ells, so that the fire will not be able to run back, each one then beginning to set fire to the grass, which is mightily ignited, so that the fire travels away, in towards the center of the circle, which the Indians follow with great noise, and all the animals which are found within the circle, flee from the fire and the cries of the Indians . . . now the Indians have surrounded the center with a small circle, so that they mutually cannot do each other any harm, then they break loose with guns and bows on the animals.

Loskiel described a similar hunt among the Delawares who had removed to Ohio in the last decade of the eighteenth century. In the northern part of New Jersey, lines of huntsmen were used to drive deer to and off cliffs. Birds were also avidly hunted. Even young boys were taught to shoot them on the wing with a bow and arrow.

Fishing, according to Loskiel, was "one of the most favorite diversions of the Indians next to hunting. . . ." This was carried on in several ways, either individually or in groups. Weirs, nets, bows and arrows, spears, harpoons, clubs, and hooks and lines were among the implements used.

Individuals always carried hooks and harpoons along on hunting expeditions. Hooks were of bone, the line was of wild hemp or milkweed, the bait an earthworm or a grasshopper. On May 30, 1715, John Reading's surveying party met "an Indian called Nepuck and his sons a fishing," in the Musconetcong. They did their fishing with bows and arrows.

Group fishing activities were of several types. On July ninth of the same year that Reading's party met Nepuck, they witnessed Indians in canoes on the Delaware fishing for eels. For this purpose the Indians employed lighted torches to attract the eels at night, and struck them with clubs when they approached the canoes. Another widely used device was the fish weir. This consisted of a V-shaped dam placed across a stream, with the point of the structure facing downstream. The fish would be driven upstream from a point well below the weir by a party of Indians dragging either a brush net made by lashing branches together, or a knotted net of wild hemp weighted with stone sinkers. The fish would be clubbed or speared upon attaining shallow water on the flanks of the weir.[25]

The arrival of European settlers in eastern North America during the seventeenth century brought increasing contacts between European and American Indian cultures. In general, relations between European settlers and the Indians of New Jersey were relatively good. In the province of West Jersey especially, according to Smith, the aborigines "manifested an open hospitable disposition to the English, and were in general, far from any design to their prejudice." In large part this was due to the Quaker influence in the area.[26]

Unfortunately, the Indians were adversely affected by European diseases and alcoholic beverages, and declined greatly in numbers in the seventeenth century. An additional factor adversely affecting the Munsis was warfare with the Dutch in the middle of the seventeenth century. By 1685 the aborigines of the southwestern portion of the state were "but few in Number," [27] and in the northern part of the state were "sparce at the beginning of the eighteenth century." [28] In 1758, by means of a treaty with the Munsi signed at Easton, Pennsylvania, all Indian claims to the northern part of New Jersey were relinquished. For the most part, however, the aboriginal inhabitants of present Morris, Hunterdon, Sussex, and Warren counties had left by the middle of the eighteenth century.[29] John Reading, for example, regularly encountered Indians in his travels through the Highlands in 1715, but in 1743 John Lawrence encountered only "an Indian Wigwam" approximately one mile north of Waterloo, and mentioned no inhabitants. A few Indians remained behind after their fellows had left for the west, and mixed with Europeans or carried on a precarious living on marginal land. Two Indian families maintained themselves until the fifth decade of the nineteenth century on Schooley's Mountain in Morris County.[30]

Contact with Europeans affected Lenape culture in several ways. Politically, there was more unity after conflicts with Europeans. Economically, a dependence on European trade goods often replaced traditional enterprises. Europeans provided a ready market, especially for skins and pelts, that had not existed before. Later observers noted that the numbers of many game animals, especially deer, increased noticeably immediately after the departure of the Indians from the Highlands.

The Lenape also adopted certain of the domesticated plants and animals introduced by Europeans. As early as 1631 the Swedes planted orchards on the lower Delaware, and Pehr Kalm indicates that by the early eighteenth century the Indians had a great love for the apples and peaches found in Swedish settlements. In the nineteenth century it was claimed by one observer that apple, plum, and cherry trees planted by the aborigines could still be seen in Sussex County. Possibly as a result of stimulus diffusion, at least some of the Lenape turned toward the planting of native trees. Schoepf, writing of eastern Pennsylvania in 1783, noted that the Delawares planted "wild red plums [*Prunus americana*] . . . [and that they were] very fond of this insipid fruit, which grows wild in the wood, and plant the seeds wherever they stay for any time. And so these plums, not much bigger or better than sloes, are called Indian Plums." [31]

The only domestic animal possessed by the Lenape before contact with Europeans was the dog. The value of European domesticates was soon seen, however, and in the mid-eighteenth century, according to Kalm, "some Indians . . . bought hogs of the Swedes and raised them. They taught them to follow them like dogs, and whenever they moved from one place to another their pigs always went with them." Later in the eighteenth century, Loskiel indicated, horses were raised, "which feed in the woods without a keeper," and cows, chickens, and cats were also kept.[32]

Aboriginal influences upon Europeans were manifold. Indian crops were adopted by the early settlers, and initial settlement often took place in Indian old fields, where the task of clearance had been accomplished by the aborigines. Early surveyors sought out these clearings and were often opposed, as was John Reading in 1715, for doing so. "We came to one of our Indian plantations where the owner of the same opposed our surveying and would not let us proceed in the same."

Europeans, at least at first, adopted Indian methods to attain certain ends, often with marked success. In 1680, Mahlon Stacy wrote a letter to his brother indicating that he and several other Englishmen had trapped large numbers of fish in the Delaware "after the Indian fashion. . . ." [33] The fact that Indian fish weirs continued to exist long after their original builders had left the province and that fish drives reminiscent of aboriginal practices were carried out by settlers in Bucks County,

Pennsylvania, in the nineteenth century, may also indicate aboriginal influences.[34]

With the exception of certain plant domesticates, it is, perhaps, in the field of transportation that Indian influences were longest felt. The Lenape were a water-conditioned people who often traveled by means of the dense network of natural waterways. Canoes were of two types—dugout and bark. The dugout was fashioned of tulip poplar, white cedar, or sycamore, and was hollowed out by means of adzes and fire. Bark canoes were made of elm, black oak, or hickory bark. European settlers adopted especially the dugouts for traveling the inland waters of the state, and were to be seen using them on such rivers as the Raritan as late as 1800.[35]

Perhaps the most lasting influence of the aborigines on the European settlers of New Jersey, as well as on the landscape of the state, has been the extensive network of Indian footpaths, since these "Indian trails finally became, in most instances, the crooked highways up hills and down dales for use of the wagon traffic of the white man." [36] Indeed, "in nearly every instance the Indian paths were followed in the location of the roads that are to-day [1880] the great thoroughfares of the State." [37] In addition, Indian routeways often determined lengthy portions of county boundaries, and of township boundaries as well. Thus the maps of New Jersey are still replete with the effects of aboriginal occupance, which for all practical purposes ended over two centuries ago.

Major Indian footpaths served to link the interior camp and village sites with the shellfisheries of the Atlantic coast. Large shell middens still attest to the seasonal movement on the part of many groups to the seaboard during the spring and summer months. Major trails also served to link interior village sites with one another.

Minor trails branched off the major paths and led to favorite hunting and fishing grounds, camp sites, garden plots, and rock shelters. There were so many of these lesser trails, in use and fallen into disuse, that a great deal of confusion has always attended efforts to unravel their exact locations and destinations.

The Indian paths were usually sinuous in their courses, being designed to follow the lines of least resistance to travel on foot rather than to facilitate travel in a straight line. In general, considerations in selecting the line of travel included dry land in relatively low terrain, the absence of rocks and stones in the pathway, and easily ascended grades. The Minisink Path, for example, was located for a great part of its length on the Wisconsin terminal moraine. Another consideration was the

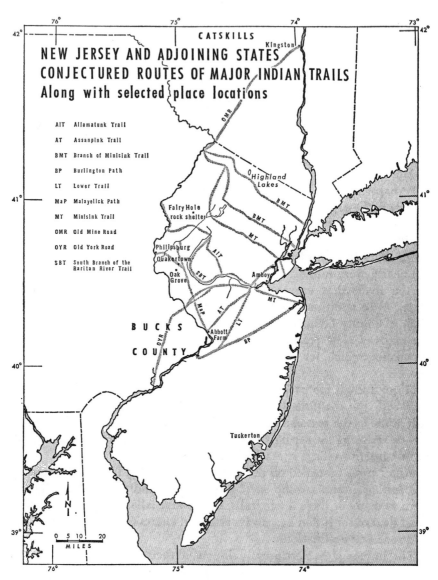

NEW JERSEY AND ADJOINING STATES
CONJECTURED ROUTES OF MAJOR INDIAN TRAILS
Along with selected place locations

AIT   Allamatunk Trail

AT   Assanpink Trail

BMT   Branch of Minisink Trail

BP   Burlington Path

LT   Lower Trail

MaP   Malayelick Path

MT   Minisink Trail

OMR   Old Mine Road

OYR   Old York Road

SBT   South Branch of the
       Raritan River Trail

Compiled from various sources.

crossing of streams. The Indian preferred locations with shallow, uniform depths and firm bottoms.

Major Indian routeways were well-beaten paths that could be easily located. They were perhaps two or three feet wide and were kept clear by the regular travel of Indians throughout the year. An idea may be gained of the ease of access to the interior of the state afforded by these paths in examining the journal of John Reading, one of the early surveyors of northern New Jersey. Reading and his party traveled widely in sections of the Highlands in 1715 and 1716 on horseback, and rarely had any difficulty of access to any area in which they had an interest.

On the other hand, since the Indian always walked in single file and thus, according to Haines, "disturbed as little as possible the foliage along their footpaths," many of the minor, seldom-used paths were difficult to locate. Smith, writing of the New Jersey Indian population in 1765, mentioned that "to know their walks again, in unfrequented woods, they heaped stones or marked trees." John Reading, in 1715, had difficulty finding a path to the village of "Penungachongh" and required the services of a local Indian to put him in the proper trail. In another instance his party moved along a path but "it being very blind we could not keep it. . . ."

The withdrawal of the Indians from the state before the entrance of whites in numbers into certain areas probably served to obscure many formerly well-frequented trails. Richard Smith, in 1769, described a path, once used by the Delaware Indians, that led from the Susquehanna to the Delaware in the vicinity of Deposit, New York, as being "a blind Indian Path," and complained of it as being "in many parts blocked up by old trees and Brush. . . ." [38] There were only a few impoverished Indians left in the locality at the time.

A summary of the locations of many of the major Indian paths in the northern part of New Jersey has been compiled by Lane. In addition to these, several other important aboriginal routeways served the northwestern portion of the state. These included the Malayelick Path, the South Branch of the Raritan River trail, the Allamatunk Trail, northern branches of the Minisink Trail, and the Old Mine Road from Kingston, New York. Several minor trails served to connect the major routeways. Not a few of these eased access to the Musconetcong Valley. [39]

Many of the toponyms (place-names) of the Highlands are aboriginal in origin. The suffix *ong*, written and pronounced as *unk*, or *onk* in the eighteenth century, is especially evident in toponyms of Indian origin in the region. In the Munsi dialect this apparently meant either "in," "in the," "on," "out of," [40] or "place where there is." [41] In the case of northern New Jersey the latter meaning is probably the more accurate one.

Unfortunately, the Munsi dialect is imperfectly known and various meanings are assigned to the Indian terms. "Musconetcong" is itself a Munsi term, the meaning of which is not clear. Interpretations have included "a rapid running stream," "clear running stream," or "stream running along the base of a mountain," and "place where bass fish are caught with fish spears." Musconetcong, or as it was often spelled in the eighteenth century "Musconetkonk," refers most likely to a locality instead of a stream. The Munsi had no terms for individual streams per se prior to the arrival of Europeans. When asked for the names of streams by the early surveyors and settlers, the Indians generally replied with a term referring to an important event that had taken place nearby or to an economic activity that was regularly pursued in the area. The contention that a vicinity instead of a stream was referred to by the term "Musconetcong" is borne out by the fact that pioneer European communities used the term in this sense [42] and the fact that the highest upland area in the vicinity came to be known as Musconetcong Mountain.

Another important Indian term of which the corrupted form, "Hopatcong," is still in use, refers to the largest body of water in the Musconetcong drainage system. The early eighteenth-century orthography appears to have been "Huppakong" or "Hapakonoesson." There are several suggested meanings of this term, the most popular of which alludes to the supposed former shape of the lake: "a pipe to smoke out of." Other possible interpretations include "place of very deep water," and "stone water."

Two other aboriginal toponyms in use in the Musconetcong Valley include "Netcong" and "Pohatcong." "Netcong" may mean "place of a stream" and "Pohatcong" may mean "place of a stream outlet in a split in the hills." [43]

Aboriginal effects on the flora of New Jersey were long in evidence. The use of fire by the Indians on a large scale, for a variety of reasons, greatly modified the natural vegetation. Fires were set in order to drive game, to prevent young trees from gaining a foothold in open areas, to encourage the growth of grasses instead of brush on the forest floor, to clear high grass in open areas so as to remove the cover sought by pursued game, and to encourage a new crop of succulent grasses after the previous crop had withered.

The effects of widespread burning were much in evidence at the time of first European settlement in many localities. This was a fortunate circumstance for many settlers, who at first had great dependence on livestock. In 1685, Budd wrote of southwestern New Jersey: [44]

> The *Trees* grow but thin in most places, and very little under-Wood. In the *Woods* groweth plentifully a course sort of *Grass,* which is so proving that it soon makes the Cattel and Horses fat in the Summer. . . .

Early settlers and travelers also found park-like landscapes in other areas of former aboriginal occupance. In 1684 Gawen Lawrie, in writing of the vicinity of Amboy in the east central part of the state, mentioned that the trees "grow generally not thick, but in some places ten, in some fifteen, in some thirty upon an acre, this I find generally, but in some particular places there is one hundred upon an acre; but that is very rare. . . ." [45] In the middle of the eighteenth century, in the southwestern part of the state, Pehr Kalm found that he could "ride on horseback without inconvenience in the woods, and even with a cart in most places. . . ."

In addition to grass for the stock, the open forest floors were also rich in mast for the ubiquitous hogs of the pioneers. In 1765 Smith noted that "the Indians, before the European settlements, used every year regularly to burn the woods . . . this practice kept the woods clean, so that pigeons regularly got acorns, which then not being devoured by hogs, were plenty almost every where. . . ."

Burning also served to expand grasslands. If near water and relatively small in extent, perhaps being at least in part the remnant of an old field, grasslands were termed "meadows" by the early settlers and were much prized and avidly sought by the early surveyors. Many poorly drained meadows lapsed back into forest after seasonal Indian burning ceased: [46]

> There is a story related, that in a certain law suit in which a large tract of "meadow," then swamp was in dispute, a witness, an old lady of three score and ten, testified that when she was a child the whole tract was treeless, except one small tree, naming the kind and its location. Curiosity, mingled no doubt with a desire to impeach the old lady's testimony, led some persons to search for the tree, which they found, so accurate was her description, and, on cutting it down and counting its rings of yearly growth, they found it confirmed the old lady's story.

When wide areas were denuded of trees, eighteenth-century surveyors termed them "plains" or "barrens." In 1715 John Reading, approaching the vicinity of Hackettstown, related that "about two miles short of Muskonetkong we entered a very large plain but barren, we went across the same which is better than a mile over. . . ." The next day Reading's party explored both banks of the stream southwest of Hackettstown and found "the aforesaid Plains on the upper side of the same Musconetcong about six miles by computation." The area covered by this grassland corresponds very closely to the droughty slaty-shale uplands southwest of Hackettstown, where aboriginal burning could be expected to have been especially effective.

A larger area of grasslands and degraded forest vegetation existed south of the river on the gneiss uplands southeast of Bloomsbury, in the middle of Alexandria Township. This grassland was termed the "Barrens" by early settlers and was more than fifty square miles in extent. Even in the late eighteenth century, a little to the south of this area, it was said that one could see all the way from Oak Grove to Quakertown, a distance of over two miles, because of the dearth of trees. Local tradition assigns the responsibility for the lack of forest cover in the area to Indian burning. After such burning ceased, the area, although still termed the "Barrens" grew up in a forest composed almost exclusively of chestnut.[47]

The lack of trees in many areas was considered a favorable rather than an unfavorable circumstance for early settlement, since clearance was generally viewed as an onerous task, especially by English settlers. In 1684, a report on the upper Raritan Valley included the intelligence that "so far as we went, was very rich land, and yet that above it is said to be richer; a great deal of it is naturally clear of wood, and what is not so, is easily cleared, the trees being but small and at a good distance from one another. . . ."[48] The early English settlers of Quakertown, approximately ten miles southeast of the Musconetcong, chose the vicinity, according to a later county history, "on account of the richness of the soil, the beauty of its situation, and *the absence of forests, the last, as is usually the case in new countries being considered a great advantage to the settler.*" (Italics mine.)[49]

Aboriginal burning also probably affected the species composition of the forests. Trees such as the oaks, hickories, and chestnut were more fire-resistant than maple, yellow birch, and hemlock.[50] Considering the value of the nut bearers to both aborigine and European pioneer, this was a most favorable result of burning. To the later charcoal-iron interests, however, such was not the case. They complained of the lack of dense forests and of the poor quality of the charcoal made from the fire-damaged, immature trees.[51]

Another and more subtle influence of the Indians on the area was their effect on the native fauna. Although the Indians are often cited as natural conservationists, in some cases they may have caused certain species, which existed in a fragile equilibrium, to become extinct. The presence of the tooth of the giant beaver, and bones of the porcupine and elk at the Fairy Hole rock shelter indicate that at least the latter two were widely hunted in the state. Giant beaver remains have been found in other nearby caves in Pennsylvania and New York associated with post-Pleistocene deposits. The tooth associated with the artifacts of historic Indians at the Fairy Hole rock shelter many indicate that they had a hand in causing its extinction. In historic times elk were rare even in eastern Pennsylvania and were unknown in New Jersey, and the porcupine has been exterminated in historic times.[52]

CHAPTER 3

Pioneer Agricultural Settlement

Ca. 1720–1790

The initial settlement of northwestern New Jersey by pioneers of European descent was concerned mainly with subsistence agriculture and thus depended on the availability of land, in one form or another, for such pursuit. As natural increase and the swelling tide of European immigrants encouraged settlers to look outside the areas of older European occupance, a growing tide of pioneers entered the northwestern part of New Jersey, including the Musconetcong drainage system. In northwestern New Jersey, land for agricultural settlement was obtained in three ways: (1) outright purchase, a situation rare for the average pioneer in the days of earliest settlement; (2) tenancy, which involved the paying of rent to, or sharecropping with, a landowner or proprietor; and (3) squatting, or occupance without payment of rent. The latter form of tenure was often possible because of the lack of knowledge on the part of distant landowners that the practice was taking place, and the unsettled conditions, especially insofar as law enforcement was concerned, on the frontier.

Agricultural settlement generally followed in the wake of surveying parties, which were active in the Highlands during the first years of the eighteenth century. Only on occasion did squatters precede even the surveyors into favored areas. Surveyors were hired by proprietors or, in the case of John Reading and his son, were themselves proprietors. The proprietors held shares in the companies that owned the lands of, and encouraged settlement in, East and West Jersey. East Jersey included, for the most part, the portion of the Musconetcong drainage system northeast of Waterloo; West Jersey the valley southwest of Waterloo (Appendix I). The proprietors of each division of the colony periodically declared dividends, which were in the form of warrants for unlocated lands. These warrants could then be taken up by the proprietors themselves and the lands surveyed and held, or later sold. Often, however, the warrants were sold to speculators or, on occasion, to actual settlers, although the latter practice was rare in early days.

The early surveyors moved into the wilderness by way of the network of Indian paths already described, or by way of the major river valleys, which, as we have seen, were easily penetrated. The first lands to be surveyed were selected carefully with several criteria in mind. In value, waterpower sites and outcroppings of ore, especially of iron, surpassed agricultural land, and were thus first surveyed. The most valuable of agricultural lands were the cleared areas lying near a source of water, and near the network of Indian paths.[1]

> It is a circumstance which has not failed to impress itself upon those familiar with the records of the proprietors of East Jersey that among the first lands to be taken up or purchased especially in the northern part of the county [Morris] were the lots containing waterfalls, and where veins of ore cropped out on the surface, afterward pieces of natural meadow, and last of all the surrounding hills.

The same could be said for West Jersey. John Reading, the younger, was mainly interested in surveying "natural" meadows and Indian plantations. These generally lay contiguous to Indian paths and so were of relatively easy access in addition to having pasture available for the pioneer agriculturist's stock during the critical first few winters.

On occasion, the surveying of advantageous parcels of property brought great competition on the part of early purchasers. An early legend provides an example of such activity in the Musconetcong Valley: [2]

> When John Bowlby was running the boundaries of his land, Col. Daniel Coxe was also laying out a tract to the east of him. There seems to have been some strife between them as to who should get his survey entered upon record first, and at the same time get as much of the creek [Musconetcong] as possible.
>
> Coxe became alarmed, mounted his horse and rode towards Burlington as fast as he could, while Bowlby ran his lines so far as to take up the whole stream, keeping Coxe out of every foot of it. He then mounted a horse and followed Coxe, who rode one horse to death, and borrowed another, and thus reached Burlington first. But Bowlby "kept him out of the creek" and that was all he desired, for now he had a mill site, and the most valuable portion of the land.

The early deeds and returns of surveys extant show that the metes-and-bounds system of survey was in general use (Appendix V). This system made use of natural features as corners rather than any systematic earth grid. Trees, streams, Indian paths, and an occasional cairn built by the surveyors served to demarcate the different tracts of the early landholders. This casual, inaccurate method of survey, depending as it did on impermanent features, often led to difficulties when later, more accurate surveys were made. In 1771 Garret Rapalje, an important capitalist of the day, sold thirteen and six-tenths acres of his land at the outlet of Lake Hopatcong which, it had been found, had been included "within the bounds of a former survey," to James Parker, President of the Council of Proprietors for the Eastern Division of New Jersey, for six-pence, "in Order to Obtain a Certificate for Locating so much Land Elsewhere." [3] In 1762 William Coxe, one of the great landholders of Hunterdon County (Appendix VI), wrote to his agent and surveyor, John Emley, that the bounds of his lands "were never done with care," and asked him to be cautious in selecting chainbearers, and especially not to select relatives of purchasers for the task.[4] Boundary difficulties, apparently, were almost universal in later days.

The metes-and-bounds system allowed the early surveyors to work quickly, if not well, and they were generally far in the van of actual settlement. In much of Warren County, for example, the best lands had already been located by 1730. Unfortunately, many of the proprietors, and most of the speculators who bought large tracts of other proprietors, held onto their lands in anticipation of rising values. In Sussex County "the best locations were generally entered before any immigrants had arrived . . . and they had to cultivate the soil when they did come as tenants or trespassers." [5] This could be said of much of northern New Jersey. Such a situation was naturally resented by the pioneer agriculturist, whose resources were slight and who could not hope to buy a small parcel of land at a reasonable price.

Allen and Turner, capitalists of Philadelphia, had a great deal of trouble with squatters on their lands in northern Hunterdon County in 1749. Harassment on the part of the aforementioned Allen and Turner backfired when the adamant pioneers went so far as to destroy much of an iron furnace that had been erected by the Philadelphia partnership.[6] In Sussex County, a few years later, lands were taxed not according to ownership, but according to the improvements made by the settlers actually living thereon. This was done in order to collect taxes from the settlers present, who often did not hold titles to the land upon which they were located.

The widespread practice of squatting and the large number of settlers engaged in the practice caused many landowners and speculators to be cautious in their treatment of the impecunious pioneers. After conditions had stabilized and legal pressure could be judiciously applied, most of the squatters later agreed to become tenants. This occurred mostly after the middle of the eighteenth century. Settlers refusing to sign leases were either ejected or finally left the area of their own volition. Tenancy probably became the common form of tenure in a large portion of northern Hunterdon County in the middle decades of the eighteenth century.

In Sussex County, also, tenancy was quite widespread, and one author even indicated that the rapid settlement of that county was the result of landholders' eagerness to improve their lands and their offering tenants extremely generous terms. This, however, did not work out quite as well as expected and, finally, "instead of holding on, in the hope of ultimately getting large prices, the owners sold out to as good advantage as they could, ere the virgin soil of their respective tracts should become completely exhausted; and every portion of our county soon felt the beneficial influence of the change." [7]

In addition to the landowners' fears that tenants would ultimately ruin the land and decrease its value, subdivisions of the large tracts apparently often occurred because of the imposition of high taxes. Some owners were forced to sell unused lands at a low price in later days. Such was the case for John Bowlby of Hampton. [8]

> John Bowlby sold many hundreds of acres of land for 2s,6d. per acre, because he did not wish to pay the tax on it. . . . Parties now living at the Junction [Hampton] can remember hearing their grandfathers tell about the time when they could have bought land from Bowlby for 50 cts. per acre. It must be remembered that in those days taxes were high in proportion to the value of the land; and while land was plentiful, money was scarce.

Unfortunately, there are few data extant on the relative importance of the types of land tenure involved in early days in northwestern New Jersey and on the availability of lands for pioneer agriculturists. The best source for this information, and for the general course of agricultural settlement and improvement of the land lies in the eighteenth-century newspaper advertisements, as reprinted in the *New Jersey Archives*. [9]

In general, the early advertisements, beginning in the 1730's, reflect the purchase and disposal of large tracts, often of a thousand or more acres, by land speculators. Later advertisements show that tenancy was an important form of tenure, and remained important until after the Revolution. During the 1760's many smaller, unimproved properties of less than three hundred acres became available. In many cases, however, land was difficult to sell, especially since many farmers were poor and were accustomed to tenancy. As late as 1774, William McAdams reported to Samuel Barker, owner of a 7,308-acre estate in Alexandria Township (Appendix VI), that his land "would be very difficult to sell . . . at any rate for Cash as it is rare that such chaps [tenants] offer hit. . . ." [10]

The economic dislocations caused by the Revolution generally served to discourage tenancy and to increase ownership by dirt farmers. Even wealthy patriots met with heavy losses. One of these, William Alexander, lost thousands of acres of tenanted farmland in the Musconetcong Valley alone in 1779 and 1780. The seizure of Tories' property by county governments also rendered much formerly tenanted land available to small freeholders. As late as the last decade of the eighteenth century, some locations in the fertile limestone portions of the Musconetcong Valley lay unused because they were held by large landholders, but most plots had been sold to individual settlers by that time. [11]

In any areal study involving culture-historical geography a knowledge of the ethnic and cultural origin or origins of the population is essential. In regard to the origins of the settlers of northern New Jersey, the remarks of John Rutherfurd in 1786 are generally pertinent. In his words: [12]

> Morris County is partly New England descent, and a few from West Jersey. . . . Part of Morris . . . were from the north of Ireland, but all the most valuable lands in Somerset County are possest by the low Dutch, also the large township of Reading in Hunterdon. Sussex is settled and is a mixture from all the other Counties.

Of West Jersey it could be said:

> the chief Proprietors were Quakers, who made fine settlements in the Counties of Burlington, Gloster [*sic*], Salem, Cumberland, Cape May, Hunterdon and half of Sussex and the many Settlers among them were of different Persuasions, yet the Quakers held the chief Property and Management.

And finally:

> dispersed in both Divisions are many laborious, ingenious and parsimonious Germans, who came here late and poor, but are daily acquiring Estates, especially in the large Counties of Hunterdon and Sussex.

It can generally be asserted that the pioneer population of much of northern New Jersey was quite a polyglot one. Indeed, the local historians have been most eager to accentuate the polygenetic nature of their subjects. [13]

no county [Hunterdon] in the State had so mixed a population, composed, as it was of Huguenots, Hollanders, Germans, Scotch, Irish, English, and native Americans.

In general, the Musconetcong Valley as a whole reflects the same mixture of ethnic stocks to a greater or lesser degree. Unfortunately, it is often difficult to ascertain exactly ethnic affiliations and dates of settlement for individual localities. It could be said, at the time the first local histories were being written, that "few, if any, of the early settlers survive, and their representatives have not preserved the traditions of their ancestors. It is, therefore, almost impossible for the historian to obtain a sufficient number of facts to make a record of the early settlement interesting or valuable." [14] It will be necessary, then, to draw upon many sources and often trace early population movements by inference.

A common misconception in dealing with the early settlement of the southern Highlands is that [15]

> It is well-known history that northwestern New Jersey was settled by two distinct streams of emigration: one from Ulster County, New York, consisting of Huguenot and Hollander stock, and another from Philadelphia, consisting of Quakers, Germans and Scotch-Irish and Irish.

In fact, the situation was far more complex. Pioneer settlement in the Highlands was influenced, and eased, by the existence of a relatively dense network of Indian paths. These provided ready access to the major river valleys of the Highlands not only from Philadelphia and southern New York, but also from Trenton, New Brunswick, Elizabeth, Newark, and the Jersey shore of the Hudson.

Major routeways of the first settlers included the Old York Road leading north from Philadelphia, the Malayelick Path leading north from Trenton and crossing the Old York Road at Ringoes, the trails leading west and north along the South Branch of the Raritan from New Brunswick, the Allamatunk Path leading northwest from New Brunswick, and the various paths called the "Minisink Trail" leading northwest from the settlements of Elizabeth, Newark, and Bergen.

An additional factor easing initial European access to the interior was the open nature of the woodlands, especially in the major river valleys, so that forested areas in early days were not so serious a barrier to settlement as they later became. In this connection, we might mention that in some localities tradition asserts that early settlers had to "cut their way" in order to attain their lands. This might have referred to the obliteration of Indian paths by forest growth after they had fallen into disuse and also to the thickening of the forest understory because of the discontinuance of aboriginal burning.

All available information indicates that the southwestern portion of the Musconetcong Valley was settled before the middle or northeastern portions were. There is a possibility that the earliest pioneers had arrived by the beginning of the eighteenth century. Snell [16] cites the records of an early surveyor, Daniel Leeds, in this connection. According to Snell, Leeds recorded encountering a blacksmith, "William Titfoot," settled in the vicinity of present Riegelsville, New Jersey, in 1710. Snell felt that this proved prior agricultural settlement. However, Snell also mentioned that Leeds referred to the river in the locality as Maghaghtmeck Creek. This is suspiciously like the term used contemporaneously for the Neversink River in the vicinity of Port Jervis, New York: Maghagkemek in 1689, Maggaghkamieck in 1694 and Mahekkomack in 1719. Also, a blacksmith by the name of William Tietsort or Titsoord located in that vicinity as early as 1689 and did not remove until 1713.[17] Thus, it is quite possible that Snell was mistaken in locating settlers in the Musconetcong Valley at such an early date. The will of Andrew Heath of Hopewell Township, which was filed in 1717, included a listing of "600 acres, on the Muskanickcunk Branch of Delaware River, *farm,* bo't of Thomas Truss." [18] (Italics mine.) The listing of the property as a farm may indicate that agricultural settlement had occurred as early as the second decade of the eighteenth century.

The settlers who first arrived in the southwestern portion of the Musconetcong Valley were most likely of English stock. Dutch settlers were located to the north, near Port Jervis, but they were few in number and had not penetrated very far southward in the early eighteenth century. To the south, however, there lay a great reservoir of Englishmen and their descendants. The Hunterdon County Tax Roll of 1722, which includes the names of the taxpayers of the present area of Hunterdon, Morris, and Sussex counties, illustrates this point by an almost entire absence of non-English names.[19]

Since Trenton in 1726 consisted of "hardly more than one house," [20] we must look elsewhere for the major source of these early English settlers. This source can be found in the old Quaker settlements of Philadelphia and southwestern New Jersey. Indeed, English Quakers had already begun to explore the Highlands by way of the Delaware River as early as 1685.

Dispersed settlement was the rule as the English Quakers pushed north. John Reading, for example, a former resident of Burlington, located his homestead far from any neighbor in the vicinity of the present city of Lambertville (Stockton?) in 1703 or soon thereafter. Others had joined him in this vicinity by 1707.[21]

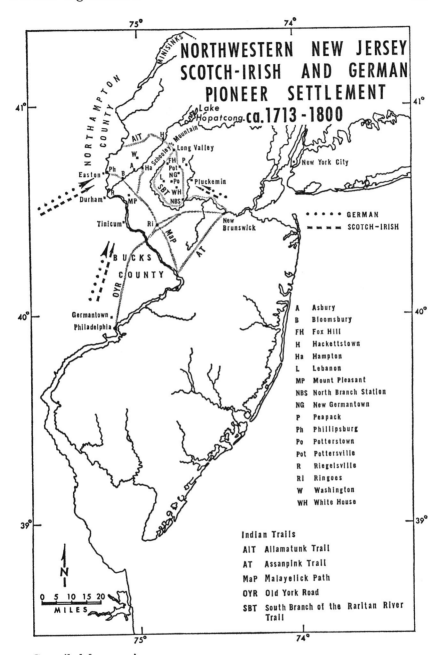

NORTHWESTERN NEW JERSEY
SCOTCH-IRISH AND GERMAN
PIONEER SETTLEMENT
ca.1713-1800

· · · · · GERMAN
– – – SCOTCH-IRISH

A	Asbury
B	Bloomsbury
FH	Fox Hill
H	Hackettstown
Ha	Hampton
L	Lebanon
MP	Mount Pleasant
NBS	North Branch Station
NG	New Germantown
P	Peapack
Ph	Phillipsburg
Po	Potterstown
Pot	Pottersville
R	Riegelsville
RI	Ringoes
W	Washington
WH	White House

Indian Trails

AIT	Allamatunk Trail
AT	Assanpink Trail
MaP	Malayelick Path
OYR	Old York Road
SBT	South Branch of the Raritan River Trail

MILES
0 5 10 15 20

N

Compiled from various sources.

Reading had probably used the Malayelick Path as his means of access to this new home, but others could well have come north from Philadelphia via the Old York Road. Quakertown, lying ten miles south of the Musconetcong Valley, was settled by Englishmen having an early relationship with the Burlington Quarterly Meeting. Settlement in this vicinity may have occurred before 1700 or perhaps "about 1725" but surely had taken place by 1733.[22]

Lack of concensus by the authorities concerned with the actual date of settlement reflects the general paucity of early historical data. At any rate, Quakertown also could be most easily reached via the Malayelick Path.

Another English Quaker, of whom we have more definite information, was John Axford, who settled in the vicinity of the present Oxford, New Jersey, approximately five miles north of the Musconetcong, *ca.* 1730. Axford was formerly a resident of the vicinity of Trenton. It may be noted that Axford's land could be reached from Trenton most easily by the eastern branch of the Malayelick Path.[23]

Other Englishmen in West Jersey were associated with the Church of England. Episcopalians were located in Hopewell Township as early as 1703 and built a log church at Ringoes in 1725.[24] Both of these localities were serviced by the Old York Road and the Malayelick Path.

Evidence of the early origins of English settlements in the southwestern portion of the Musconetcong Valley and vicinity is also found in the statement of the Reverend William Frazer, a missionary associated with the Society for the Propagation of the Gospel. In 1768 he wrote of his parishioners in the vicinity of present Changewater, New Jersey: [25]

> There are a great many families who call themselves Church of England people from no other principle as I can find than because it was the Religion of their Fathers. . . . I have once preached about 16 miles distant from the place I generally attend at Muskenetcunk where I was told there had been Churchmen (as they called themselves) arrived to the age of 40 who never in their lives had been to hear a church min [minister]. . . .

Frazer's statement indicates that many Englishmen had settled so far in the van of the establishment of organized religion that they had raised families with no formal religious knowledge.

Further evidence of the English origins of the earliest settlers of the lower Musconetcong Valley may be found in the names of Sir Robert Barker's tenants in Alexandria Township in 1756 and thereafter; in the names listed in the account books of the Greenwich and Chelsea forges in this locality in the 1780's; and in the John Cooley papers dealing with Alexandria Township in the 1790's.[26]

Another stream of English settlers, although much weaker numerically than those associated with the Delaware Valley, entered New Jersey by way of the Raritan Valley and quickly pushed to the interior, using the Raritan, its tributaries, and associated Indian paths to reach their lands. Many of these people ultimately settled in West Jersey.

Earliest settlement on the Raritan and vicinity was in 1667, involving Presbyterians and Episcopalians from Massachusetts and Connecticut settling in Woodbridge, and Baptists from Maine and New Hampshire settling Piscataway Township.[27]

The subsequent movements of these settlers and their descendants are not well known. There is a good possibility that some of them moved north along the Allamatunk Trail into the vicinity of present Oldwick at an early date. It is certain that Englishmen preceded Germans into this vicinity. The plot upon which the Zion Lutheran Church was built in 1749 had been owned by Ralph Smith, who is described as a "Yankee" and was a member of the Lamington Presbyterian Church. It is certain that English-speaking settlers remained numerous in the area as late as 1753, since Henry Muhlenberg preached a sermon in English to a large crowd of Dutch and English after his regular German service in that year.[28]

New Englanders and their descendants also worked their way inland along the branches of the Minisink Trail leading northwestward from Newark and Elizabethtown (Elizabeth). By 1710 a few families had settled in the vicinity of "Whippenung" (Whippany), and they established a Presbyterian Church not long after. Other New Englanders, in the course of time, became interested in this locality and the surveyor John Reading records meeting "with some New England men who came to treat about purchasing of lands," at Whippany in 1715.

Emigrants from the Long Island communities of New England descent began locating in the area peripheral to the Minisink Trail approaching Lake Hopatcong from the southeast as early as 1737. Additional emigrants from Long Island joined them in the 1740's and thereafter.[29]

A scattered population of New England origin probably was already located in the environs of Lake Hoptacong and the northern portion of the Musconetcong Valley as early as the 1740's. In 1743 John Lawrence, in running the partition line between East and West Jersey, mentioned leaving his work of the day six miles north of the Musconetcong and going "to a house belonging to Richard Green." [30] In a survey of land adjoining the "Great Pond" (Lake Hopatcong) in 1759, Daniell Cooper used the "Dwelling House that was formerly Stown [?] Bishops" as a bound.[31] A list of "Names of Settlers Living on Lake [Hopatcong] Shore Prior to Year 1800," [32] included names that are all of English derivation except for two that are Dutch. The prevalence of English stock in the area is further supported by the list of freeholders of Morris County, which included "township of Roxberey [sic]" names.[33] These are all Anglo-Saxon in appearance. Even after the establishment of the iron industry in the area, there remained a general prevalence of English names.[34]

The Dutch and their religious brethren, the Flemish, Walloons, and Huguenots, also appeared in northern New Jersey at an early date. Their chief means of access to our area of interest lay in a movement northward and westward from the Raritan Valley, movement westward along the branches of the Minisink Trail from Bergen and associated settlements on the Hudson, and a movement down the Delaware from Kingston, New York, via the Old Mine Road.

In numbers and influence, the "Dutch" settlers moving along the Raritan, its tributaries, and associated Indian paths were most important. Their origin lay in the older Dutch settlements on Long Island, Manhattan, and Staten Island, and at Bergen on the Hudson. As early as 1683 Pierre Ballou settled southeast of present Bound Brook at what later became Fieldville. Dutch Huguenots had reached the North Branch of the Raritan in 1685 and a Dutch church was established in Somerville in 1699.

The era of Dutch migration lasted until about 1735. Hundreds of families came by sloop to the present site of New Brunswick and then ascended the river above Raritan Landing by flatboats of shallower draft. Shortly after 1700 the Dutch became preponderant in the vicinity of what is now New Brunswick, which had hitherto consisted only of a ferry site. A congregation was organized in 1717 and by 1735 counted 110 families as members. The influence of the Dutch was strong enough to affect the English settlers of Piscataway, and by 1735, north of a line from Raritan Landing to New Market, there were twenty-one Dutch and Huguenot families and only seven English families. The latter attended Dutch churches and soon used Dutch as their language.

Land hunger served to drive the Dutch farther and farther into the interior. The "Scotch Proprietors" of East Jersey thought of them as "their best customers." Many settled the region between Pleasant Run and the South Branch from 1710 to 1720, and the vicinity of White House had been reached by 1724. Estimates place the numbers of Dutch and Huguenots in Somerset County in 1740 as high as ninety per cent of the 4,505 inhabitants.

The rapidly advancing Dutch swept northward and westward and accounted for many of the earliest pioneers of present Hunterdon County. Bethlehem Township, which includes a portion of the southwestern Musconetcong Valley from Hampton to Bloomsbury, traditionally was first settled by Hollanders. As this township may have been organized as early as 1724, Dutch settlement may have occurred at that time.[35]

The branch of the Minisink Trail serving the old Dutch settlements in Bergen County also afforded access to the New Jersey Highlands. By 1700 four or five Dutch families, which had originated on Long Island, Manhattan, and at Bergen, had penetrated the Pompton Valley near the present town of Pompton. Another area of Dutch settlement, apparently, was in the vicinity of present Mountain View, where John Reading visited George Ryerson in 1715. By 1718 Dutch settlers were penetrating the valleys of the Pequannock and Wanaque rivers.

It is apparent, however, that Dutch settlers never entered the vicinity of Lake Hopatcong in great numbers from this or any other source. The early family names in the area are all English, as established above, and even in the late eighteenth century only a few Dutch names appear in store accounts, and the bearers of these could well have been living at a distance. According to the list of "Names of Settlers Living on Lake [Hopatcong] Shore Prior to year 1800," only two of the nineteen families in the area were of Dutch descent.[36]

In addition to the Dutch moving up the various Indian paths and stream courses connecting with the Raritan Valley, and the Dutch moving into the Highlands via the Minisink Trail, other Dutch families had penetrated the northwestern portion of the state via the Neversink Valley from Kingston, New York. This route is locally known as the Old Mine Road. Snell places the Dutch in scattered settlements from the Delaware Water Gap northward to Ulster County, New York, prior to the year 1700. This, however, is far too early a date for settlements in the Delaware Valley south of the vicinity of Montague, New Jersey. The best evidence for this is mustered by John Reading's journal. In traversing the area from Manunka Chunk to the Water Gap in 1715, he found only Indian settlements. In 1719, when he and his party traveled northward to help survey the boundary between New York and New Jersey, they first met with a settler, Solomon Davis, in what must have been a location north of the present Montague, New Jersey. Dutch settlements were located approximately six miles north of Davis's land. In 1725, Nicholas Dupui, a Huguenot, settled in the vicinity of Shawnee, Pennsylvania, which is just north of the Water Gap. His means of access was by way of the Old Mine Road. More Dutch and Huguenot families must have been lured into the region at this time, since by the year 1737 four Dutch Reformed Churches had been organized to serve residents on both sides of the Delaware from present Port Jervis to the Delaware Water Gap. A parsonage for the minister serving these congregations was built in Sandyston Township, New Jersey, in 1741. This probably marked the approximate geographical center of these settlements at that date.

John Lawrence, surveying the East and West Jersey boundary line in 1743, emerged at the Delaware south of present Bevans, New Jersey. He mentions Dutch families as residing in the vicinity on both the New Jersey and Pennsylvania sides of the river.

There is little evidence to substantiate the movement of sizable numbers of Dutch from these northwestern settlements into the Musconetcong Valley. Several Dutch names are recorded as having been among the earliest settlers of Mansfield Township, but they could just as easily have been a result of the general movement of Dutch families northward from the Raritan Valley. About 1760, however, there is record of a Dutch family which originated in New York State settling in Greenwich Township. They may well have been a result of the Dutch movement southward.[37]

Large numbers of Ulster Scots, or as they are generally known in the United States, Scotch-Irish, began to arrive at Philadelphia between the years 1710 and 1720 and thereafter. Although the general movement of these pioneers was west and south from southeastern Pennsylvania, many may be traced northward into Bucks and Northampton counties in Pennsylvania, and into present Hunterdon and Warren counties, New Jersey. The general absence of New England stock in West Jersey and eastern Pennsylvania eases the identification of Presbyterian churches as being associated with Scotch-Irish population movements. Indeed, in the case of Warren County "they were the founders of all the early Presbyterian churches in the county." [38]

In East Jersey, tracing Scotch-Irish movements is much more difficult, because of the affinity of New Englanders in New Jersey for Presbyterianism and because early Scottish settlers at Perth Amboy and vicinity also established Presbyterian congregations. There does seem to have been a movement of Scotch-Irish up the Raritan Valley, but their origins and numerical strength are unknown. In the case of the movement northward from Philadelphia, there is better evidence. The movement was rapid, as is indicated by the fact that Scotch-Irish Presbyterian congregations had been organized at Tinicum and at Durham, Bucks County, by 1739. Also, the minutes of the Presbytery of New Brunswick in 1739 contain "a supplication for supplies of preaching in Mr. Barber's neighborhood near Musconnekunk." [39] This, apparently, was a

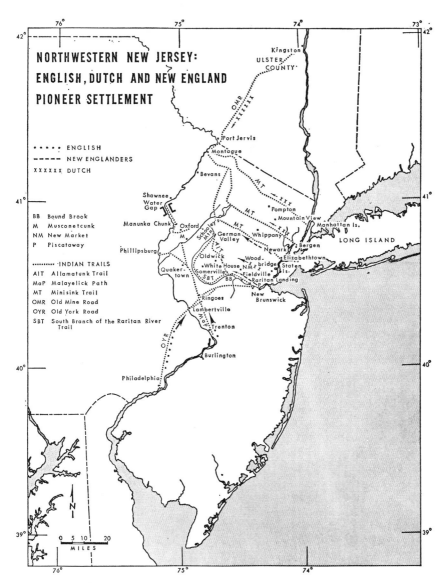

Compiled from various sources.

congregation made up of Scottish and Scotch-Irish settlers. Their church was located a short distance west of present Bloomsbury on the Musconetcong, or near Asbury, and was built of logs, probably *ca.* 1740. One source indicates this church as functioning in 1738. The same preacher served other nearby Scotch-Irish congregations at Durham, Pennsylvania, and at Greenwich [Phillipsburg?], New Jersey, in 1740. Still another Presbyterian church serving the spiritual needs of the Scotch-Irish may have been located at Mansfield Woodhouse (Washington, New Jersey) as early as 1730.

Local historians, recognizing the influence of the early Scotch-Irish settlements, have stated that the vicinity of Phillipsburg was a strong center of Scotch-Irish Presbyterians after 1735 and that the "larger and for a time controlling element [of Greenwich Township] was Scotch-Irish." [40]

That many of these Scotch-Irish may have arrived in New Jersey by way of the Old York Road from Philadelphia, and then followed trails northward into West Jersey is indicated by the Reverend William Frazer's complaining in 1768 that "the Dissenters have now got such a footing here [Amwell Township] especially Presbyterians," and that they had three places of worship within ten miles of his Episcopal church.[41]

A further Scotch-Irish increment occurred somewhat later than the original settlement because of the turbulent conditions on the Pennsylvania frontier: [42]

> The French and Indian war had an important effect on the character of the population of Warren and Northampton [Pennsylvania] counties. The population of Northampton up to that time was prevailingly Irish [Scotch-Irish]. . . . When the Indians drove out nearly all the inhabitants from the county above Easton, these fled mostly to Warren County, and many stayed here permanently.

Other Scotch-Irish continued to trickle in in later years. The Kennedy family, for example, came from the north of Ireland to Bucks County after 1730. In 1771 they moved to Greenwich Township, New Jersey, from Tinicum, Bucks County, Pennsylvania. Other Scotch-Irish settlers were still arriving in Greenwich Township from the same locality as late as 1793.

The lesser numbers of Scotch-Irish who penetrated the interior of northern New Jersey via the Raritan Valley may have traveled via the Old York Road from Philadelphia to New Brunswick or may have actually debarked at New Brunswick. They were preceded in the Raritan region by Scottish, English, Dutch, and German settlers, and this probably accounted for their small numbers. We do know that Scotch-Irish settlement did take place, since the Lutherans at Pluckemin were "bereft of their glebe through the artifices of English and Irish people who had settled around them." [43] This occurred in 1743 or 1744 and we can thus date the Scotch-Irish as being there at the time.

Unfortunately, it is extremely difficult to determine whether the early Presbyterian congregations of the region serviced by routeways northward from New Brunswick were chiefly of New England, Scottish, or Scotch-Irish derivation. At any rate, we may postulate that since Scotch-Irish were definitely in the area, they may have formed at least a portion of the congregations established. Presbyterian congregations were formed at New Brunswick in 1726; at Lebanon, Peapack, and White House in 1740; and in Fairmount, or Fox Hill, before 1746. The initial settlement of Hackettstown in the Musconetcong Valley is generally attributed to Scotch-Irish, New England, and Scottish stock. A Presbyterian congregation was established at an early date and a frame church built in 1764. This may well indicate that the Scotch-Irish joined with their fellow Presbyterians in moving northward along the Allamatunk Trail and its branches. [44]

German settlement in northern New Jersey is generally fixed at a much later date than that of other ethnic stocks such as the English, Scots, Dutch, or Scotch-Irish. Rutherfurd's statement that the Germans "came . . . late and poor," is true for most parts of the state. An exception to this rule is found in the valley of the Raritan, where scattered German settlers were to be found quite early in the eighteenth century. There is evidence to indicate that Germans may have joined the Raritan Dutch in their movement to the interior as early as 1713. These were almost certainly disgruntled remnants of the 1710 Palatine emigration to the Hudson in New York.

These early Germans, and many Dutch as well, were Lutherans. Justus Falckner, a Lutheran minister from New York City, ministered to the needs of these Lutherans on the Raritan and to other congregations as well, on the Millstone, the Hackensack, at Middlebush, and at Piscataway. In all, the Dutch and German congregations numbered a total of one hundred communicants in 1715. Between 1715 and 1720 these Dutch and German Lutherans had formed a congregation "in the Mountains near the River Raritan," the members of which were the widely dispersed residents of northern Somerset County. Between 1725 and 1730 another congregation was formed by the Lutheran inhabitants of western Hunterdon County. This indicates the rapidity of dispersal of these early Dutch and German settlers. The latter congregation had the appellation "Rockaway Lutheran Society."

The approximate centers of the dispersed Lutherans of the day may be indicated by the sites of the churches they established. The "congregation in the Mountains" built a church near present-day Pluckemin. The Rockaway Lutherans built their own church in the hamlet of Potterstown in 1731. The former was large enough to call its own minister in 1731–34, and included the "Hanover district," which referred to all of Morris County at that date and probably specifically to the scattered Lutherans of Black River north of Pottersville. Since Dutch and German speech were used both in the temporal and spiritual dealings of these congregations as late as 1735, both ethnic stocks must have been well represented.

After 1735, apparently, there came an in-migration of Germans to this general area. Most likely, Philadelphia, instead of New York City as in former days, supplied the new settlers. It is instructive to note that the early Lutheran congregations on the Raritan and its tributaries had close relations with New York City during their formative period, suggesting that a movement of Germans from that city by sea to the Raritan was involved in their origin. Their minister, Falckner, for example, who served in the second decade of the eighteenth century, was a German from New York City. Until 1743 all advice on spiritual and temporal matters was sought in New York. Thereafter, however, these congregations turned toward the German Lutherans of eastern Pennsylvania for guidance.

This change of orientation on the part of the Raritan Lutherans probably reflects a change in the source of Lutheran migration. An oft-recorded legend in New Jersey recounts the movement overland, *ca.* 1717, of Palatine Germans whose ship had been blown off its course for New York and had landed in Philadelphia instead. These people, supposedly, wished to join their brethren in New York and set out to do so overland through New Jersey, but became so enamored of the area in the vicinity of Long (German) Valley that they settled there. This, of course, is far too early a date perhaps by thirty years or more for the settlement of Germans in this area, and a movement overland at this time to hostile New York would have been highly unlikely, to say the least.

The legend, however, may well be based in fact. The Old York Road is mentioned in an early source as the actual route of the migrants. This certainly would have been the most logical overland route of that day. It is instructive to note that German settlers are recorded at Ringoes in 1721, and they surely must have come in via the Old York Road. Also, in tracing the movements of Johannes Moelich, a member of the Zion Meeting House in New Germantown (Oldwick) in 1749, we find that he remained in the vicinity of Philadelphia for ten years after debarking there and then settled on a farm between the present White House and North Branch Station, New Jersey, before 1750. It is most logical to assume that he reached his property via the Old York Road. Moelich became a member of the congregation of German Lutherans at New Germantown in 1749. New Germantown traditionally owes its settlement to an overland movement from Germantown, Pennsylvania. Again, the Old York Road is the most logical means of entry. In 1759, when Henry Muhlenberg came from Pennsylvania to preach to the Raritan Lutherans, he definitely traveled via the Old York Road.

When the Zion Lutheran church was built at New Germantown in 1749, the trustees were all German and included Moelich. Germans were certainly in the majority in the area by 1753, as the Reverend Muhlenberg preached in English, after the German service, to Dutch and English in the vicinity. The German influx is also reflected in the names of communicants of the United Societies of Zion and St. Paul's in Pluckemin in 1767. Of 111 names there is not one that is English, Irish, or Scottish, and only eight or ten are surely Dutch and not German.

Other German Lutherans were moving along the South Branch of the Raritan River and Allamatunk trails at the same time, and by 1749 another congregation, that of Fox Hill, had formed. It included residents of Fox Hill, Long (German) Valley, Spruce Run, and Schooley's Mountain.

The numbers of Germans moving into the Raritan Valley at this time may be judged by Pehr Kalm's statement in regard to New Brunswick in 1749, that "the German inhabitants have two churches, one of stone and the other of wood." [45] The descendants of these people, if not the early Germans themselves, often filtered northward over Schooley's Mountain and took up land in the valley of the Musconetcong. Some Germans settled in the environs of the valley after residence in New Brunswick.

In western New Jersey, unlike the Raritan Valley, the initial German settlers came from Philadelphia. In speaking of Warren County, New Jersey, the arrival of German settlers is often dated as beginning about 1740 and ending at about the time of the Revolution. Large numbers of Germans, however, were entering the port of Philadelphia in the second decade of the eighteenth century, and some of them began to appear in the vicinity of Ringoes as early as 1721. This would indicate a movement into New Jersey via the Old York Road at a rather early date. By 1755 Germans had penetrated the far northwestern portion of the state, as is shown by an article in the *New York Mercury* for that year: "A List of the People killed, and Houses burnt, by the Indians at the Minisinks . . . Several Palatines, and their Families, supposed to be about . . . 20. . . ." [46] There were sufficient German settlers to erect a church at Mt. Pleasant before 1760 and to build a church at Phillipsburg by 1762. German settlers in the vicinity of the Musconetcong Valley are recorded as early as 1738 "in the vicinity of Riegelsville" and "shortly after 1750" in Phillipsburg. Lists of the tenants on Sir Robert Barker's land in Alexandria Township begin to contain German names as early as 1765, with direct proof of the German origin of at least one of the families (Fine) in 1767. In 1774 an agent of Sir Robert Barker mentioned that the settlers on Barker's Pohatcong tract "are of German extraction and very Industrious." [47] Several of the names included in the account book of Greenwich Forge in the 1780's and in the Chelsea Forge journals for the same time period are also most likely of German origin. [48]

As lands became available in northwestern New Jersey in general, and in the Musconetcong Valley in particular, many additional settlers flocked in to establish farms. Comparative county population figures give some idea of the rapid increases in numbers. In 1737, Hunterdon County, which then included present Morris, Sussex, and Warren counties, boasted 5,507 inhabitants. In 1745, Hunterdon had a population of 9,151, and Morris County, which had been separated from Hunterdon in 1738, had 4,436 of its own. In 1784 Hunterdon had 18,363 inhabitants, Morris 13,416, and Sussex (including present Warren), which had been separated from Morris in 1753, had 14,187.

The rapidity of settlement in northern New Jersey was so great, especially after 1765, that the Board of Justices and Freeholders of Sussex County was forced to apply to the Provincial Legislature for funds to supply sufficient wheat to the new settlers. Settlement had outrun the local food supply. Before 1765 the situation in Sussex County had been far different. At that time it was "a frontier . . . not much improved, [having] but few inhabitants. . . ." [49] In similar fashion, Morris County also experienced rapid development, and between 1740 and 1775 "the whole county had been opened up by the actual settlers. . . . Only the roughest hills and the large lakes or little "gores" of land overlooked by the surveyor were left to the proprietors." [50]

This is not to say, however, that all localities were developed and settled equally. Unfortunately, there are no complete data on the relative density of population in northwestern New Jersey during the eighteenth century. It is indicative, however, that when taxes were assessed during the Revolutionary War in Sussex County (present Warren and Sussex), Greenwich Township, which bordered the Musconetcong to the north and extended to the Delaware, was third in total valuation of the ten townships existing in the county at that time, showing that it was a relatively well-developed township. At virtually the same time, Thomas Anburey, who traveled through Hackettstown and vicinity in 1778, lamented the fact that he had seen only the "back settlements." [51] Before the advent of the nineteenth century, only nineteen families were enumerated by Stephen Shaffer as living on or near the shores of Lake Hopatcong. [52]

After the initial occupance of the Musconetcong Valley, many subsequent population movements took place. We have already noted a continuous movement of Scotch-Irish settlers from Bucks and Northampton counties, Pennsylvania, into the region. An additional movement, probably much larger in total numbers, involved Germans from Pennsylvania. Many came in the 1780's and 1790's as land became available, especially from nearby Bucks and Northampton counties. This migration was still taking place in the first two decades of the nineteenth century. That Germans from Pennsylvania were good customers for lands available in the Musconetcong Valley can be seen in many of the letters written by James Parker to his agent John Cooley in the last decade of the eighteenth century. [53]

> I now inclose you forty advertizements for the Sale of the Lands in Greenwich and Alexandria townships *which I would have you set up chiefly in Pennsylvania* and at the different places of crossing the Delaware—and *I think you had best go out yourself into Pennsylvania as farr as you can.* I have sent you forty with my name signed to them which *I think will be best to put up in Pensylvania.* (Italics mine.)

Joshua Gilpin, in writing of the people living in the vicinity of Easton, Pennsylvania, approximately eight miles north of the mouth of the Musconetcong, in 1802, described a situation probably very much like the one obtaining in the Musconetcong Valley and much of northwestern New Jersey, when he said: [54]

> I never knew before the total want of a Language for in this respect we might quite as well have been in the middle of Germany. J. Nevins being vexed at one of the houses we called at with their speaking only a foreign tongue instead of the American giving travellers no information got to talking Spanish to them.

Other later migrations involved German families from Schooley's Mountain settling in the vicinity of Hackettstown in the early nineteenth century and families of probable New England descent continuing to enter the same area in the late eighteenth and early nineteenth centuries. [55]

Natural increase also served to swell the valley's population after

initial settlement had taken place. In 1794 Theophile Cazenove estimated the average number of children per farm family in the area as
being from five to eight. Some families were even larger. One is recorded
as having included fourteen children. As early as the last decade of the
eighteenth century, members of the younger generation began leaving
the area for the less densely settled agricultural frontier of Ohio and
central New York, thus ending the pioneer period in northwestern New
Jersey. Those farming the more marginal and worn-out farmlands joined
the exodus at this time.[56]

As could be expected, by the beginning of the nineteenth century the
population of the Musconetcong Valley was quite mixed as to cultural
traditions and ethnic stock. In general, the western portion of the valley
was composed of people of German, Scotch-Irish, English, and Dutch
origin, probably in that order. The middle portion of the valley, center-
ing at Hackettstown, was composed of New England, Scotch-Irish, German, and Dutch stock, and the vicinity of Lake Hopatcong by New
Englanders and a few Dutch families.

The naming of physiographic features in and near the Musconetcong
Valley reflects the English origin of most of the earliest settlers. Uplands
are labeled "hills" and "mountains," both terms of English origin. The
two portions of Lake Hopatcong, which existed prior to impoundment
in the nineteenth century, were known as the "Great Pond," and the
"Little Pond." [57] The term "pond" is of English origin, and is especially
used in New England, from where many of the first settlers of the area
north of the terminal moraine had come.

The Musconetcong itself is often termed a river or a creek in early
advertisements. Both terms are of English origin. A problem presents
itself, however, in the name applied to the chief affluent of the Musconetcong, Lubber's Run. One writer has proposed that it "derived its name
from some early settler whose name was Lubbert, a name quite common
in the early records of the Dutch." [58] The Dutch, however, arrived
later in the area than did New Englanders, and Lubbert is not a family
name that is known in the area. In 1769 the term "Lubbers" Run was
in use, as is shown on the Faden map (Appendix I). Perhaps this was in
error, but "Lubber's" seems to have been the spelling used since that
time. Also of interest is the fact that the term "run" as used to designate
small streams, has been attributed to Scottish or Scotch-Irish influence.
The term is comparatively rare in New Jersey, and the settlers of the
region involved were not of Scotch-Irish derivation. However, in eight-
eenth- and early nineteenth-century surveyors' notes dealing with the
area, the term "run" is often applied to very small streams, despite the
diverse ethnic origins of the surveyors.[59]

CHAPTER 4

Pioneer Agriculture

Ca. 1720—*Ca.* 1800

With the exception of a few scattered hunters and trappers who may have preceded pioneer agriculturists into some portions of the Musconetcong drainage system, the first settlers were in most cases subsistence farmers. It has been stated, and often repeated, that in much of the New Jersey Highlands "the pioneers . . . were rather manufacturers than agriculturists," and that "the forge was uniformly the precursor of the farm. . . ." [1] Although this may be true for many northeastern Highlands localities, it certainly is not true for most of the limestone-floored valley of the Musconetcong. The earliest ironworking establishment founded in the Musconetcong Valley was that at Changewater, built *ca.* 1741. It has been established in the previous chapter that agricultural land use in the southwestern portion of the valley probably preceded the erection of the forge at Changewater by two decades. The traditional and inferred dates of agricultural settlement elsewhere in the valley are contemporaneous with or slightly earlier than the known dates of the erection of ironworks.

One of the best examples of the contemporaneity between the establishment of ironworks and of pioneer farms is that to be found in the vicinity of original Lake Hopatcong, which in the eighteenth century consisted of two smaller lakes. The area is rugged and the soils much poorer for agriculture than those found southwest of the Wisconsin terminal moraine. A forge was erected *ca.* 1760 at the outlet of the lake, yet in 1759 a survey of a parcel of land adjoining the larger (southern) of the two lakes included the "Dwelling House that was formerly Stown [?] Bishops" [2] as a bound. There is no evidence to indicate that Bishop was an agriculturist. Tradition has it that the area was first settled by hunters and trappers, and Bishop may have been one of these. There is,

53

however, definite proof of agricultural settlement before 1762. In that year, the executors of George Eyre's estate offered for sale [3]

> a valuable Tract of Land, lying in the Township of Roxbury, in Morris County, West New Jersey, at the Head of Muskennecunk River, adjoining a certain Pond, called the Little Pond [the northern lake] containing about 943 Acres, the greatest part of which is extraordinarily well timbered, and about 90 Acres of this Tract is cleared, and under good Fence, with a good Log House on it. . . .

Thus, even in this rocky, glaciated area, agricultural occupance was at least contemporaneous with ironworking.

The most arduous task facing the majority of pioneer agriculturists besides housing their families, which will be treated in the following chapter, was clearing and improving the land. Many of the earliest settlers chose to settle properties where "meadows," existing mainly because of Indian burning, were located. Others settled in Indian old fields. In both cases the necessity for immediate forest clearance was obviated and this, as will be seen, was a definite advantage at the time of earliest settlement.

The later pioners were not quite so fortunate. Most of the northwestern portion of the state was forested and later settlers had to clear away the trees for their initial subsistence plot. Although the earliest New England and Dutch immigrants in East Jersey preferred to clean-cut their new lands, later pioneers in the northwestern portion of the state were a bit more casual and followed methods that had possibly been suggested by aboriginal precedent.[4] If friendly neighbors were available, the pioneers [5]

> would proceed to the forest with their axes and grubbing hoes and set to work felling the smaller trees and cutting them up for rails and firewood, and girdling the larger ones to prevent the circulation of the sap, thus causing their death, and these after a year or two were to be cut down and converted into fence rails and firewood. With the grubbing hoe the small saplings and under brush were taken out by the roots, cut up, and the brush piled into heaps, and when dry, burned; the ashes of which helped to fertilize the virgin soil.

Although the foregoing passage refers to the practice of German settlers in Sussex County, elsewhere in the state pioneers of other origins used the same general methods. Within four or five years after clearance, the stumps that dotted the landscape would have decayed to a point where they could be beaten to pieces and plowed under.

Gradual improvements in transportation allowed a shift from what had been primarily subsistence agriculture to the production of commercial grain crops. In many cases the local millers acted as middlemen and forwarded grain to market in manufactured or raw form. Since mills were being established in the area as early as 1737, commercial agriculture in the Musconetcong Valley was probably in development before 1750. At any rate, the advertisement of a mill at Hackettstown in 1777, including a pair of stones for "merchant" work, indicates that a considerable trade in flour had developed by that date. The establishment of ironworking enterprises in the valley as early as the fifth decade of the eighteenth century also served to stimulate commercial agricultural production. In 1763 a proprietor advertised lands in the "Center of the County of Sussex" and stated that "on Account of the great Number of People employ'd at the Iron Works in that Neighbourhood, there is generally as good a Market for Grain, and other Produce as at New-York." [6] Elsewhere in the glaciated Highlands, agriculture was also stimulated by the iron industry.

The produce of pioneer farms in the Musconetcong Valley, as well as in all of northwestern New Jersey, varied quite considerably from the period of initial occupation to the period of commercial farming. In general, at first, because of the small amount of cleared land and the poorly developed transportation network, emphasis was on subsistence crops such as buckwheat, rye, and flax, and also on freely roaming livestock. Later, with the extension of cleared land and improvements in transportation, the cash cropping of grains such as wheat and rye became the major economic activity of most pioneer agriculturists.

The first subsistence crop was planted before the stumps had decayed. The newly cleared earth was disturbed by drawing a knotty log over its surface, and buckwheat was broadcast and then harrowed in with heavy brush. Sowing took place in July, harvest in September. When ripe, the stalks of this first crop were cut with sickles; threshed on ground made hard by horses hoofs, by driving the horses again over the grain; and then winnowed by "a good stiff breeze." [7]

Buckwheat had several distinct advantages as an initial crop. It was easily grown, requiring a minimum of effort, equipment, and farming skill, yet yielded extremely well on newly cleared land. Also, buckwheat was a much preferred grain, especially among the English. Kalm found that buckwheat cakes and puddings were in wide use throughout New Jersey in the middle of the eighteenth century. An additional use for the crop lay in its being a valuable feed for the animals kept by the farmer, especially during the winter. Chickens and hogs, apparently, were especially fond of buckwheat and throve on it.

Buckwheat remained important throughout the eighteenth century. Local stores in the Musconetcong Valley bought and sold it frequently.

It was not so much a commercial crop as wheat and rye, since trading took place mostly on a local level where buckwheat's value as a poultry and swine feed could be realized and where buckwheat cakes were appreciated by the settlers. Buckwheat also furnished excellent pasture for bees, which were quite common throughout the state. During the 1780's, on occasion, a prudent tenant could pay his rent with the produce of his hives—honey, mead, and beeswax.[8]

Although wheat became the most important cash crop later in the eighteenth century, rye was probably more important during the first days of commercial farming in many areas, and even later in the eighteenth century remained a strong competitor of wheat. Some ethnic groups, such as the Swedes in southern New Jersey and the Germans generally in Pennsylvania, grew rye as a preferred grain, especially for bread flour.[9] Rye was often the first of the major grains to be grown by settlers of other ethnic affiliations in northern New Jersey because it did better than wheat on new ground and yielded better on poor soils. In many localities, where the first grain crops "all grew to straw," rye could be used for thatching. Rye remained a competitor of wheat in later days, as local store accounts testify in the Musconetcong Valley. Also, for several years after 1786, crop losses caused by the Hessian fly encouraged farmers to substitute rye for their usual sowings of wheat.[10]

In most cases, however, after initial occupation, clearance, and cultivation had taken place, the most important cash crop in the Musconetcong drainage system was wheat, as, indeed, was the case generally in the Middle Colonies during the eighteenth century. This was due to the fact that wheat was a preferred crop, especially among the British and Dutch, and also could readily be sold, in either finished or raw form, at first in the West Indies and southern planter colonies, and later in New England.

The wheat and rye grown in New Jersey in the eighteenth century was almost invariably sown in the fall and harvested in the spring. Moderate snowfalls in winter served to shield the crop from severe temperatures, and winter wheat and rye could be harvested before the occasional killing droughts of the summer season.

In the Musconetcong Valley, wheat must have been the leading crop in acreage during the eighteenth century. The records of local merchants contain far more entries of wheat credited to farmers' accounts than of any other farm product.[11] Also, when James Parker offered Samuel Barker's extensive property in Alexandria Township for sale in 1790, he advertised it as being located "in the Heart of a fine wheat Country. . . ."[12]

Maize, or Indian corn, was of much less importance than the two major grain crops, wheat and rye, possibly because the initial methods of cultivating it were more laborious than those required for wheat or rye. Kalm, writing in 1748, described the cultivation of maize in southwestern New Jersey: "The corn is planted as usual in squares, in little hills so that there is a space of five feet and six inches between each hill, in both directions." [13] Similar methods were followed by James Parker on his estate in Hunterdon County in 1778, and Schmidt, drawing on other sources, found that much the same practice existed for many years in Hunterdon. Since the seeds of wheat, rye, and other small grains of European origin could be simply raked in by hand or scratched in with a simple harrow, maize cultivation was more difficult. An additional factor discouraging cultivation of corn during the pioneer phase of settlement in northwestern New Jersey may have been the prevailing belief that the area was too cold for Indian corn to ripen. As late as 1784 maize was grown in Hunterdon County for sale in Sussex County.[14] An advertisement in 1779, of property lying six miles northwest of Hackettstown, includes the statement that the "meadow is good for hemp, rie [*sic*], indian corn, &c." [15] Local stores were buying maize on many occasions in the 1780's, perhaps indicating that the crop was being grown locally at the time.

Barley and oats, although of widespread secondary importance during the eighteenth century in the state, apparently were but seldom grown in the Musconetcong Valley, according to early store accounts. One entry of "Oats" has been encountered [16] but no reference to barley has been found. Oats had a great value as a horse feed, and may have been grown for use on the farm without being traded locally, and barley was used primarily for beer and whiskey, which were apparently not produced in quantity during the eighteenth century in the Musconetcong Valley.

Flax was one of the initial crops planted in northwestern New Jersey. Its cultivation was almost universal among pioneers, since clothing was a necessity, and wool was difficult to obtain locally both, no doubt, because of a lack of money on the part of the pioneer, and because of the depredations of wolves in days of earliest settlement. Flax also was easy to cultivate and grew extremely well on newly cleared land. An estimated one acre or so would serve to supply the average family with clothing for an entire year. Although flax was most likely a universal crop among pioneer agriculturists, the plots remained small, through time, because backbreaking labor was necessary in harvesting and processing enough linen just for family use. Flax maintained an important position throughout the eighteenth century despite its limited acreage. The Reverend Uzal Ogden, an early missionary, reported in 1771 to the Society for the Propagation of the Gospel in Foreign Parts, that "Flax-seed" was one of the most important products of Sussex County. "Linen" and "tow" are mentioned occasionally in Musconetcong Valley store accounts, and one entry refers to a charge of "Flax ground" [17] in 1781, perhaps indicating the local production of linseed oil. Linseed oil was quite valuable for its use in paints and much was exported through the port of New York during the eighteenth century. Linen and tow (tow being the coarse fibers of flax before spinning) were produced throughout the state in the eighteenth century to answer the local demand for clothing.[18]

The appearance of orchards also marked a further development in agriculture after subsistence had been attained. The earliest fruit trees planted in almost every case were apple trees. Casper Schaeffer planted an apple orchard within a few years after he settled at Stillwater in the 1740's. Eighteenth-century advertisements of property in the vicinity of the Musconetcong Valley indicate that apple and other orchards were almost universal, and were established during the days of earliest settlement. Surviving agreements between tenants residing on the Barker tract in the latter days of the eighteenth century and James Parker, reflect the early importance of fruit trees. One tenant in 1793 agreed to "plant out in some convenient place one hundred thrifty apple trees and keep up the number and also suffer not creatures to damage them." [19] In southern Hunterdon County orchards were thought small unless they occupied at least nine or ten acres. The trees were planted in rows about six or seven yards apart, to allow convenient tillage with a plow, and many trees were placed by the side of the road for the refreshment of travelers. Perhaps the same conditions obtained in the Musconetcong Valley during the waning days of the eighteenth century.

The early importance of apples in the farm economy stemmed from the fact that New Jersey cider became famed throughout the colonies at an early date. Kalm, writing in 1749, lavishly praised the beverage. "The *best cider* in America is said to be made in New Jersey and about New York, hence this cider is preferred to any other. I have scarcely tasted any better cider than that from New Jersey." [20] Cazenove, writing in 1794, mentioned the existence of many apple orchards in northern Morris County. According to him, sixty-five to seventy trees could be planted per acre and would yield two hundred and fifty bushels of apples.[21]

As early as 1773, stills began to be imported from England into Morris County for the production of applejack or "Jersey lightning." One acre planted to apple trees would ultimately yield 125 gallons of spirits, which could be sold for seventy-five cents per gallon in 1794. This was a good return, as the wages of a laborer engaged during the harvest season averaged only seventy-five cents per day. Apples apparently were also valued for eating, as relatively small amounts are occasionally mentioned in early store accounts in the Musconetcong Valley. In the eighteenth century oven-dried apples were considered a delicacy, and many were exported to the West Indies in this form.[22] It may be that this trade also influenced the establishment of large apple orchards in northern New Jersey.

Other fruits besides apples were undoubtedly grown in the area, as New Jersey was well known for the variety and quality of its fruits during colonial days. Peaches, cherries, and plums were grown throughout the state.

Vegetable gardens made their appearance at an early date. Many advertisements list "paled" gardens as distinct assets to the farmstead. Vegetables produced by these gardens were a welcome addition to the family larder. Kitchen gardening was mainly women's work. An eighteenth-century writer noted that the "Wives and Daughters of the Farmers and poorer Inhabitants . . . make good Gardens of a variety of good Vegetables which is half the support of their Families. . . ."[23] Although this was said of East Jersey, the more developed portions of the western part of the state revealed a similar picture as reflected in the eighteenth-century land advertisements.

Vegetables mentioned in store accounts during the eighteenth century in the Musconetcong Valley included potatoes, turnips, and cabbages. These were common garden crops during this period in most of the state. Although most vegetables probably did not have particular affiliations with certain ethnic groups, cabbages did. The sauerkraut of the German settler and the *Kohl-salat* of the Dutchman necessitated large numbers of cabbages in the gardens of these settlers.

Other garden vegetables, most likely present in individual eighteenth-century garden plots, but not available through local merchants, perhaps because they kept poorly, were asparagus, cauliflower, parsnips, carrots, onions, cucumbers, pumpkins, watermelons, muskmelons, squashes, beans, radishes, peas, beets, spinach, parsley, leeks, and endive and other salads.[24]

Although the pioneer was, for the most part, a farmer, his chances of successfully growing and marketing a cash crop were exceedingly small. His initial clearing was too small, the demands on his time too great, and the means of transportation available to him in early days too primitive and costly to allow him to carry on agriculture much in advance of the subsistence level. Self-sustaining though pioneer agriculture was, however, certain items as, for example, salt, firearms, and gunpowder, were needed from the outside. A product was needed, therefore, that would require relatively little labor or investment but that would yield the cash or exchange value necessary to obtain goods not available locally.

The solution to this problem was an early emphasis on livestock. Cattle, horses, and hogs required little care, yielded a relatively high return, and could be driven or even ridden, by way of the primitive Indian paths, to market. The importance of livestock in the days of early settlement is reflected in the early tax records, in which a man's holdings in livestock are listed often to the exclusion of any mention of land ownership. The true wealth, especially of the squatter or tenant, lay in his livestock. Great numbers of livestock were to be found in the Musconetcong Valley in early days, as is shown by an advertisement in 1766, which, in listing the advantages of a certain tanyard, mentioned that it was "situate on the great road leading through the county to Hacket's, from whence a great quantity of hides may be had yearly. . . ." [25] Since "Halketstown" appears as a misnomer on a map as early as 1769 (Appendix I), "Hacket's" most likely referred to the environs of present Hackettstown.

The importance of livestock also served to magnify the importance of the "meadows" and old fields so sought after by the early surveyors and settlers. The advantages here were relative, however, as the forests, because of their open nature in early days, also furnished abundant native American grasses for livestock. This use of wooded land was so important to the early settlers that they would burn the woods every spring to remove the overburden of several inches of fallen leaves, so that the native grasses would be freed for immediate growth. Kalm spoke unfavorably of this practice in eastern Pennsylvania, where it was so widespread that the state government tried unsuccessfully to get the settlers to abandon the custom.[26] Undoubtedly, the practice of spring burning was widespread in New Jersey at the same time, since the *New York Journal* in 1768 stated: [27]

> The cold dry weather we have lately had, has been attended with bad Consequences to many in the Country, by the Loss of Cattle, &c. but the usual Practice of burning of Woods and Meadows in the Spring, has been more so than usual; for we are assured, that near Mount Holly in Burlington County, [New Jersey] three Dwelling-Houses, and much Fencing have been destroyed by Fire on Wednesday last, besides other great Damages; And in the Event has been detrimental to those who would probably have been out of the Reach of such Fires otherways.

The keeping of livestock in New Jersey in early days was strongly influenced by the traditionally casual practices of the English, who prevailed numerically in most areas. Pehr Kalm, in 1749, noted that the Swedes, who had originally built barns for their cattle, had become completely acculturated to the English practice, which was to let the cattle roam free, with little or no shelter even during the winter. Hogs, and to some extent horses also, were allowed to wander almost at will at the time of first settlement.[28]

It is probable that the early emphasis on livestock encouraged some settlers to acquire lands that were marginal for agricultural purposes, but which, with little labor, could serve to support cattle and hogs. The advertisement of a property near Andover, north and east of the Wisconsin terminal moraine, in 1773, indicates that this may well have been the case.[29]

> Besides the meadows above mentioned, it contains a considerable quantity of good swamp, which may be easily cleared and brought into grass; so that upon the whole there are few (if any) lands in that part of the country better calculated for raising stock. The advantages of raising hogs thereon are also very considerable, on account of the great quantity of oak timber and acorns on it and many thousands of acres of unimproved land, contiguous thereto afford, where they may be fattened with little or no expense to the owner. . . .

In Jefferson Township, where agricultural clearing was minimal because of arid rocky soils, the first town meeting, on April 9, 1804, fixed a reward of "two shillings per head on cattle drove into town and not owned by the inhabitants thereof. . . ."[30] Thus, in areas north of the Wisconsin terminal moraine, where clearing was less extensive and farming more marginal, the existence of loose stock lasted well into the nineteenth century.

The lack of supervision given livestock at the time of pioneer occupance created several problems. It was not at all unusual for animals to wander off and perhaps cause damage to another's crops. The early settlers coped with this problem in several ways. First, a property right was established by notching the ears of cattle and hogs in a distinctive manner, and by notching the ears of, or branding horses. The distinctive earmark and brands of the owners would be duly registered in the township's records and any strays originating outside the township were impounded until the owner appeared, who was required to pay all charges arising from any damages caused by his animal, and for the cost of keeping the animal at the township pound. The records of Bethlehem Township are especially interesting in this connection. An entry on November 20, 1760, is typical. One Bairfoot Brundson apprehended a stray bull and the animal was described as being of a "dun colour, supposed to Be marked in the Near ear with a half Crop and half penny Aged three years. . . ." Other earmarks, registered by residents of the township in 1762, were listed as follows: [31]

> Mary Clifford's ear-mark is a crop off the off ear and a slit in the near ear. Joseph Beaver's ear-mark is a crop off the near ear. Peter Case's ear mark is a half-penny under each ear and a slit in the near ear. Robert Biggers' ear-mark is a 'croop of the off ear, and a nick in the croop and a nick in the fore part of the near ear near his head.' James Biggers' ear-mark is a 'croop off the near ear, and a swallow fork in the off ear, and a half-penny in the fore part of the near ear.' John Beaver's ear-mark brought from old book, record there in the year 1753; his mark is a half penny under side each ear, and a slit in each ear top the ear.

Despite the emphasis on grain production, livestock retained an important economic position throughout the latter part of the eighteenth century. Oxen were of special importance once commercial agriculture began. Of a more steady nature and stronger than horses, oxen were less likely to break plows and harness on the imperfectly cleared fields of the first days of commercial crop production. In the Musconetcong Valley and vicinity, oxen were being used at an early date. A contract dating from 1754 mentions the purchase of yoked oxen and a farm cart.[32] After fields had been brought under more thorough cultivation, horses began to replace oxen as draft animals. This was because of the greater speed of the horse, which could be used for relatively rapid transport, as well as for farm work.[33] By 1786 a knowledgeable Jerseyan was able to state that "unfortunately few Oxen are used for Draught except in Morris and Essex Counties, which are a great Advantage to them, and deserves to be imitated."[34]

Despite the waning interest in oxen, cattle remained important in the local economy. Cattle and butter were major products of Sussex County in 1771, reaching the Philadelphia and New York markets in large quantities in that year.[35] Cowhides, calfskins, beef, veal, and butter are mentioned frequently in the accounts of stores in the Musconetcong Valley during the 1780's. As late as 1794, Theophile Cazenove remarked that farmers in the vicinity of the Musconetcong Valley "buy as much land around here as they can, not so much for cultivation as to . . . send their cattle and horses to pasture in the uncultivated woods."[36] This may have been the result of the presence of numbers of German settlers, as "a noticeable feature in a German settlement was a fondness for cattle. . . ."[37]

Cattle in use in New Jersey during the eighteenth century were a mixture of Dutch and the more hardy English stocks. In 1786, Rutherfurd stated that New Jersey cattle were smaller than those of Rhode Island or Connecticut, "and the Cows weigh from four to six hundred Weight the Quarter. . . ." [38]

As has been mentioned, horses began to take over the draught functions of oxen at an early date, and horse breeding aroused great interest because of the prestige value of owning a good animal. Horses in use on most farms in the eighteenth century were of medium size, suitable for both farm work and riding.

Although not raised at the time of first land clearing, because of wolves, sheep rapidly became an important feature of many farms in the Musconetcong Valley. Mutton was a common item credited to the accounts of farmers in local stores during the 1780's. New Jersey became famous for its wool a few years before the onset of the Revolution and Hunterdon County alone had approximately twenty thousand head of sheep at that time. It is interesting to note that "wool" or "mutton" is omitted from a list of the leading products of Sussex County in 1771, perhaps because of the frontier conditions still prevailing at that time.[39] Despite the relatively large numbers of sheep found in the state before the Revolution, one writer lamented the fact that "we keep so few Sheep, owing to our not providing Winter and Spring Food for them, otherwise nothing more profitable." [40]

Eighteenth-century sheep in New Jersey were the result of crossing Swedish, Dutch, and English stocks, with characteristics of the latter, larger breeds predominating.

Of all the livestock kept by farmers in the eighteenth century, swine were probably the most profitable. In 1786 Rutherfurd stated that "I have known a sow to cost four Dollars and within the Year she and her Broods have amounted in Value to eighty-two Dollars, with very ordinary keeping." [41] "Hams" are mentioned as one of the important products of Sussex County in 1771,[42] and local store accounts in the Musconetcong Valley list credits for *fresh* pork quite frequently.

Hogs were allowed to run about almost at will in many cases and subsisted on the abundant mast of the forest. When confined they were fed maize and buckwheat and allowed to run about the orchard to eat the fallen fruit. During the winter hogs fared rather poorly. They were kept in small enclosures, fully exposed to the cold weather. Occasionally, pig drovers would pass through the back settlements, on their way to market, and purchase hogs from the farmers.

Eighteenth-century hogs were mostly descendants of English stock, and were slaughtered at an age of from twelve to eighteen months, by which time, if well kept, they weighed at least two hundred pounds. The hogs running about in the forest rapidly assumed the "roachback" or "razorback" form: narrow body, long snout, arched back, and large bones.[43]

Of great importance, but little mentioned in early sources, were the domestic fowls. Of these, chickens were the most important. Chickens were allowed to run about the farmstead at will, perching in nearby trees or in the orchard at night. An occasional "poultry house" was built by wealthy farmers in more heavily settled areas,[44] but farmsteads in northwestern New Jersey apparently did not possess such specialized structures, as references to them are totally lacking. At the Schaeffer farm in Stillwater, chickens were commonly kept in coops built on the lower floor of the barn during the winter season. This practice may have been followed elsewhere, especially where bank barns were in use.

The chickens found in New Jersey during the eighteenth century left much to be desired. Only in the mid-nineteenth century was the stock improved by crossing with imported fowls.

Another domestic fowl of some importance was the goose. The Greenwich Forge store bought thirteen geese from a farmer in 1780, indicating their presence in the environs of the Musconetcong Valley at that time. Geese were useful for both their meat and their feathers, which were used for bedding. At Stillwater they were large and of a gray color, but varied considerably elsewhere. Geese were also allowed to roam freely about the farmstead but were restrained from damaging field crops by three or four sticks, fastened crosswise about their necks, which prevented them from creeping through the casual fencing of the day.

In many localities in northwestern New Jersey turkeys were raised. They were of a smaller size than the wild stock found at the time and were a much preferred food among the farmers. Their origin in this region is obscure. Other commonly kept fowls in northwestern New Jersey included ducks, pigeons, and guinea fowls.[45]

Although the pasturing of herbivorous stock in local woodlands persisted well after initial occupation of the Musconetcong Valley had taken place, the establishment of permanent pastures with European grasses began at an early date. Soon after first settlement, settlers noted the decline of native annual grasses, caused, no doubt, by overgrazing, especially before the plants produced seeds for the following year. In many areas, perennial English grasses had appeared during the seventeenth century, probably introduced accidentally, and had begun to force out the native grasses. "English grasses" appeared before 1770 in the Musconetcong Valley. These most likely included timothy and red clover.[46]

European travelers in the Middle Colonies, as well as elsewhere in North America, were generally unimpressed by the agricultural practices of the average farmer. Pehr Kalm, an especially competent observer who had visited wide areas in western New Jersey and eastern Pennsylvania, indicated that a lack of sound agricultural practices was not the exclusive trait of any single nationality or ethnic group.[47]

Here . . . one can travel several days and learn almost nothing about land, neither from the English, nor from the Swedes, Germans, Dutch and French; except that from their gross mistakes and carelessness of the future, one finds opportunities every day of making all sorts of observations, and of growing wise by their mistakes. In a word, the grain fields, the meadows, the forests, the cattle, etc. are treated with equal carelessness. . . .

One of the poorest practices, insofar as pioneer agriculture was concerned, was the rotation of land instead of crops. It was customary to crop the land continuously after clearance without fertilization until it was exhausted, then turn it into pasture for cattle or abandon it, and clear yet another plot. This casual practice, as well as many others, differentiated the easygoing New Jersey farmer from his European contemporaries and ancestors. Land was easily obtained; labor was dear.

Especially ruinous in their agricultural practices were the squatters, who made up a large proportion of the early settlers in the Musconetcong drainage system. Sir Robert Barker, owner of a 7,308-acre estate in northern Alexandria Township, Hunterdon County, bounding on the Delaware and Musconetcong rivers, received a letter from his agent, John Emley, in 1764, complaining of settlement on the tract by squatters. In 1765 another of Barker's agents reported on the lack of improvements on the property. "We found the Houses in a miserable situation and very few Barns that were fit to preserve their grain or shelter their cattle . . . the fences in very bad repair. . . ." A later report by the same agent indicates the ruinous land use of the forty families of squatters residing on the tract in 1764.[48]

[The squatters,] from the uncertainty of their tenure had no object in view beside getting whatever they could by constant ploughing where they had any prospect of reaping and by cutting down the Timber to convert it into Charcoal for the two Neighbouring Forges—had they not been restrained the Bulk of the Timber would have been destroyed and the bare hills naturally unfit for cultivation would only have remained at this day. . . .

These practices were probably typical for squatters in that day.

Barker, cognizant of the troubles other landholders had had with squatters in the same general area, wrote his agents to persuade the squatters to become tenants. "My desire is that you may use your best endeavour, by gentle and persuasive means, to get the livers on the estate to come under lease for one year or, at most, three." [49] His agents, William McAdam and the aforementioned John Emley, then approached the settlers individually and had good success, in most cases, in persuading them to sign leases. These two agents later reported to Barker that they "used every means that might tend to promote peace and Industry among our new tenants, who still retained doubts concerning our Title. . . ." Their efforts, however, were not made without some difficulty.

> [Resistance to coming under lease was] . . . supported by the Art and malevolence of that Firebrand, Mary Gamman who was now presecuting [*sic*] Mr. Thos. Richie for Trespass which he had made on her on our Acct. by turning her out of her House by Force—In this distress we found it necessary to assist to endeavour to get her away for our own Interest which was effected with considerable Expense.

After the squatters had been persuaded to accept leases, and were impressed with the activity of Barker's agents, there was a general improvement in their land use and in the appearance of the farms and farmsteads. A similar problem on a tract owned by Barker a few miles north, in the vicinity of present Phillipsburg, was solved in a similar way. The tenants there were "of German extraction and very Industrious," and when sure of their tenure repaired their houses and barns and did not cultivate so ruinously as before.

In later years landowners attempted to assure suitable use of their properties on the part of tenants by carefully stipulating what should and should not be done with the property in a lease which was signed by the tenant. In 1790, after James Parker had taken over the ownership of Barker's large Alexandria tract, a tenant promised the following: [50]

> to cut no green Timber but for the use of the Premises: not to cut any green Timber or Wood for Fire-Wood while there is dry to be had on the Premises; not to plow any Part of the Premises, more than once in four years for winter grain and that he will plow for the present year the field or fields that come next in course at the Rate that he will lay the fences that were division fences between him and the neighbouring Farms on the Division lines as they are now run out and bounded.

Additional conditions imposed in some indentures included plowing winter grain once in three years and keeping a meadow "properly enclosed." Constant vigilance was required to make the tenants live up to their part of the agreement. Especially difficult to control was timber thievery, which was prevalent in most of northern New Jersey. In 1789 James Parker found much of his tract "very bare of Timber." [51]

That difficulties with tenants and poor use of the land on their part were the rule rather than an exception is seen in the fact that, as mentioned before, landowners sold out in Sussex County before "the virgin soil of their respective tracts should become completely exhausted. . . ."

Farm management among freeholders was not far different from that of the tenants and squatters. In 1794, Cazenove noted that farmers in the Musconetcong Valley, who by this date were mostly freeholders, used "little manure." Although lime was known to be a suitable fertilizer in the eighteenth century and "a good convenience for burning lime to manure the land" [52] was advertised as being on the Squire's Point Forge property in 1773, the practice of burning lime for fertilizer does not seem to have been widespread in the area before the early years of the nineteenth century, after the passing of the pioneer period. It is no wonder, then, that Cazenove wrote of a farmer's land in Long Valley as being "overworked and cannot produce any more." The use of animal manures also was not widely followed.

In the last years of the eighteenth century, many farmers began to follow the practice of crop rotation. The systems varied according to the individual farmer and his location, but in general involved a four-year and four-field system in which a summer grain would be grown the first year, a winter grain the second, grass the third, and in the fourth year the field would lie fallow. James Parker's leases indicate that he required this system on the part of many of his tenants in 1790. Practices in East Jersey at the same time were similar. Planting occurred in the spring and harvest in the fall during the first year. The crops grown in this way included maize, oats, flax, and buckwheat. The field lay fallow during the second year. In the third year a winter grain, wheat or rye, was grown, and in the fourth year the field was seeded in grass. [53]

It is instructive to note the contrasts in land use, productivity, and value between the limestone-floored valley of the Musconetcong southwest of the terminal moraine, and similar land in the German area of Pennsylvania in 1794. In that year the average per acre yield in the Musconetcong Valley was ten bushels of wheat, twenty of maize, or fifteen of buckwheat. In the vicinity of Allentown, Pennsylvania, an area heavily inhabited by Germans, twelve to eighteen bushels of wheat were harvested per acre, forty bushels of maize, and twenty to twenty-eight of buckwheat. A four-year rotation was the rule. Wheat was grown the first year; oats, maize, or buckwheat the second; clover the third; and clover (apparently used as a green manure) the fourth year. Lime was universally used as a fertilizer, and forty bushels per acre were applied.

The more sophisticated land use of the Pennsylvania-German farmer was reflected in land values. A two-hundred-acre farm in the Musconetcong Valley brought a maximum of £800 in 1794. A similar acreage near Allentown would bring at least £2,000 and perhaps as much as £3,000, in the same year.⁵⁴ The difference in land values between the Musconetcong Valley and similar property in eastern Pennsylvania largely reflected the fact that the German agriculturists were especially able, and as *freeholders,* were very industrious. Joshua Gilpin, writing in 1802 of the area lying about Easton, Pennsylvania, only a few miles north of the mouth of the Musconetcong, indicated the success of German farmers. "Many farmers of our own country [i.e., those of English stock] would lay by nothing where these [Germans] collect handsome estates. . . ." ⁵⁵ In many locations in Pennsylvania the Germans arrived late, but prospered where the others had worn out their lands. In 1794, Cazenove noted that "8 miles from here [Bethlehem, Pennsylvania] is the Irish [Scotch-Irish] settlement, where the Irish came in 1740, while the Moravians settled at Bethlehem; but the Irish became poor and their places have been gradually filled by Germans who are thriving there." ⁵⁶ As we have already seen, in the later years of the eighteenth century there occurred a gradual influx of Pennsylvania-Germans into the worked-out, cheaper lands available in West Jersey.

Farm acreages in West Jersey tended to be larger than in the eastern portion of the state. In northeastern New Jersey the size of the earliest grants was normally between one hundred and two hundred acres. In West Jersey, grants of two hundred to five hundred acres were not rare. The Hunterdon County tax roll of 1722 indicates that the most typical size at that time was two hundred acres. A list of the tenants and the acreages that they leased on the Barker Alexandria Township property, which antedates 1776, indicates that of twenty-nine individual parcels, eighteen were from two to three hundred acres, two from three to four hundred acres, one slightly over four hundred acres, and only eight were from one to two hundred acres in size.⁵⁷ As the property was said to have forty families of squatters resident in 1764, and as Barker desired the property to be used wisely, the two hundred or more acre size may have been considered the ideal for that time. In 1794, when Theophile Cazenove traveled across the valley of the Musconetcong in the vicinity of present Penwell, he indicated that the typical farm acreage was two hundred acres.

Farming tools in use during most of the eighteenth century in northwestern New Jersey were not as primitive as in many areas of pioneer occupation. The nearness of sources of supply made it possible for most farmers to have an inventory of well-made tools. The well-equipped farmer possessed iron-toothed harrows, plows, plow tackling, scythes, hoes, spades, and forks. Plows had points or shares of iron, and moldboards almost entirely of wood. Harrows were triangular, with heavy wooden frames. Cradles were used in harvesting before 1740 in Hunterdon County, and by 1750 in Sussex County. Flails were used for threshing, or occasionally, as with buckwheat, horses trod out the grain. Fans composed of willow rods were used to clean grain before 1750 but after that date the fanning mill came into use.[58]

The ubiquity of loose stock during the days of first settlement caused fencing to have an early importance among the pioneers. In northwestern New Jersey, as was the case elsewhere in the colonies, fences were erected rather to keep stock out than in. The first fencing used in the Musconetcong drainage system was probably made out of the stumps of trees, as was the case in nearby Bucks County, Pennsylvania. The uprooted stumps were rolled together, roots outward. The use of this crude type of fencing lasted only a short while. The fence most in use after substantial clearing had taken place, and the pioneer turned seriously to the erection of fencing, was the snake or worm fence. This became an integral part of rural landscapes throughout the area and lasted well into the nineteenth century.

Worm fences were built of rails approximately ten feet long. These rails were piled one on top of another and interlocked with other rails at either end at an angle of approximately sixty degrees. Although the rails were cut about ten feet long, the need to zigzag the panels of the fence so that they would interlock, shortened the actual linear distance enclosed by a panel to seven or eight feet. These fences were about four feet high, which generally required eight rails. The appellation "worm" or "snake" applied to the fencing came as a result of its distinctive sinuous course over the landscape. (See illustration section.)

An early improvement of the worm fence was the stake-and-rider fence. This was developed because of the ease with which cattle could push over the rails of an ordinary worm fence. The stake-and-rider fence solved this problem by setting two stakes into the ground in the form of an "X" over the intersection of the panels of the worm fence, thus steadying them, and then placing one or more rails in the crotch of the stakes as "riders." The stake-and-rider fence was well known in New Jersey before 1780.

There were several disadvantages in using the worm fences even with stakes and riders. The sinuous course of this fence removed much land from easy cultivation, and a great amount of timber was needed to erect and maintain it. These, however, were not major problems during the days of first settlement, when the land was used extensively instead of intensively and large amounts of wood were available.

On the other hand, there were several advantages in using the worm fence. Construction was relatively easy, requiring little in the way of specialized equipment or skills. Also, these rail fences were easily reconstructed after storm damage, and lasted longer than other forms of fencing which, by extended contact with the earth, soon rotted away and had to be replaced.

Worm fences were apparently unknown in both the British Isles and Sweden. The only European precedent for this fence type to date is an example encountered in the Austrian Tirol in 1897.[59]

In addition to fencing, there were other means to control livestock so that they would have difficulty disturbing tilled crops. Hobbles, yokes, and heavy drags were used where appropriate. In 1748, Pehr Kalm noted that near Philadelphia [60]

> The fences were in some parts low enough for the cattle to leap over with ease; to prevent this the hogs had a triangular wooden yoke and this custom was, as I have already observed, common all over the English plantations. To the horses neck was fastened a piece of wood, which at the lower end had a tooth or hook which would catch in the fence and stop the horse just as it lifted its fore feet to leap over; but I know not whether this is a safe invention with regard to horses. They were likewise kept in bounds by a piece of wood, one end of which was fastened to one of the fore feet, and the other to one of the hind feet. It forced them to walk pretty slowly, and at the same time made it impossible for them to leap over the fence. To me it seemed that the horses were subject to all sorts of dangerous accidents from this contrivance.

Since many of the early settlers of the Musconetcong drainage system were English, and had come from the southwestern portion of the state, we may infer that these devices were in use there also. Yokes were most certainly used to control stock in the valley during the mid-eighteenth century, but in northern New Jersey dairy cattle and horses were generally hobbled at this time, and bulls were restrained by means of heavy logs dragging from their horns. These methods probably remained in use as long as unconfined stock remained in northern New Jersey.[61]

Another form of fencing, although not nearly as popular as the worm fence, emerged as clearings were extended and wealth accumulated. This was the post-and-rail fence, consisting of posts six or seven feet long set into the earth ten or eleven feet apart, containing three or four rails, inserted one above another in holes cut into the posts. The construction of such a fence, especially before the invention of the thread auger in 1809, was much more difficult than construction of the worm fence. In addition, maintenance problems were greater with the post-and-rail fence since posts had to be straightened every spring after the heaving of the earth during the winter season. For these reasons, post-and-rail fences were probably not to be found in newly cleared areas. Later, when one wished to impress neighbors or travelers with the neatness of one's farm, a post-and-rail fence might be built along the public road, and the more utilitarian worm or snake fence used elsewhere. Post-and-rail fencing existed in New Netherland before 1650, and had come into use in the Musconetcong Valley by the end of the eighteenth century.[62] John Emley, in 1792, recorded paying for the making of "50 posts" and "150 flat rails," to be used on the Barker Tract in Hunterdon and Sussex Counties.[63] Apparently these were to be used for fencing.

Another type of fencing, which probably followed the use of wood, especially in areas north of the Wisconsin terminal moraine where the soil was quite rocky, was the stone-wall fence. As many early advertisements of lands newly cleared north and east of the terminal moraine mention that fencing was in use, we can infer that this referred to the worm or snake fence, as stone-wall fences could not be erected so quickly. The use of stone for fencing is not the obvious result of the presence of a large amount of glacial boulders in the vicinity, as Zelinsky[64] has ably demonstrated. That the pioneers of

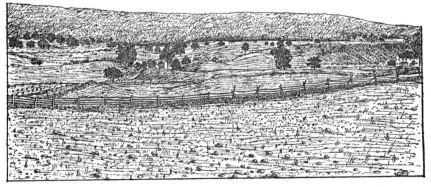

Post-and-rail and worm fencing, late nineteenth century. Near Oak Ridge, New Jersey. Source: Salisbury, *et al., The Glacial Geology of New Jersey.*

the Highlands did build stone fences there can be no doubt. Such fences were in wide use in the later nineteenth century before the building of macadamized roads. Macadam pavement required a crushed stone foundation, which was in many cases furnished by the old stone walls.

In many cases nineteenth- and early twentieth-century fences in the Highlands were constructed of both stone and rails. The stones acted as a foundation for the rails, which were placed on top and often staked and ridered. It may be that in some instances stone fencing originated through the placing of boulders found in the fields along the line of the rail fences, and the resulting stone walls finally became high enough to replace the rails.

The charcoal iron industry was also associated with, and influenced pioneer agriculture in the Musconetcong Valley in several ways. Since it existed side by side with agriculture in many areas, it provided a nearby market for the produce of the farmers, who dealt with the company store or with individual ironworkers. The gristmills and sawmills associated with most ironworking establishments provided needed services for the agriculturists. Also, many farmers were employed seasonally by the iron interests as woodchoppers, colliers, or teamsters. The iron industry also often turned to farming on its own, using the land available after the cutting of portions of the forest to provide wood for charcoal production had taken place. The creation of meadows was a primary consideration, since the working livestock had to be provided with fodder. Later, grain and other crops were planted, and stock might be kept for food or milk, in addition to their use as work animals. The combination of iron and agricultural in-

Stone-wall fencing without rails, late nineteenth century. Near Oak Ridge, New Jersey. Source: Salisbury, *et al., The Glacial Geology of New Jersey.*

terests was not peculiar to the New Jersey Highlands; "Iron Plantations" played a large role in the development of Pennsylvania's charcoal iron industry.[65]

In the Musconetcong drainage basin, as early as 1761, an iron interest located at present Bloomsbury included "a good plantation
already cleared, and a considerable quantity of meadow cleared, and
in good fence." In 1763, another nearby ironworking establishment
also had "some meadow cleared," probably also for the working stock.
Further improvements were fast in coming. A forge located at present
Waterloo in 1770, included "a good Farm, with about 50 Acres of
Winter Grain in the ground, and 25 Acres of Meadow in English
Grass." Four years later, at Changewater, a forge had "a great quantity
of very good meadow already made," and also had a barn located
on the property. In 1777 a forge located at the outlet of Late Hopatcong was advertised as "a Valuable Plantation *and* Iron Works,"
(italics mine) but in the next year the owner admitted that the property included only eighty acres of "choice meadow." [66]

The farming interests of the iron industries of the Musconetcong
drainage system are best illustrated in the papers collected by B. F.
Fackenthal on Greenwich Forge, which was located within five miles
of the mouth of the Musconetcong. In 1779, an "Inventory of sundries
delivered at Greenwich Forge by Samuel Williams for the use of
Richard Backhouse and Company, contained the following items:
"Plow with Irons Clevus &c.; a gray horse; sorrel horse; a four year old
bay horse; a wagon; a cow; a bull." Three years later Williams sold
Backhouse "eight horses, two cows and a calf, two sows and seven
shotes; a quantity of hay and straw; two plows and one harrow;" and
"about 30 Acres of Wheat and Rye in the Ground. . . ." The books
of the Greenwich Forge store for the same period show credits for such
activities as "three Days Mowing," and for "Splitting 500 Rails." The
forge owners evidently intended to be good farm managers. Still
another forge property in 1780 was advertised as being "under good
fence." [67]

Deforestation and the general depression of the iron industry after
the Revolution also encouraged agriculture. Especially in the Musconetcong and other fertile limestone valleys southwest of the Wisconsin
terminal moraine, many large tracts associated with forges "when
stripped of their timber, were subdivided among agricultural suc-
cessors. . . ." [68] As early as 1774, the Squire's Point Forge was advertised as a "plantation divided into four farms." [69] The failure of
this forge released approximately eighteen hundred acres for use as
farmland.

In some cases, the ironworkers themselves turned to farming when the forge declined. On February 24, 1790, James Parker recorded in his diary that "two forge men at Greenwich Forge send word by Fine that they would wish to buy the Lott Conrad Conell lives on. . . ." In 1790, John Smith, who had been a boss collier at the Andover Iron Works, leased the tract near the old forge at Waterloo, which was "a barren waste" at the time because of deforestation, and carried on farming operations with his three brothers for a number of years.[70]

The major effect of pioneer agriculture on the landscape was deforestation. Actual clearing was accomplished in league with the woodcutters and colliers of the iron interests, but the persistence of cleared fields was the result of agricultural occupance. Since the southwestern portion of the Musconetcong Valley was first occupied by both the pioneer farmers and the iron interests, it can be assumed that this area was well cleared by the end of the eighteenth century. Theophile Cazenove, who traveled across the valley in the vicinity of Penwell in 1794, noted that between Black River (Chester) and Penwell, "you see very few farms and everything is woods and uncultivated land, except the valley between the two ranges of mountains [the Musconetcong Valley] . . . there the land is pretty good as far as Easton. . . ." Despite the general agricultural land use in the area, Cazenove noted that his host, probably Andrew Miller, a tavern keeper, had bought his property five years earlier "where it was all woods." Also, two nearby properties totaling fifteen hundred acres were still woodland in 1794.

To the southwest of this point, however, there was more intensive land use, and woodlots were often somewhat removed from the farms, which had been entirely cleared. In the 1780's and 1790's the wills of residents of Alexandria, Bethlehem, and Greenwich Townships begin to contain specific bequests of "wood lots." [71] A popular location for woodlots in later years was the "Barrens" in Alexandria Township, which had begun to become a woodland after aboriginal burning ceased.[72] These woods were composed almost entirely of chestnut, which was the wood most valued for general farm use. In 1805 Job Thatcher of Alexandria Township left his daughter "2 small lots in the Barrans." [73]

Other farms had their woodlots on land too rugged to cultivate. Although much of this land was cut off by the iron interests, the forest soon regrew from stump sprouts. In 1794 Cazenove noted that in the vicinity of Penwell one-third of the typical farm was "on the mountain." This was probably the land set aside for woods; whereas the soil of the limestone valley was intensively tilled, and almost entirely deforested.

North and east of the terminal moraine the difficulty of agricultural endeavors kept most areas not cut over by the iron interests in woodland. Marginal agricultural activities served to keep some areas cut over by the iron interests free of forest for several years, but as in the case of the Smiths at Andover [74] these activities failed and the forest soon reasserted itself.

CHAPTER 5

The Pioneer Farmstead

Occupation of the Musconetcong Valley by pioneers of European descent brought houses and farm structures in keeping with traditional European building practices. These were erected near a ready source of water, preferably a spring, a brook, or the river itself. In house construction, the use of hewn or round logs seems to have been universal among the earliest settlers. An early resident of the area recalled that during his childhood in the waning years of the eighteenth century, "there was nothing but log houses" [1] in the vicinity of Hampton. This statement is substantiated by the numerous references to log structures in the area in the latter part of the eighteenth century, contained in contemporary advertisements, and also by such references in county histories written during the nineteenth century.

This is not to say, however, that frame and even stone structures did not exist as well, after the earliest settlement had taken place and finished lumber became available. This can be seen in the case of the colony of Quakers from Kingwood Township in Hunterdon County who settled near Allamuchy in 1764 "and took along to the new location all the frames and lumber for their first dwellings." [2]

Log structures, however, remained important in most locations long after water- and even steam-driven sawmills had begun to provide finished lumber relatively cheaply. A traveler en route from Newton to Johnsonburg in 1817 noted the ubiquity of log dwellings: "The Houses in general are quite mean. More than one half of them are built of logs. . . ." [3] Indeed, log structures remained to lend a definite character to the landscapes of the Highlands well into the last years of the nineteenth century. In some areas log houses were still being inhabited as late as 1911.

Log structures were introduced into New Jersey and surrounding

76

states through the agency of Swedish and Finnish settlers on the Delaware in the early seventeenth century, and also by German and Swiss colonists in southeastern Pennsylvania in the late seventeenth and early eighteenth centuries. Settlers of other ethnic stocks adopted the trait of building with logs and spread log construction from its primary hearths in southeastern Pennsylvania and southwestern New Jersey to the frontiers of settlement elsewhere.[4] In this connection, it is interesting to note which traits of log construction reached the Musconetcong Valley, over forty miles from the hearths of their introduction.

The Works Progess Administration's survey of early log houses in New Jersey is the most complete record of log houses in the state. The houses surveyed were almost entirely in the southwestern portion of New Jersey, as only scattered data were available for other parts of the state, where the ravages of time, fires, and cannibalization had removed log structures. The survey recognized three basic types of log structures in southwestern New Jersey: [5]

(1) [This type is] constructed of round logs of oak or cedar notched together at the corners, the interstices closed with moss, chips and clay. . . . The round-log cabins consist of one room with a small fireplace at one end. Door openings were made by pinning a hewn frame to the outside face of the log wall with hard wood pins, one to one and a half inches in diameter and six or more inches long. In the small window openings the jamb frames are pinned to the ends of the logs with the hewn log over and below the opening serving directly as head and sill.

(2) The second type is the hewn plank cabin of cedar or oak with dovetailed corners and with the same type of chinking between logs as employed in the cabins constructed of round logs. . . .

The construction of the oak plank houses is similar to that of the round log with the exception that the logs at all openings are pinned together by short dowels about one inch in diameter and long enough to penetrate one log and half of the one below it. The jambs of door and window frames are pinned to the ends of the logs at those openings. There is a second floor loft, the floor of which is laid over rough hewn beams which penetrate the outside walls and extend as much as three feet beyond them. The foot of the roof rafter which has a slope of about 45 degrees rests on the ends of these beams. The logs forming the walls are roughly dressed to a face on both sides. They are from four to six inches thick and from eight to fourteen inches high. The usual inside arrangement was a stone fireplace at one end or corner and a ladder alongside of it to gain access to the loft.

In most examples, the uppermost three or four logs are corbelled out in a continuous cover to bring the face of the top or wall plate three to six inches beyond the face of the walls.

(3)   The third and most interesting type is the hewn cedar plank cabin with dovetailed corners and V joints extending the entire length of the logs or planks and requiring little or no chinking. . . .

The cedar plank houses are similar to those of oak construction, except that the planks do not exceed three inches in thickness and vary from five to sixteen inches in width. The very close V joint running the full length of the building is characteristic. . . . One of the most interesting and progressive steps in this general type of construction is . . . [an] almost . . . complete second story. . . .

Broadly speaking, on the basis of general morphology, the three log-house types identified by the survey can be grouped into two broad categories. These would be: (1) The round or unfinished log dwelling without a loft; (2) the hewn-log house of one-and-one-half stories, the joists of which penetrate and extend beyond the outside walls. The descriptions of log dwellings in northern New Jersey indicate that these two broad classifications may also be used there. In general, but not exclusively, the one-story, simpler structure seems to be associated with English or Scotch-Irish settlement, and the more sophisticated one-and-one-half-story house with German settlement.

The search for the antecedents of this house type is most difficult because of the general lack of data. It would seem, however, that the one-story, crude dwelling is probably largely of Swedish origin. Pehr Kalm, in describing the original homes of the Swedish colonists on the Delaware, stated that "the whole house consisted of one little room" and also that "the board ceilings in the first colonial houses had been covered with earth to prevent the heat from escaping through the top." [6] This, of course, indicated that the Swedes made little or no use of a loft or attic.

Log building techniques, as well as this type of house, seem to have been adopted early by pioneer settlers of other ethnic stocks who passed through the Swedish area. Kalm, in 1749, noted that "the houses of the Swedes were all of wood with clay smeared between the logs, like those now built by the Irish [Scotch-Irish]." [7] This building tradition was largely concerned with [8]

round logs from which the bark was peeled. The horizontal joints were caulked with various substances such as clay or moss. At the corners of such buildings the logs were saddle-notched with rounded cuts, and the ends of the logs projected from the face of the building to give strength to the notch.

The movement north of the English and Scotch-Irish through eastern Pennsylvania and western New Jersey extended the distribution of this construction technique. The early log structures of Stockton, in southwestern Hunterdon County, were built in this way. A very old dwelling there destroyed in 1837 has been described as having been "a log house about 20 feet square one story high . . . covered with shingles. It had a door in front with a window front and back." [9] In the vicinity stood three similar log structures. Nearby, another had a partial second story, indicating a mixture of types within the area. On all these houses the logs were notched at the ends and laid up like a crib, with their ends protruding six to eight inches beyond the notches. This kind of construction is found widely in Sweden.[10]

In nearby Bucks County, Pennsylvania, the earliest log structures are similar in description.[11]

> White oak sapling trees about ten inches in diameter, cut in lengths of 22 or 24 feet, notched at the ends, were laid up a little higher than a man's head, as the walls of the house; the roof was made on rafters hewed from smaller trees, pitched from the center each way, and covered with rived lath and shingles and the gable ends from the square with rived weatherboards running up and down.
>
> These houses were of the one-story order, and occasionally one was built more elaborately with two rooms on the floor, which lengthwise required longer logs. . . . The windows were few and small, and until glass 7 x 9 were available, the greased paper or thin linen filled the bill for window lights. In this second edition of houses [a cruder log structure was the initial dwelling] there was a great improvement in doors, for instead of a blanket or canvas to close the *Foramen magnum,* a wooden door hung on wooden hinges, the boards of which were carefully rived out of choice timber with a froe.

It may be noted that Bucks County was initially settled by the Scotch-Irish moving northward from southeastern Pennsylvania. The Morgan family, residents of Durham, Bucks County, and products of a migration from Darby, Pennsylvania (south of Philadelphia), were dwelling in a log structure when their son Daniel, the famous hero of the American Revolution, was born. The building was briefly described by a collector for the University of Pennsylvania.[12]

> As near as I could ascertain the building was twenty feet by twenty-eight, of logs, chimney running up outside, fireplace and large. John Dillon, who died in 1890, was the last child born in the Morgan house. After the death of James Morgan, ironmaster, the parents of Mr. Dillon occupied the house from 1782 to 1806; according to Mr. Dillon's evidence, the house soon after becoming leaky and thus unfit for habitation.

The house was then dismantled, some logs utilized for fencing, and the foundations finally taken up in 1863.

> In 1863 the foundation stones and the hearthstones were removed . . . the hearthstone, when in situ, had small holes cut into it for the legs of the olden-times andirons, to prevent them from slipping when heavy logs of wood were rolled into the chimney corner into the fire.

A one-and-one-half-story dovetailed hewn log house, with a projecting roof, seems to have been in early use among German settlers. In 1738, Caspar Wistar, a product of direct migration from Germany through the port of Philadelphia, erected a log dwelling approximately one mile distant from the present town of Alloway in Salem County, southwestern New Jersey. A later account of the structure described it as "built of logs neatly squared and dovetailed at the corners," and as possessing "joists . . . which at one time extended several feet beyond the first story to support the projecting roof, so common to the homes of the early German settlers." [13] This account, unfortunately, does not mention the location of the fireplace or chimney. The Reall log house, located near Friesburg, approximately four miles southeast of the Wistar log structure, possesses all the features of the latter and definitely has a central chimney. Unfortunately, the date of construction and the name of the builder are unkonwn, but the house is distinctly Germanic in type. Many of the houses of similar morphology in the area (types 2 and 3 of the W.P.A. survey) have corner fireplaces. This certainly is not a German trait. Kalm, writing in 1750 of the earliest Swedish log structures in the same region stated that [14]

> the fireplaces made at the time were built in a corner of the dwelling room . . . they are now called Swedish fireplaces here, and are said to be quite rare. The most common ones now are English, which are as large as our kitchen hearth, though the bottom of them is not higher than the floor of the room.

Waterman and Shurtleff also concur that a corner fireplace is definitely a Swedish trait. There is no evidence to indicate that this feature penetrated northwestern New Jersey, although there is mention of it in single-story log structures in Bucks County, Pennsylvania. Use of this type of fireplace in one-and-one-half-story log houses, which are probably not of Swedish derivation, does, however, indicate that there was a synthesis of building traditions at an early date in southwestern New Jersey. Further, type 3 of the W.P.A. survey reflects the distinctly Swedish technique known as the "long groove" (V joint). Thus, it is impossible to call these log house types purely German or purely Swedish.[15]

Let us turn to data that mark the occurrence of the one-and-one-half-story house in northern New Jersey. The early German settlers of Cokesbury, about seven miles southeast of Changewater, are thought to be an offshoot of the New Germantown (Oldwick) settlement, which, as we have seen, was most likely in part, at least, derived from an overland migration from eastern Pennsylvania by way of the Old York Road. The Cokesbury pioneers built log structures, according to tradition, "with hewn logs, split shingle roof and plank floor, the plank cut out with a crosscut saw." These houses differed little from each other in general form.[16]

> Single-story houses, big cellar, chimney in the middle, wide fireplace in the kitchen and store room at the other end. . . . On the upper floors a portion of the grain was kept. . . . An indispensable appendage to the German's house was the piazza [overhanging roof—integral porch] in which the saddles, bridles, and sometimes plough and wagon harness were hung up.

We have here all the features of the one-and-one-half-story houses described in southwestern New Jersey, except for the central chimney. Although a half story is not mentioned, the absence of remarks as to sleeping quarters may be taken to imply that a loft was probably included above for that purpose. Also, "upper floors" may well refer to an attic or garret. In this connection, it is well to note the statement of a historian most familiar with the early Germans of this area about a structure at New Germantown during the 1750's, which was [17]

> probably not better than the common run of dwellings of that day. It must have been built of smoothly hewn logs, and was perhaps clapboarded on its front and sides. . . . I conjecture that it was of one story only, with a low garret arranged for sleeping rooms.

Johannes Moelich, a German from Philadelphia, settled at Peapack, northern Somerset County, around 1749. Before building a stone house he erected a temporary log structure. One of his descendants, drawing on family tradition and a general knowledge of the history of the region, described the raising of this temporary structure as follows: [18]

> The ends of the logs are squared and so cut as to be let in or dovetailed together . . . the walls go up apace; by afternoon skids are necessary upon which to roll the heavy logs to their places. . . . When entirely completed it was nothing more than a square enclosure, with one story and a cockloft above. . . .

In this example of a temporary dwelling, an overhang and the hew-
ing of the logs are not mentioned, but the logs are dovetailed and a
"cockloft" is included.

Indeed, an attic or garret seems to have been in wide use among
German settlers. Peter Stryker, a Jerseyan traveling in the vicinity of
Wilkesbarre, Pennsylvania, in 1816, mentions staying overnight at the
house of John Mills, whom he describes as a German. "I lodged un-
comfortably between two feather beds in an open garret of a log-
house!" [19]

The distinctive German log house, with its central chimney, one-and-
one-half stories, and overhanging roof, is well illustrated by the Hey-
drick-Yeakle log house, which stood at Mermaid Lane and Germantown
Avenue in Germantown, Pennsylvania, until it was demolished in 1909.[20]

The most complete data available on log structures erected throughout the state during the eighteenth century are contained in the advertisements of property reprinted in the *New Jersey Archives*. The
distribution of these log structures has been plotted.[21] Excepting the
large numbers of log buildings that were associated with the ironworks
of the day and which may have no cultural significance, it can be seen
that the greatest cluster of log structures is in the southwestern portion
of the state, well within the sphere of Swedish influence. There is also
a generally continuous distribution of log structures up the Delaware
Valley and into the Highlands.

Unfortunately, the advertisements reflect a span of only forty years
(1742–1782), and give no hint as to the real age of the structures listed.
Also, the first listing of a log structure in the Highlands does not occur
until 1750, thirty years or more after the first settlers had entered the
region. These dates are much too late to indicate whether the hearth
of German log culture in southeastern Pennsylvania or the Swedish
hearth of log culture in southwestern New Jersey was largely responsible
for the techniques of log construction and the types of log structures
that entered the Highlands. The striking distribution of log structures
in the state certainly does indicate, however, that log structures did
penetrate the state from the south and perhaps from the west as well,
but not from the north or east. The well-settled eastern portions of the
state generally seem to have rejected log structures through time. It
may be noted that log structures seem to have been associated with
minimal clearance and a general lack of improvements on the property
that contained them.

Additional evidence for the origin of log building techniques in
New Jersey may be seen in the names associated with the advertisements
of log houses. These are almost entirely of Anglo-Saxon origin, suggest-

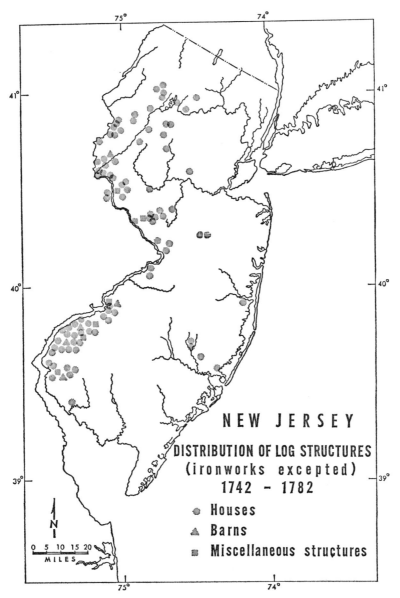

NEW JERSEY

DISTRIBUTION OF LOG STRUCTURES
(ironworks excepted)
1742 - 1782

● Houses
▲ Barns
▦ Miscellaneous structures

0 5 10 15 20
MILES

Source: William A. Whitehead, *et al.* (eds.), *Archives of the State of New Jersey: Documents Relating to the Colonial, Revolutionary, and Post Revolutionary History of the State of New Jersey* (First Series, 42 vols.; Various Places: State of New Jersey, 1880–1949); and William S. Stryker, *et al.* (eds.), *Archives of the State of New Jersey: Documents Relating to the Revolutionary History of the State of New Jersey* (Second Series, 5 vols.; Various Places: State of New Jersey, 1901–1917).

ing a movement north from the old English settlements in the south-western portion of the state.

Both the one-story and story-and-one-half log house were in existence in early days in northwestern New Jersey. The story-and-one-half house was considered to be a better dwelling and was preferred by settlers after initial occupation of the area had taken place. John Bowlby's log house, built after 1740 near Hampton, in the Musconetcong Valley, "was once considered the grandest house in the settlement. It consisted of logs hewn on two sides and notched at the ends; was one and a half stories high and had two large rooms below stairs, while the other houses had only one."[22] One source mentions Bowlby as a German pioneer, although the orthography of the name seems English.

Log houses in existence during the nineteenth century in the area seem to have been of the one-and-one-half-story type. A log house that was still inhabited in 1911 at Hardwick, in northern Warren County, approximately twelve miles northwest of Hackettstown, of which a photograph exists, looks much like the German form of log house. It was one-and-one-half stories in height, and had joists that could have supported an overhanging roof. The exact position of the chimney is unsure, but it was at the gable end, not in a central position.

A log house built by John Byerly in 1799 or by Thomas Roberts in 1803, in the section of Doylestown, Pennsylvania, once known as "Germany," may represent the German log house as it was constructed by other ethnic groups. It is very similar to the descriptions of German log houses in New Jersey and may well, at one time, have had an overhanging roof. The joists are certainly in a proper position for such an appendage. The chimney, however, is built inside, at the gable end. The corner-timbering (V notch) is definitely a Pennsylvania-German trait.[23] (See illustration section.)

After the pioneer agriculturists had completed the initial phases of developing their farms, many turned to the improvement of their habitations, and substituted structures of frame or stone for those of logs. This was especially true of those settlers who came after initial occupation had taken place and of those whose ties to Old World traditions had not been erased by several generations of life on the frontier. Settlers in Hackettstown, for example, who were of New England derivation, built frame structures at an early date. Other earlier settlers, after inhabiting log dwellings for several years, also turned to the construction of more elaborate and prestigious frame or stone structures.

As in the case of log dwellings, the later stone and frame structures reflect a blending of architectural traditions in the New World, and the process of acculturation. Unfortunately, data on the folk house types

Log house near Friesburg, New Jersey, from a photograph made early in this century. Note the one-and-one-half story height, the neatly squared and dovetailed logs, the protruding joists that carry the roof well beyond the front wall of the house, and the central chimney.

From Joseph S. Sickler, *The Old Houses of Salem County* (2nd ed.; Salem, New Jersey: Sunbeam Publishing Co., 1949).

Log house near Hardwick, New Jersey, occupied as late as 1911, characterized by the one-and-one-half story height, partially adzed logs, the appearance of joists in the front wall of the house, and the gable end (interior?) chimney.

From George W. Cummins, *History of Warren County* (New York: Lewis Historical Publishing Co., 1911).

Front view.

Byerly log house at the Mercer Museum, Doylestown, Pennsylvania. In this story-and-a-half structure, the joists plainly appear in the front wall. Note the interior chimney and the distinctive Pennsylvania German notching technique.

Gable view.

"English" house near Hackettstown, New Jersey.

Small East Jersey cottage, Beattystown, New Jersey.

Deep East Jersey cottage near Hackettstown, New Jersey. Note (original?) central chimney.

Remains of typical outdoor cookhouse, Fine homestead, Finesville, New Jersey. The stone house is of the "I" type.

English barn, East Anglia, 1965. New Jersey English barns are identical except for the steeply pitched roof, which is generally associated with thatching.

Dutch barn near Pluckemin, New Jersey, 1967.

Old barracks falling prey to suburbanization,
Hackettstown, New Jersey, 1967.

Raising a barrack roof, early twentieth century,
Warren County, New Jersey.
From George W. Cummins, *History of Warren
County* (New York: Lewis Historical Publishing
Co., 1911).

Staked and ridered worm fencing, late nineteenth century, near John-sonburgh, New Jersey.

Rollin D. Salisbury, et al., *The Glacial Geology of New Jersey,* Geological Survey of New Jersey, Final Report of the State Geologist, Vol. V (Trenton: MacCrellish & Quigley, 1902).

Remnant of the Brookland Forge dam, made of soil, boulder, and gravel fill, approximately six feet in height. This dam was responsible for greatly enlarging Lake Hopatcong after ca. 1760.

Lake Hopatcong State Park, New Jersey.

Aerial view of the southwestern portion of the Musconetcong Valley from northwest of Finesville to Riegelsville, 1964. Here the southern course of the river is original, the northern course man-made and of twentieth century provenance.

Albert C. Jones Associates, Cornwells Heights, Pennsylvania.

extant in the region today are largely lacking, except for the pioneer efforts of Thomas Jefferson Wertenbaker, some cataloging by the Historic American Buildings Survey, and a recent landmark address given by Fred B. Kniffen.[24] Also, eighteenth-century advertisements generally give few hints as to the types of houses listed for sale. Thus, it was decided to map the present distribution of house types known to have been present in the general area during the eighteenth century. This was done by car traverse of every road in the Musconetcong Valley that was in existence before the nineteenth century. Distinctive farm buildings were recorded in a similar fashion. (See illustration section.)

Throughout the greater part of the Musconetcong Valley today, the "I" house prevails. In northwestern New Jersey this house type is characterized by its rectangular form, generally with the gable end or shorter axis oriented away from the road; its two-and-a-half-story height; its simple, generally porchless exterior devoid of pent roof or ornate door hood; its doubly pitched, moderately sloping roof, which is devoid of dormers; its interior gable-end chimneys; and the presence of a full cellar. The house is one-room deep. Additions to these houses are often built in like form, sometimes as an ell, but more often in a straight line extension to one side. The material used in construction of the addition often is a variance from the original.

The "I" house is held by Kniffen to have evolved from an old English

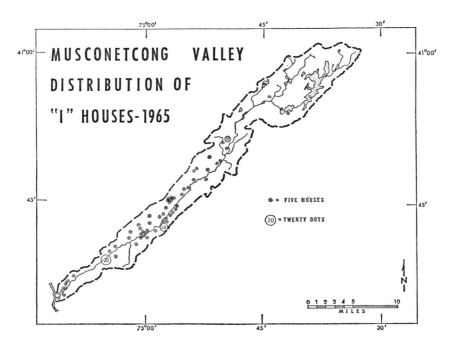

unit consisting of one room and an end chimney. Houses very similar to the "I" type may be seen today on many of the secondary roads of East Anglia. It is instructive to note, however, that not a few of the "I" houses erected in the last years of the seventeenth century and the first years of the eighteenth century in southwestern New Jersey possess corner fireplaces. This is a distinct Swedish characteristic. Since the fireplace is such a basic part of these houses, it would seem that at least in southwestern New Jersey the "I" house is not purely of English provenance.

By the end of the seventeenth century the "I" house had become established all the way from Chesapeake Bay to the lower Delaware. Although the type largely diffused to the south and west, it also advanced northward up the Delaware Valley with the tide of settlement. Culturally, the "I" house became the accepted abode in western New Jersey, of all who could afford it, early in the eighteenth century. In southwestern New Jersey, the desire for this type was so pronounced that existing gambrel roofs were altered to gable roofs so as to conform with the preferred roof line.

In many cases, the houses of the owners and managers of the local ironworks may have served as models for the farmhouses of agriculturists when the latter turned from the log structures of their pioneer days to more sophisticated dwellings of frame and stone. The managers and owners of ironworks in western New Jersey were largely of Philadelphia or Pennsylvania origin and many of them were accustomed to living in frame or stone "I" houses. Sawmills were established early at most forges to supply the lumber needed for such houses, as well as for the iron enterprise itself. Abram Evans, of Philadelphia, offered the Chelsea Forge, at what later became Finesville, on the Musconetcong, for sale in 1763. On the premises was "a good Stone House, two Stories high, with two Rooms on each Floor. . . ." [25] Another advertisement of Chelsea Forge in 1780 listed one of the dwellings on the property as being of "stone, two stories high, with fire-places at each end. . . ." [26] This was probably the same house and most likely also contained a full cellar and garret—in short a perfect "I" house. Thus, at a time before most agriculturists turned from log to frame or stone construction, the "I" house existed as a model, and with it was associated the prestige of the moneyed iron interests.

The distribution of the "I" house in the Musconetcong Valley well reflects the Delaware Valley stream of diffusion of the type. For the most part, the houses are clustered in the limestone portions of the watershed, where better soils prevail. This is especially true of the "I" houses associated with farmsteads. Few "I" houses are found north of the terminal moraine. Large numbers of them are found lining the older streets of many of the agglomerated settlements such as Blooms-bury, Hampton, and Hackettstown. These are probably in large part of nineteenth-century origin, but reflect a preference, on the part of the population, for such houses. It is especially interesting to note that Hackettstown, which is well within the New England sphere of influence in the valley, has such large numbers of "I" houses.[27]

Second in numbers in the Musconetcong Valley, but with less than one-half the total of "I" houses, is the two-room-deep "English" house. The "English" house is very similar in description to the "I" type, ex-cept for its generally being near or over thirty feet in depth, whereas the "I" house is seldom deeper than twenty-two or twenty-three feet. The "I" house and the "English" house are probably ultimately related types.[28]

The "English" house appears to have diffused northward via the Delaware Valley early in the eighteenth century and also westward along with later waves of migration from New England, which entered eastern New Jersey in the first half of the eighteenth century carrying along a similar house type based on Georgian lines.[29] The present distri-bution of the "English" house in the Musconetcong Valley gives little indication as to its route or routes of entry. Variations of the basic

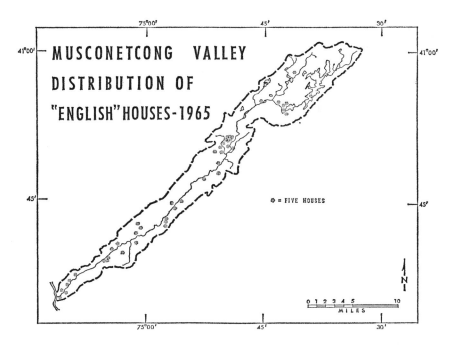

MUSCONETCONG VALLEY DISTRIBUTION OF "ENGLISH" HOUSES-1965

type probably entered by way of both the Delaware Valley and routes
from the east such as the Minisink Trail. Variations from the distribution of the "I" house include the fact that the "English" house is not
particularly oriented to the better soils, as is the "I" house, and the fact
that a significant number of them is located north of the Wisconsin
terminal moraine. Also, the "English" house is, in terms of relative
numbers, far more of an urban house than is the "I" type.

The East Jersey cottage has been described by Wertenbaker: "The
typical house was perhaps forty-five feet by eighteen, one story high
with loft, with few or no dormers . . . the chimneys usually, though
not always, at either end and invariably placed in, not on the outside
of the wall, the roof often sloping down behind to cover a narrow
annex to the rear." [30] Wertenbaker held that this house type had
evolved from a cottage found widely on Long Island and Connecticut.
The primary cultural influence causing the evolution from what had
been a two-room-deep house with a central chimney to a one-room-deep
house with a gable-end location for the chimney was most likely Flemish.
Flemings were especially numerous in northern Morris and Essex counties and generally on the north bank of the Raritan in Middlesex
County. These were all sources of the settlers of New England cultural
antecedents who penetrated the Musconetcong Valley.

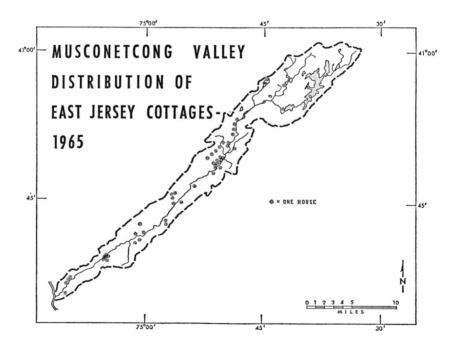

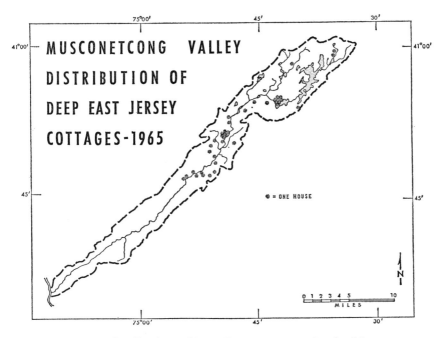

MUSCONETCONG VALLEY
DISTRIBUTION OF
DEEP EAST JERSEY
COTTAGES-1965

● = ONE HOUSE

The present distribution of East Jersey cottages in the Musconetcong Valley, as well as their occurrence now and then along the older roads from the east penetrating the valley, tend to confirm this. They are especially numerous as farmhouses in the portions of the valley influenced by both the Dutch and New Englanders. The generally scattered distribution of East Jersey cottages south of Stephensburgh (except for Bloomsbury) can best be explained by a diffusion of the type from the Raritan Valley, perhaps by means of the South Branch of the Raritan River trail. A similar one-room-deep cottage has also been recorded for southwestern New Jersey in the early eighteenth century. This, however, had a gambrel roof, which is unknown in the northwestern portion of the state.[31]

Closely related to the East Jersey cottage is a structure we might term the "deep East Jersey cottage." This house type is closer to New England precedent than is the East Jersey cottage, except for the general gable-end location of the chimney and the frequent use of stone as a building material. These, again, are probably Flemish influences. The deep East Jersey cottage can be followed from its sources in northern Essex and Morris counties with greater ease and continuity than can its shallower relative. In the Musconetcong Valley the type is confined to the area of New England settlement and is a diagnostic feature of such cultural influence.

The need for structures auxiliary to the main farm building soon manifested itself, as additional land was cleared and the pioneer families grew in wealth and numbers. Specialized structures were needed for baking, storage, odd jobs, and the housing of farm animals. These additional structures arose as soon as need or inclination permitted. Logs, stone, frame, and brick were used as building materials, depending on purpose, local availability, and cultural preference.

One of the first additions to the original farmstead was a separate kitchen. These were often erected before the dwelling was improved by switching from log to frame or stone construction, as can be seen by James Ellison's advertisement in 1767 of one hundred and fifty acres in Gloucester County including "a square Log House and Kitchen, with a good stone chimney in each. . . ." The outside kitchen seems to have been almost universal in much of western New Jersey and had lasted as an important feature of the farmstead until well into the latter part of the nineteenth century in the northwestern part of the state.[32] A property offered for sale in Hackettstown in 1777 included a "frame kitchen." Apparently, the outside kitchen was also known at an early date in the eastern portion of the state, as a house with "a Kitchin adjoyning" was advertised for sale in Elizabethtown in 1737. Outside kitchens are frequently associated with Dutch barns in eighteenth-century advertisements. The dimensions of these early structures may have been similar to one in Princeton in 1775, which was listed as being "22 feet long and 16 wide," or to one at Middlebush during the Revolution, which was twenty-four feet square.[33]

The present term applied to outside kitchens is "outdoor cookhouse," and older residents of the Musconetcong drainage system remember their mothers' using them all day long. The remains of a typical cookhouse on the Fine Homestead at Finesville built after 1811 has a foundation of brick with a length of 13 feet, 11 inches and a width of 11 feet, 10 inches. The cookhouse itself was of frame construction, with a gable roof, a door on each long end, and a built-on porch on one side, where the family's clothes were washed. The large fireplace, still standing, has outside dimensions of 8 feet, 2 inches in width and 4 feet, 10 inches in depth. Inside dimensions are 5 feet, 4 inches in width; 2 feet, 10 inches in depth at the bottom, 2 feet, 5 inches at the top; and a height of 4 feet, 9 inches. The chimney is approximately 14 feet high. Another cookhouse, near Asbury, also a frame structure, is 12 feet, 3 inches square on the outside. The distribution of existing cookhouses in the Musconetcong Valley closely corresponds with the areas of Dutch and German settlement in the western portion of the valley.

A later and not quite as universal addition to the farmstead was the

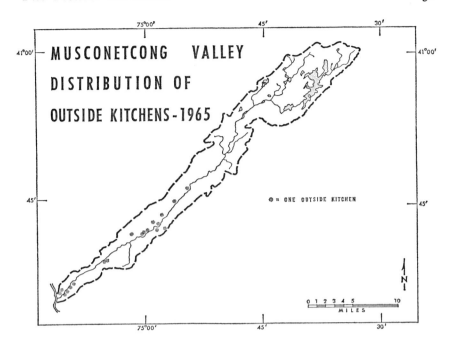

springhouse. These are to be widely seen in northwestern New Jersey and nearby eastern Pennsylvania and are often still in use. They are apparently always built of stone and have [34]

> small windows one on each side, with outside stationary blinds or shutters made of wood. They differ mainly in size. . . . sometimes the roof is a stone arch covered with sod, and sometimes it is made of wood covered with shingles. They are built over a spring or springs.

The earliest known occurrence of a springhouse in the Musconetcong Valley was in 1774, at Greenwich Forge, but they date back to at least 1727 in nearby Bucks County, Pennsylvania, and probably entered northwestern New Jersey also at an early date.

In 1749 Pehr Kalm recorded springhouses as being common north of Philadelphia.[35]

> Pennsylvania abounds in springs. . . . The people near such springs, besides making the usual use of the spring water, also conduct it into a little stone building, near the house where they can confine it. In summer, they place their milk, bottles of wine and other liquors in the water, where they keep cool and fresh.

Kalm's discussion of these structures elsewhere indicates their general absence among Swedish and Dutch settlers in early days. The Pennsyl-

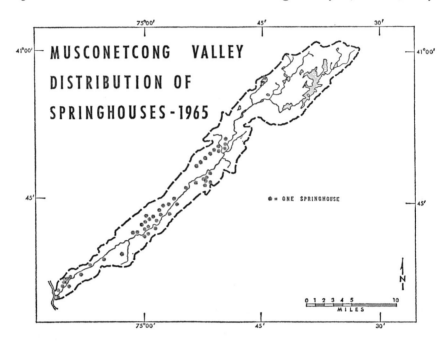

vania-Germans, however, were well acquainted with their use, and springhouses were built by them at an early date.[36] In the Musconetcong Valley the distribution of springhouses most closely correlates with that of the "I" house, suggesting that both of these structures are parts of a complex that diffused into northwestern New Jersey by way of the Delaware Valley.

Miscellaneous structures, most often of frame, but sometimes of stone construction, joined the house, outside kitchen, springhouse, and barn at a later date, depending on the prosperity and need of the farmer. These later structures might include a shop "for weaving, mending tools, and doing odd jobs," a "Smoak House," and an individual "Wash House" built on a stream where the water for the laundry could most easily be obtained. The shop was often joined to the farmhouse, and the other buildings were separate, but nearby. Occasionally, an auxiliary building would combine several functions, as in the case of a structure in Reading Township, Hunterdon County, in 1755, which housed "a large Store-House and Shop with an Under-ground Kitchen and Oven. . . ."[37]

The use of extra buildings probably became more widespread later in the history of settlement, after the farm was entirely won from the forest and the barn was no longer large enough to accommodate the miscellaneous additional farm functions undertaken once the pioneer period had passed. As has been seen, the sheltering of farm stock was not a major concern among most pioneer agriculturists. Also, since the produce of the initial farm clearing was small, it could easily be stored in the farmhouse itself. With the improvement of the farm, the clearing of additional land and the increase of stock, came the need for additional farm buildings. In some cases, multipurpose structures were erected. In most cases, however, the barn served to house the stock, store the grain, and protect the farm implements.

Undoubtedly, the first barns were primitive affairs. Most likely, the original log dwelling often served to house cattle after a better house had been built. Schmidt, after intensive research into the pioneer agricultural settlement of Hunterdon County, came to the conclusion that the first barns of the settlers were "usually of logs and built somewhat like their cabins." [38] The above-mentioned Morgan log dwelling, built at Durham, Pennsylvania, only a short distance from the mouth of the Musconetcong, in 1732, had a stable associated with it. In later years the foundation of the latter structure was described as being "a small affair, sixteen by twenty, and loosely laid, also of logs."

Log barns were occasionally mentioned in advertisements of property in northwestern New Jersey during the eighteenth century, but were probably more prevalent than their listing indicates. The tax records of Bucks and Northampton counties in Pennsylvania, which border northwestern New Jersey, indicate that in 1798 well over sixty per cent of the barns in those counties were entirely of log construction, and many more contained logs as at least a portion of their structure. The typical log barn in Pennsylvania at this time was "a rectangular building, without a foundation or only a simple stone one, and it was one or one-and-one-half stories high." [39] Most of these structures were between thirty and forty feet long, but a good number also ranged from forty to fifty feet in length. At least some of the log barns in the Musconetcong Valley must have been of this size in early days, as William Frazer reported holding religious services in such structures as early as 1768.[40]

Although log barns were an important feature of the pioneer farmstead, frame structures appeared at an early date. Indeed, in many cases the erection of a frame barn preceded the erection of a frame or stone farmhouse. In 1751 William Gammon, an inhabitant of Bethlehem Township, was dwelling in a log house while his cattle were housed in a frame barn. During the latter portion of the eighteenth century the association of log farmhouses and frame barns was quite common elsewhere in the Highlands. As late as 1817, an observer from Connecticut, traveling from Newton to Johnsonburgh, noted that "more than one half of the houses are built of logs, yet they have large Barns universally thatched with straw. . . ." [41] Apparently, these barns were of frame construction.

Unfortunately, there are few references to the types of barns that were to be found in northwestern New Jersey after building in frame became common. That distinct types did exist, however, is evident from occasional references to English barns and frequent references to Dutch barns in contemporary newspaper advertisements. English barns are mentioned only occasionally in eighteenth-century advertisements. A "tollerable good English barn" [42] was offered for sale in 1780 at Flanders, by Mary Mills. This was most likely the rectangular, gable-roofed structure, with high doors on its longest side, that was common in New England, whence many of the settlers of Morris County had come. English barns thus probably entered the northeastern part of the Musconetcong Valley along with the New England settlers of that area. New Englanders had been forced, through harsh continental winters, to give protection to their cattle. Pioneers directly from the British Isles, who settled the southwestern part of New Jersey, followed a more casual practice of wintering their stock outdoors. By the middle of the eighteenth century, Kalm indicates, they had influenced the descendants of Swedish settlers, who at first had built barns to house their cattle, to do the same. Thus, the barns of English type now found in the Musconetcong Valley probably did not come along with the earliest tide of English migration into the valley.

Dutch and German settlers, coming from regions in which winter temperatures were more severe, and in which the care of farm stock was more seriously pursued, were not acculturated to the casual ways of the English and, even in milder southwestern New Jersey, in Kalm's words, "preserved the custom of their country, and generally kept their cattle in barns during the winter." [43] The barns used by the early settlers of Dutch and German origins were described by Kalm, who saw many of them in traveling between Trenton and New Brunswick in 1748. [44]

> The barns had a peculiar kind of construction in this locality, of which I shall give a concise description. The main building was very large almost the size of a small church; the roof was high, covered with wooden shingles, sloping on both sides, but not steep. The walls which supported it were not much higher than a full grown man; but on the other hand the breadth of the building was all the greater. In the middle was the threshing floor and above it, or in the loft or garret, they put the unthrashed grain, the straw, or anything else, according to the season. One one side were stables for the horses, and on the other for the cows. The young stock

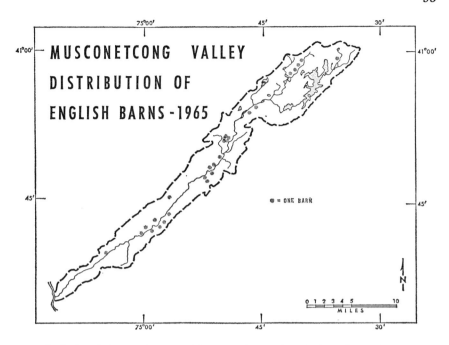

MUSCONETCONG VALLEY
DISTRIBUTION OF
ENGLISH BARNS - 1965

● = ONE BARN

had also their particular stables or stalls, and in both ends of the building were large doors, so that one could drive in with a cart and horses through one of them, and go out at the other. Here under one roof therefore were the thrashing floor, the barn, the stables, the hay loft, the coach house, etc. This kind of building is used chiefly by the Dutch and Germans, for it is to be observed that the country between Trenton and New York is not inhabited by many Englishmen, but mostly by Germans or Dutch, the latter of which are especially numerous.

Thomas Anburey, a British prisoner of war, in traveling through western New Jersey and Lancaster County, Pennsylvania, in 1778, described Dutch barns in a similar fashion. Advertisements, and an account book listing the damages done by the British army during the Revolutionary War, indicate that the typical Dutch barn was square, or almost so, ranging from forty to fifty feet on a side.

The origin of the Dutch barn is held to be in the Lower Saxon peasant house that centers in the basin of the lower Elbe River. These houses are quite common today in this region and generally in rural portions of the northern Netherlands.[45] Dutch barns must have entered the Musconetcong Valley with the early Dutch settlers of the area and possibly with Germans as well. In 1769 "a good new large Dutch barn" [46] was located within three miles of Squire's Point Forge on the Musconetcong, so that surely such structures were known in the area by this time.

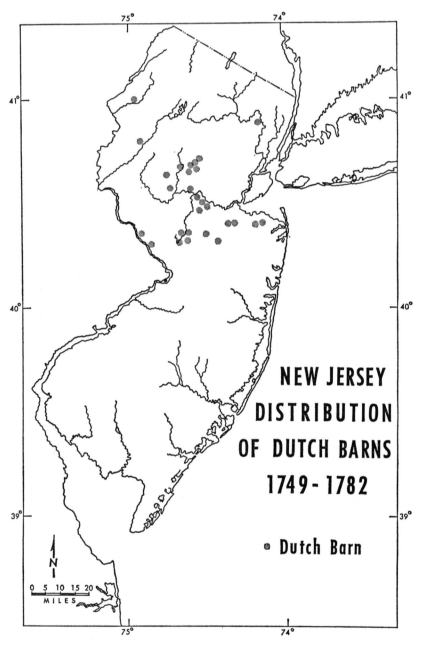

NEW JERSEY
DISTRIBUTION
OF DUTCH BARNS
1749-1782

● Dutch Barn

Source: Whitehead, *et al.* (eds.), *Archives of the State of New Jersey,* First
Series; and Stryker, *et al.* (eds.), *Archives of the State of New Jersey,*
Second Series.

According to eighteenth-century newspaper advertisements, the hearth of Dutch barns in New Jersey was the Raritan Valley. Dutch barns appear to have had a limited acceptance insofar as non-Dutch cultural groups were concerned and were generally associated with large, prosperous farms owned by settlers of Dutch extraction. The Dutch barn type has entirely disappeared from the Musconetcong Valley but occasional relict barns are still to be found in the environs of the Raritan Valley.

The accounts of early settlement and the newspaper advertisements of the day do not mention the barn type dominant in much of northwestern New Jersey today. This is the "bank barn" or "Pennsylvania barn," which today dominates the Musconetcong Valley southwest of Hackettstown. Locally, where there are English barns extant, the term is "overshot barn," in opposition to "undershot barn" for those of English type.

The bank or overshot barns that are found today in northwestern New Jersey are almost universally of frame construction lying over fieldstone foundations, and have two levels, the second level being used for grain, hay, implement, and vehicle storage, and also for threshing. The first level is primarily used to house the farm stock, today mostly dairy cattle. The bank barn is often built into the side of a "bank" or hill, so that one can enter the second level, the doors of which face the road, at ground level. In some cases a ramp is built to facilitate entry. In many cases the second level of the barn projects over the first level. The entrance to the first level almost always faces south, to take advantage of as much sunlight during the winter months as possible.

Many scholars have associated the Pennsylvania or bank barn with German settlement in the Middle States. Wertenbaker has sought its origin in the great peasant houses of the Black Forest, the Jura, and upland locations in Switzerland and southern Germany. The superiority of German methods of animal husbandry, especially in relation to the casual attitudes of early English and Scotch-Irish settlers, has by many writers been associated with the use of the bank barn. Later investigation has shown, however, that as late as 1798, the barns of Germans and other settlers in Pennsylvania did not differ markedly. It would appear that the bank barn, so often attributed entirely to the Germans and Swiss, also partially owes its origins to English influence, and perhaps to frontier innovation. The bank barn is of much later origin than earlier investigators realized. The first use of any term to delineate this most distinctive barn type appears to have been in York County, Pennsylvania, in 1796.

A prosperous late-nineteenth-century farmstead. Lopatcong Township, Warren County, New Jersey. Note especially the presence of the "I" house, the bank barn, with side in view (front) facing south, and the springhouse. Source: James P. Snell (ed.), *History of Sussex and Warren Counties, New Jersey* (Philadelphia: Everts & Peck, 1881).

In northwestern New Jersey, where this barn is so prevalent today, its appearance also must have been relatively late. Although advertisements of the 1740's through 1780's often mention "Dutch" barns and occasionally "English" barns, there is never a mention of any other kind in the state. The earliest recorded occurrence of a barn that may have been a bank barn, or an embryonic bank barn, is at Stillwater in 1792 or 1793. The barn was described as having been of frame and having two levels, an upper level, where the hay was stored, and a lower one, where the animals were kept. The general inference is that this was a bank barn. It apparently was the first barn erected by a German family, the first member of which had settled there in 1741 or 1742.

The most significant difference between bank barns in Pennsylvania and those of northwestern New Jersey is in terms of size. In Pennsylvania such barns are often of great size, perhaps forty by one hundred feet in floor plan.[47] In northwestern New Jersey such structures might average thirty by forty feet, and serve to house only six to eight cows.

It is probable, then, that the major route of entry of the bank barn into northwestern New Jersey was by way of eastern Pennsylvania, perhaps by the agency of the later German emigrants from eastern Pennsylvania to the cheaper land of northwestern New Jersey. In the Musconetcong Valley the present distribution of the bank barn correlates most closely with those of the "I" house and springhouse, indicating that these structures are culturally related.

A common feature of the eighteenth-century agricultural landscape in northern New Jersey was the barrack. This was a device that was used both to store hay and protect one or two head of cattle. It consisted of four stationary posts, and a simple gable or pyramidal thatched roof that could be adjusted to the height of the haystack by moving it up and down the posts. Barracks were encountered by Pehr Kalm in 1748 while he was en route from the Swedish settlements on the Delaware to Philadelphia. A description of a barrack by an English immigrant to Hunterdon County in 1787 is very similar to Kalm's description almost forty years earlier.[48]

> Barracks are a building . . . I noticed . . . at first coming into the
> country. It has four poles fixed in the ground at the distance of fifteen

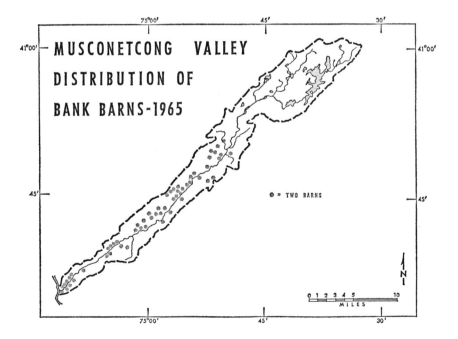

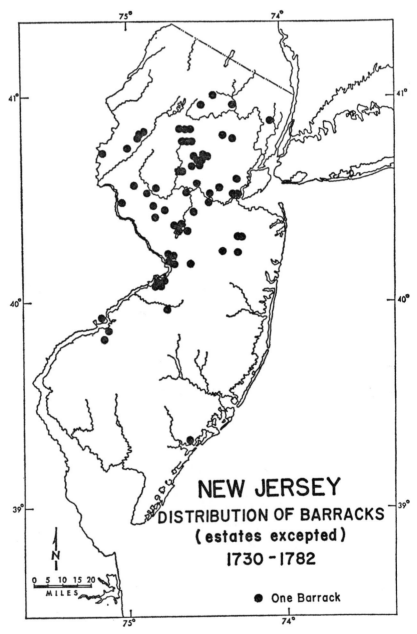

NEW JERSEY

DISTRIBUTION OF BARRACKS

(estates excepted)

1730 – 1782

● One Barrack

Source: Whitehead, *et al.* (eds.), *Archives of the State of New Jersey*, First
Series; and Stryker, *et al.* (eds.), *Archives of the State of New Jersey*,
Second Series.

feet in a square. The poles are square fifteen feet or more at top and five feet at bottom unsquared. This is all above ground. In the square part of the poles there are holes bored thro at the distance of twelve inches big enough for a strong iron pin to be put thro to support four wall plates which are tennanted at the ends, then some light spars are put upon the wall plates and thatch upon them. When it was only five feet from the ground, the room can be raised at pleasure 21 feet or any distance from the ground between that and five feet. These are to put hay or any kind of grain under and the roof is always ready to shelter it from hasty rains which is common hear in summer. Those that have only two cows have the bottom part boarded at the sides and a floor laid over and the hay at top and the cow stable under.

On more than one occasion the erection of barracks preceded the building of a barn in northwestern New Jersey. In 1761, Richard Shackleton offered a farm located approximately six miles north of Easton for sale, which included "a good Log-house, two good Barracks,"[49] but no mention of a barn. These barracks were probably also utilized as animal shelters. Later, however, most barracks were mainly used to store hay, and there was no inclusion of a shelter for stock. Occasionally, barracks were used to store grain. Silas Chesebrough, en route from Newton to Johnsonburgh in 1817, noted "very large stacks of grain with roofs thatched with straw."[50] Barracks in use in the Musconetcong Valley in the early twentieth century were approximately twenty feet square and were enclosed with boards when the roof was halfway up.

The origin of the barrack in New Jersey is surely Dutch. Such structures are still important features of the rural landscape in the northern Netherlands. They have largely disappeared from the rural landscape in New Jersey, however, which prompted Wertenbaker to assert in 1938 that "in searching through the Raritan and Passaic valleys I have never seen a sliding-roof haystack outside of the regions of original Dutch settlement. Apparently it has been a tough bit of inheritance for the melting pot."[51] An examination of the early advertisements of farms, however, shows that barracks were adopted as early as 1730 by other ethnic groups. The distribution of barracks in the state as reflected in eighteenth-century advertisements shows them to have been far more widely diffused than Dutch barns. It is probable that during the eighteenth century the barrack was more widely distributed in the Musconetcong Valley than were the settlers of Dutch ethnic origin. At the present time an occasional barrack is still to be found in the valley, notably in the vicinity of Hackettstown, Port Colden, and Asbury.

CHAPTER 6

The Charcoal Iron Industry

The charcoal iron industry entered the Highlands at an early date, perhaps at the very beginning of the eighteenth century; and for over a hundred years exerted a most powerful economic influence in the region. Many portions of the Highlands were settled first by ironworkers, who later gave way to agriculturists after deforestation occurred. This fact was not overlooked by the early historians of the region. Gordon, in 1834, wrote that the first settlers of the Highlands were [1]

> rather manufacturers than agriculturists; and the narrow valleys of the mountain region, which contain many and excellent mill seats, were only partially tilled for the subsistence of wood cutters and bloomers. The forge was universally the precursor of the farm. The iron master occupied large tracts of land, which, when stripped of timber, were subdivided among agricultural successors, operating on the smallest scale.

In the Musconetcong Valley, however, and possibly in other broad limestone valleys in the Highlands, agriculturists preceded ironworkers by perhaps two decades. The first agriculturists were small in number, however, and the charcoal iron industry probably wrought more significant changes for many years in the landscape than did farming.

Three main resources influenced the location of the various eighteenth-century iron enterprises of the Highlands: (1) readily available iron ore, (2) abundant power in the form of rushing streams, and (3) a large supply of fuel (charcoal), which could be made from the rich deciduous forests of the region. Of the three resources, the latter two were most important. The Highlands were rich in deposits of hematite and magnetite, and even in the early days of the charcoal iron industry it was feasible to transport the rich ores overland for many miles, especially to the small extractive forges. On the other hand, waterpower in most

102

cases could not be transported far from streamside, nor could bulky loads of charcoal fuel be transported as cheaply as could rich iron ore.[2]

The iron industry, because of its requirements of fuel and power, generally became established in the van of dense agricultural settlement. Where millers had preempted the best power sites, or where deforestation had taken place because of agricultural clearing, the charcoal iron industry simply was not economically viable.

In addition to the need for certain raw materials, the establishment and viability of the charcoal iron industry of the Highlands was affected by the general economic conditions of the day. An important economic influence on the iron industry of the Highlands emanated from the British Isles. British iron interests were antagonistic to the ironworks of the American colonies and, as early as 1719, sought by legislative means to prevent the manufacture of iron wares from raw iron and the erection of forges to convert raw iron into refined iron by American companies. This legislation, and similar measures advocated by British iron interests ten years later, did not become law, but resentment toward the American iron interests did not cease until the Revolution. The basis of the hostility of British interests was a fear that cheaper American bar and pig iron, produced with the abundance of inexpensive charcoal not readily available in the British Isles, would flood the English market. This fear was well founded, as American iron began to enter the British Isles in quantity in 1735.

A major encouragement to American producers appeared in 1750. Because of an unfavorable balance of trade with Sweden, which was a major supplier to the English ironmongers, a law was passed eliminating all the duties that had been imposed on iron from the colonies. Construction of facilities in the colonies to fabricate iron beyond its refined stage was forbidden, however. Official encouragement spurred iron exports from America to the British Isles, and in 1771 they rose to a peak of five thousand tons. In reality, this was a small proportion of the total iron imported from all sources at the time, perhaps forty to fifty thousand tons a year. Despite the poor showing of American iron in relation to the imports from Sweden and Russia, a great many forges and furnaces in the Highlands were erected to exploit the steady market for their products that existed in Britain and the colonies.

Toward the end of the seventh decade of the eighteenth century many Highland iron interests fell upon bad times. This difficult period was felt by many other enterprises of the day, and is probably attributable to the difficult and deteriorating political situation.[3] A typical victim of the hard times was Thomas Reading, who was interested in the Squire's Point Forge property on the Musconetcong.

Reading made public his plight in an advertisement in the *Pennsylvania Gazette* on August 30, 1770.[4]

> Whereas the subscriber has been concerned in trade, and carrying on iron-works, for a number of years past, by which, meeting with many losses, and, by the hardness of the times, is unable to procure money to pay the debts contracted at said works, whereby they, and the lands belonging to them, which cost several Thousand Pounds, have been sold, by execution, for only as many Hundreds, as also a large estate besides, sold nearly in the same proportion to its value; I am therefore under the disagreeable necessity of giving my creditors notice, that in order to free my body from confinement, I intend to petition the legislature of the province of New-Jersey, at their next sessions, for relief in the premises.

In 1773 a group of New Jersey ironmasters issued an invitation for others associated with their industry to meet with them at Morristown in order to consider measures necessary to the better fortune of the iron business, but there is no record of any agreement having been reached.

The Revolution further served to depress the iron industry in many areas. British markets, which had consumed a large percentage of the iron produced, were closed, loyalist ironmasters had their property confiscated or closed down their works, and competent managers and workmen, who were always in short supply, found their way into the army. Forges and furnaces remaining in operation also suffered financially, despite the heavy demand for their products. The lack of hard currency often caused iron interests to expedite the sale of their iron through barter.[5] The lack of cash on the part of forge owners along the Musconetcong at this time is illustrated by the fact that in 1780 the proprietor of Greenwich Forge wrote the proprietor of Durham Furnace that he "would be very glad to get cash . . . as soon as posable [*sic*] as we are much Distressed for want of cash to pay for a Night's Lodging. . . ." [6]

Conditions did not improve after the war. There was, rather, a period of retrogression in which the industry reverted from an export-commercial focus to a primarily local market. In addition to the loss of the English market, foreign iron began to undersell the domestic product in America, primarily because American labor was so costly, and because widespread deforestation in the environs of established furnaces and forges had made fuel much more expensive than it had been in the past.[7] Also, the quality of American iron was often not as high as that of the competing foreign product. In 1785, the firm of Jones and Lownes, in Philadelphia, informed Richard Backhouse, then lessee of Durham Furnace, that the iron produced by his New Jersey forges (Greenwich and Chelsea, on the Musconetcong) was "very flawey" and that "Neat Sound Iron will take the Preference here." In addition, Backhouse's product had been sold to them for £29 per ton, whereas the competitors of Jones and Lownes were able to buy "furrin [*sic*] Iron" for £25 per ton, which was "very Neatly Drawn. . . ." The concluding statement of Jones and Lownes' missive could have been profitably considered by most Highland iron manufacturers of the day: "It will be very necessary for us to have our iron better manufactured very few forges but what hath Room for improvement. . . ." [8]

The charcoal iron industry of the New Jersey Highlands consisted of three different types of ironworking enterprises. Of primary importance were the furnaces, which were producers of metallic iron supplied to the often independent forges, which refined the raw iron of the furnace to the "bar" or wrought iron of commerce. Independent of both forge and furnace were the bloomeries, or extractive forges, which manufactured wrought iron in small quantities directly from the ore.

Of all American furnaces, those of Pennsylvania and New Jersey were especially noted for their advanced design. There are few data extant to indicate the type of furnace erected in the Musconetcong Valley and its environs. The inference is that they were similar to those of nearby eastern Pennsylvania, since Pennsylvania interests were responsible for their construction. These furnaces were, apparently, immediately derived from English precedent. This, in turn, depended on developments in continental Europe during the Middle Ages. French and German terms associated with the operations of both forges and furnaces in England and the colonies offer abundant testimony in this vein.

The typical eighteenth-century iron furnace of Pennsylvania and West Jersey consisted primarily of square stacks of stone or brick, broad at the base and narrow at the top, and reached heights of twenty feet or more. The widest portion of the inner part of the stack was termed the "bosh," and usually reached nine feet in diameter. The interior of the stack was lined with a refractory material, perhaps firebrick, and the outside with blocks of limestone or other locally obtainable rocks. The stack was open at both ends, and rested on a square chamber called the hearth, built of firebrick, or of sandstone. On each side of the stack were arches that extended into the masonry and helped to support the structure. Through one of these the tuyère penetrated the stack, in order to admit a blast of air.

Most furnaces were built into the sides of hills in order to facilitate the placing of fuel, flux, and ore in the stack. In front of the furnace, protected by a simple roof, or an enclosed building, was the casting or molding shed or house. On the floor of this structure were located the sand molds into which the molten iron was channeled from the hearth of the furnace.

Additional structures were grouped around the furnace. Typically, according to newspaper advertisements of the day, these would include the mansion of the ironmaster, other more humble structures for the workmen, coal houses for the charcoal fuel, a store, perhaps a gristmill and sawmill, a blacksmith shop, and other miscellaneous structures. If agriculture was also carried on, as was often the case, buildings devoted to grain storage and the protection of stock would also be found.

The reduction of iron ore to metallic iron in the eighteenth century was through methods much the same in principle as those employed today. Layers of charcoal, iron ore, and limestone were alternated in the stack of the furnace. Charcoal was used as fuel because it was the only fuel known in America that attained temperatures high enough to melt iron ore. Mineral coals were not utilized for the reduction of ores in North America until the nineteenth century. Limestone was included in the charge because of its value as a flux, a material that would combine easily with impurities in the iron ore.

Once a furnace had started operation or had been "blowed in," its

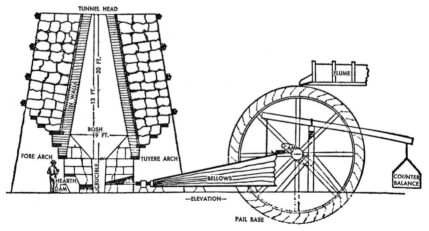

Eighteenth-century charcoal iron furnace. Eastern Pennsylvania. Source: Arthur Cecil Bining, *Pennsylvania Iron Manufacture in the Eighteenth Century* ("Publications of the Pennsylvania Historical Commission," Vol. IV; Harrisburg, Pennsylvania: Pennsylvania Historical Commission, 1938).

use was continuous. A stream of air entered the stack through the tuyère, bringing the oxygen needed for combustion of the charcoal and reduction of the iron. The air was forced through the tuyère by bellows, which were activated by a waterwheel. The high temperatures induced by the blast of air and the combustion of the charcoal liquified both ore and limestone, which tended to drip down into the hearth. The liquid iron was heavier than the slag that formed through the combination of impurities in the ore with the flux, and thus settled to the bottom of the hearth chamber.

Twice a day, or more often, depending on circumstances, the molten iron was run into the casting house from the hearth. The main stream of iron, and the molds lying on each side of it, were reminiscent of a sow and her sucking piglets, thus the terms "sow" and "pig iron" for the iron cast.

The production of metallic iron by a typical Pennsylvania furnace in the eighteenth century was about twenty-five tons per week. Durham Furnace, which supplied many forges along the Musconetcong, turned out three tons every twenty-four hours. The average furnace employed a little over a dozen men, who worked in two twelve-hour shifts. In most cases the furnace did not operate during the winter months, because freezing weather prevented the waterwheel from operating the bellows to provide the air blast necessary for smelting.[9]

Several furnaces were erected at an early date in or near the valley of the Musconetcong but not, as we have seen, before the first agriculturists began entering the area. These establishments included Durham Furnace (1727), Oxford Furnace (1741), Union Iron Works (1743), Norton Furnace (*ca.* 1743), Johnston's Furnace (1753), Andover Furnace (1760), and a small furnace erected at Changewater Forge before 1774.[10]

Although the eighteenth-century furnaces could sell and export much of their pig iron, many turned to the establishment of forges where pig iron could be processed into bar iron, which sold for three and a half times the price of ordinary pig iron. The forges in the Musconetcong drainage system, and in West Jersey in general, were often erected by Philadelphia interests, so it is probable that English methods of construction and ironworking were in use there as they were in Pennsylvania.

Eighteenth-century forges in the Highlands varied in size, small ones having but one hearth and one hammer, the largest including perhaps four fires and two hammers. Pig iron, in the form of rough bars five or six feet long and about six inches wide, was brought to these forges from the furnaces. The pig iron was fabricated into bar

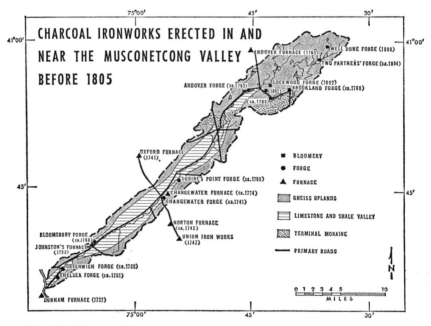

CHARCOAL IRONWORKS ERECTED IN AND NEAR THE MUSCONETCONG VALLEY BEFORE 1805

Compiled from various sources.

iron at the forges. The first step was to place the pig iron in the first hearth of the forge, which was termed the "finery." After the pig had softened into a lump, it was removed from the hearth with a hook and tongs and placed on an anvil under a great iron hammer activated by a waterwheel. After having been pounded by the hammer, the iron was replaced in the hearth, and heated to a bright red color. It was then again placed under the hammer. The result of this treatment was an "ancony," a bar of wrought iron which was flat, thick, and had a rough nob at each end. The anconies were usually reheated at another hearth, known as the chafery, and reworked under the hammer to form the "bar iron" of commerce.

Individual pieces of bar iron varied greatly in size, but were often drawn about fourteen feet in length, two inches in breadth, and half an inch thick. In 1783, John Stotesbury, then manager of Chelsea Forge on the Musconetcong, sent Richard Backhouse at Durham Furnace two one-ton batches of bar iron. One contained sixty-eight, and the other seventy-one individual pieces.[11]

The processing of pig iron into bar iron was necessary because of the brittle nature of the iron produced by the early charcoal blast furnaces. Pig iron was actually an alloy of iron with carbon, which had been introduced by charcoal; and it also contained a varying amount of slag. The processes employed by the eighteenth-century forge-men served to drive out the carbon and to extend the slag throughout the bar in a fibrous structure. This strengthened the metal but did not alter its chemical composition.

Both the finery and the chafery consisted of open hearths covered with heaps of coals, which were surmounted by huge chimneys. As was the case in a furnace of the day, a blast of air was supplied to the hearth by bellows activated by a waterwheel.

Forge hammers were truly massive, four to six hundred pounds in weight, and were mounted on oak beams running parallel to the shaft of the waterwheel. A waterwheel measured twenty-five feet or more in diameter and activated the hammers by means of trunnions catching the oak beams immediately behind the hammer heads.[12] Waterwheels in use at the forges were most likely of the undershot type in early days, as Peter Hasenclever is generally credited with introduc-ing the use of the overshot wheel for the working of iron in New Jersey in the middle of the eighteenth century. The idea was still thought novel as late as 1768.

Hasenclever, a German who operated the Ringwood Iron Works, introduced other advanced ideas for ironworking into the state. He was credited by contemporaries with being the first to use "shafts with strong cast-iron rings, whose arms served as cogs to lift the hammer handle," and also was "the first person that we know who has so greatly improved the use of the great natural ponds of this country as by damming them to secure reservoirs of water for the use of iron works in the dry season, without which the best streams are liable to fail in the great droughts we are subject to."[13]

Indeed, drought and an increased rate of evapotranspiration during the warm months were common problems throughout the Highlands, causing many smaller streams to run too low for the operation of a waterwheel. This problem affected ironworks on the Musconetcong less than it did on other streams. Eighteenth-century advertisements constantly referred to the Musconetcong as "a never-failing stream of water," and as being "noted for a fine constant stream of water."[14]

Another problem affecting forge and furnace operations alike was freezing in the winter. Forges generally operated during periods of open water during the winter. Not being continuous operations, as were the furnaces, forges could operate in a stop-and-go fashion, taking advantage of the periods of high water in winter. The problems of winter operation are illustrated by letters emanating from some of the Musconetcong forges. On January 10, 1784, Thomas Wright of Greenwich Forge wrote Richard Backhouse at Durham Furnace: "We are entirely Froze up for some days past or else you should have had a Tun of Barr Iron this day . . . Our Race is . . . much Damaged, by the Snow and Ice. . . ." [15]

Eighteenth-century charcoal iron forges in both England and America were generally somewhat removed from the furnaces from which they drew their raw material. This was chiefly because both operations utilized waterpower, and suitable sites for the same were limited, often effecting a distance of several miles between forge and furnace. Another consideration was the fact that both forge and furnace used large quantities of charcoal, which may not have been available in amounts to allow both operations in the same locality.

Eighteenth-century forges varied in productivity. In Pennsylvania, a small forge might produce about two tons of bar iron a week, whereas a larger forge, with three or four hearths and two hammers, working doublehanded, could produce three hundred to three hundred and fifty tons per year. In 1777, Brookland Forge, located on the Musconetcong near Lake Hopatcong, which possessed four hearths and two hammers, was said to be able to produce three hundred tons of bar iron per year,[16] indicating a similarity in amount of production to the forges of Pennsylvania. On the other hand, Greenwich Forge, also on the Musconetcong, and also having four hearths and two hammers, produced only 147 tons of bar iron in the period from April 6, 1780 to July 1, 1782.[17] This low rate of production may have been the result of the exigencies of wartime, however.

The shrunken local market that existed at the end of the eighteenth century encouraged at least some forges to produce quite diverse goods, in addition to turning out bar iron. Greenwich Forge frequently produced nails in the 1780's. Other products included "RINGERS' BARRS for hoops," "Shear moles," "Land Slides," "Anchonies," "Plow Shares," "Ladol molds," and a "Sledge Mould weighing twenty pounds." [18]

According to eighteenth-century newspaper advertisements, forge communities in the Highlands generally, and in the Musconetcong Valley particularly, varied considerably in their constituent parts. Most contained some sort of relatively pretentious dwelling for the proprietor or manager, smaller dwellings, often of logs, for workmen, the building or buildings containing hearths and hammers, which were built of stone or frame construction, and a coal house, often built of stone, for storing large amounts of charcoal. Other buildings housed services necessary to or convenient for the forge workers and also for the subsistence agriculturists who lived nearby, but who were independent of the forge company. The services included a company store, a smithy, and often a sawmill and a gristmill. The latter two frequently occupied the same structure.

The labor utilized by the forge owners varied from place to place. In many cases, Negroes or redemptioners were used. When Greenwich Forge, on the lower Musconetcong, was offered for sale in 1768, the owner indicated that "there will also be rented with the works, seven negro men, who have been employed for many years past in the Forge, and understand the making of iron." [19] Negroes remained a large part of the labor force at Greenwich Forge as late as the 1780's. In 1770, Negroes were also represented among forge laborers in the north-eastern part of the Musconetcong drainage system. In that year, Andover Forge employed "six Negroe Slaves . . . who are good Forge-men, and understand the making and drawing of Iron well. . . ." [20]

The redemptioners, who were employed by the majority of forges, were often dissatisfied with their working conditions, and attempted to escape. The plethora of forges in the Musconetcong Valley ad-vertising rewards for runaway redemptioners in the eighteenth century illustrate the universality of this problem. Names and descriptions included in the advertisements for runaways indicate that the ma-jority in the Musconetcong Valley were of English or Irish descent.

Whether the workman was a slave, redemptioner, or wage laborer, he often fared poorly at the iron forges. According to William Kirby, who worked at the Andover Iron Works in 1762: [21]

> The wood chopper piled his wood so as to cheat the collier. The collier put his charcoal into baskets in such a manner as to deceive the iron master; and the iron master, not to be outdone, sold his provisions to the men at an extortionate price.

The result was that very little in the sense of real wages was ever seen by even the free workman, and that the work of the forge was carried on in a more slipshod manner than obtained in northwestern Europe at the same time.

The erection of forges at suitable sites in the Musconetcong drain-age system soon followed the establishment of the charcoal iron furnaces, which assured a ready supply of pig iron. In many cases, furnace and forge were erected by the same companies. Forges erected in the Musconetcong Valley during the eighteenth century included Changewater Forge (*ca.* 1741), Greenwich Forge (*ca.* 1750), Chelsea Forge (*ca.* 1751), Brookland Forge (*ca.* 1760), Squire's Point Forge (*ca.* 1760), Andover Forge (1763), and Bloomsbury Forge (*ca.* 1766). [22]

The charcoal iron industry of the Highlands included not only the interrelated forges and furnaces but also bloomeries, which produced bar iron directly from the ore. Most eighteenth-century bloomeries in northern New Jersey consisted of one or more hearths constructed very much like a blacksmith's forge, except larger. Air was introduced by means of a tuyère and was forced into the bed of hot coals by means of bellows activated by a waterwheel, as was the case with forges and furnaces.

The production of bar iron at a bloomery involved the acquisition of relatively rich ore from nearby mines, breaking it into small pieces, and then placing it in the heated hearth along with limestone and large quantities of charcoal. As the ore softened, it was worked with a long bar by the forgemen, until a lump of metallic iron, known as the "bloom," or "loop" was formed. This pasty ball of iron, when of a suitable size, was withdrawn from the forge and was placed on an anvil to be pounded under a heavy hammer, as was done in the refinery forges. Successive heatings and hammerings drove out most of the impurities, and the resulting bar iron was appropriate for the use of local smiths and artisans.

Most bloomeries were relatively small enterprises, consisting of but one or two fires and one hammer. The maximum production of most bloomeries was one ton of bar iron per week. Bloomery bar iron sold for approximately three times the price of ordinary pig iron, but was not valued as highly as the refined bar iron of the typical forge, which brought a slightly higher price. This was probably because of the relatively larger amounts of impurities in the bloomery iron. Bloomeries were often simply called "forges" in eighteenth-century accounts, since their operations were quite similar to those of the forges, which refined the pig iron of the furnaces. Thus, it is often difficult to identify a bloomery as such.[23]

Despite their less advanced technology and independent nature, bloomeries generally succeeded rather than preceded the forges. The reason for this is to be found in the fact that the loss of the English market made the larger iron enterprises increasingly uneconomic, whereas the independent bloomeries could better adjust their production to the shrunken local market. Also, in many areas, deforestation had removed the fuel supply so badly needed by the larger iron enterprises. The bloomeries located, for the most part, in relatively rugged, glaciated areas, where large-scale, economic production of pig and bar iron was impossible, but where there was a good supply of wood available, and where a sufficient demand existed.[24]

Several bloomeries were established in the Musconetcong Valley during the latter part of the eighteenth century and the first few years of the nineteenth century. These included a relatively early one associated with, and on the site of Andover Forge (1763), two in the environs of present Stanhope (*ca.* 1780–1801), two on Weldon Brook (1800–1805), and one on Lubber's Run (1802).[25]

In order to obtain iron ore for the furnaces established at Bloomsbury and Changewater and for the bloomeries that were established at Andover, Stanhope, and on Weldon Brook and Lubber's Run, many mine pits were opened. Since there was not the demand for the large quantities of ore that characterized later nineteenth-century operations, and since quite rich ores outcropped at the surface in many locations, mining was a casual affair in that little in the way of technical knowledge was needed to remove the ore. An observer in 1783 mentioned that "any knowledge of mining is superfluous here [Pennsylvania] where there is neither shaft nor gallery to be driven, all work being at the surface, or in great, wide trenches or pits." [26] A similar situation obtained in New Jersey. When a pit became too deep for efficient operation, or a high water table caused flooding, the miners simply began to dig elsewhere.

The value of iron mines was well known to the early surveyors of the Highlands, who had staked out most of the productive mines of the area before the Revolution. The earliest mine in operation seems to have been the Dickerson Mine at Succasunna, the ore of which was being utilized as early as 1700. This was one of the richest mines ever opened in the state, and in early days supplied many extractive forges located at a distance.[27]

The earliest mine located in the Musconetcong Valley appears to have been the one owned by Martin Ryerson, who in 1750 possessed a body of ore "on ye North East Side of a Brooke that Runs in the Most northerly Branch of Maskinitkonck river [Lubber's Run]. . . ." [28] By 1761, Johnston Furnace at present Bloomsbury was making use of ore "carted from the south side of Musconetcong Mountain." [29] This ore lay "within a quarter of a mile of the furnace. . . ." [30] Andover Forge worked up ore from the Rossville Mine, which lay approximately two miles to the northeast of the forge.[31]

"Iron Mines" are shown prominently to the northwest of Changewater on the Faden map of 1769 (Appendix I). It is possible that it was from this location that the small furnace at Changewater drew its ore. Later bloomeries were most likely supplied by outcroppings of ore, which were locally abundant, or by the extremely rich ore from the Dickerson Mine at Succasunna. Lockwood Forge, on Lubber's Run, was supplied by the Stanhope or Hude Mine, opened in 1802.[32]

An extremely important activity upon which all iron interests depended was the burning of charcoal. Forges in the Musconetcong Valley employed both woodcutters and colliers. Much of the work probably was done by local farmers on a part-time basis, since the account books indicate that forges paid woodcutters by the cord, and also paid daily wages for "coaling." Much of this work was done during the cold part of the year, when agriculturists had time to spare.

The open-pit process of producing charcoal in use at this time varied only slightly from place to place in the Middle Colonies. Wood was cut in approximately four-foot lengths and piled tightly, on end, in a hole dug in the ground. The conical stack resulting varied in circumference and height according to the number of cords in the charge. The center of the stack was occupied by a shaft in which small pieces of kindling were placed. Large sheets of sod and several inches of earth were used to cover the entire mass, with the exception of strategically placed vent holes. A fire was then started in the central shaft, and by carefully regulating the air supply by opening and closing the vents, the wood was evenly charred. A fifteen-cord charge required approximately two weeks before the charcoal could be used.[33]

Forge account books indicate that open-pit charcoal kilns were constructed on the sites where cut wood was available, and the charcoal was then hauled to the forges. The presence of sufficient wooded land to allow the production of an ample supply of charcoal was vital to the continued operation of forge, furnace, and bloomery alike. Unfortunately, the general policy on the part of the owners of ironworks seems to have been to clear-cut the forest as rapidly as possible without thought as to regeneration. This practice was universally denounced by European travelers, who were cognizant of the more enlightened forest management carried on in their homelands. The remarks of Johann Schoepf in 1783 are of special note in this regard: [34]

> The business of the mines and foundries, in New Jersey as well as throughout America, cannot be said to be on as firm a basis as in most parts of Europe, because nobody is concerned about forest preservation and without an uninterrupted supply of fuel and timber many works must go to ruin, as indeed has already been the case here and there. Not the least economy is observed with regard to forests. The owners of furnaces and foundaries possess for the most part great tracts of appurtenant woods, which are cut off, however, without any system or order. The bulk of the inhabitants sell wood only in so far as to bring the land they own into cultivation, reserving a certain acreage of forest necessary for domestic consumption. The Union, a high furnace in Jersey, exhausted a forest of nearly 20,000 acres in about twelve to fifteen years, and the works had to be abandoned for lack of wood.

In similar fashion, at an early date, iron interests in the Musconetcong Valley began to experience a shortage of wood for charcoal. As early as the 1750's and 1760's proprietors of forges in the southwestern portion of the valley began buying additional property in order to secure additional woodland.[35] Owners of wooded property located near iron-works continually had difficulties protecting their timber from being cut and spirited away to be sold to the forge owners—a common practice in many thinly settled areas. In 1764, a report on the Barker tract in Alexandria Township described the incursions of timber thieves: [36]

> The Timber cut down and wasted and Three hundred Cord laying in the woods ready to be converted into charcoal for supplying the two Iron Forges [Greenwich and Chelsea] in the Neighbourhood—We had great reason to think the Owners of the forges did every thing in their power to prevent the settlers from coming under Lease which would deprive them of getting the Wood at a very low price. One Starr [Jacob Starn] who owned the larger Forge [Greenwich Forge] and was Sheriff of the County seemed to be the leading man in that part of the Country. I threatened him with a suit for Trespass and Waste, he begged hard and promised that he would neither cut himself or buy from any of the settlers on the Tract. We then found that Mr. Starr was not on good terms with his neighbours and we engaged them to watch that no timber should be cut on the Estate hereafter.

More than twenty years later, because of the turbulence of the Revolutionary War years, the same general situation existed on the tract. A report written in the year 1785 indicates that wood stealing was still a major problem: [37]

> The common Convention on this Subject is that these people are encouraged in their opposing Sir Roberts Title by Hugh Hughes who is one of the Judges of the Court of Common Pleas in the County of Sussex and is concerned in Iron works on the River Mosconetcunk [Greenwich Forge] and I think it very likely because he has no coal wood to his works and by stirring up this Spirit of opposition and keeping the owner off the Land he has an opportunity of buying wood of the Trespassers on the Tract, at a very low rate.

As woodlands became more and more depleted of coal-size trees, and the carriage of charcoal to ironworks became more expensive, the larger iron interests, which were located on fertile limestone soils, were forced to sell off their cleared lands to agriculturists. By 1774, Changewater Forge's lands had been "divided into plantations of about 200 acres each." In the same year, Squire's Point Forge was advertised as "the noted farm, late the property of Ryerson and Reading. . . ." Andover

Forge was abandoned after the Revolution because of the lack of fuel wood, and "for years thereafter the locality . . . was a barren waste." [38]

The result of the general deforestation encouraged by the iron industry was not only the encouragement of agriculture where the soils allowed, but also a change in the species composition of the forests. Wherever the land was not immediately placed in agricultural use, sprouts from the stumps of certain species of clear-cut trees began to regenerate the forest. The "piece of young timber" [39] which James Parker noted on the slope of Musconetcong Mountain in 1789 had its parallels elsewhere. Since clear-cutting encouraged sprout rather than seedling reproduction, certain vigorously sprouting and rapidly growing hardwoods soon dominated the second-growth woodlands. The chestnut and the various oaks were especially favored. [40]

Another change from the natural landscape caused by the iron industry was the impoundment of streams to provide a steady source of power during periods of low water, or to raise the head of the water and thus provide a greater fall and more power. Impoundments during the eighteenth century consisted of crude stone dams built by placing large stones in the stream at a rapids, small waterfall, or downstream from a basin or widening in the stream which would receive the impoundment. Other dams consisted of large timbers with an earth, boulder, and gravel fill. [41]

The most impressive impoundment was at Lake Hopatcong, where an earthen-fill dam raised the level of the Great Pond approximately five feet, [42] backing it up and joining it to the Little Pond to the northeast. The Faden map shows that more humble impoundments served the waterwheels at Andover and Bloomsbury. New Partners Forge was supplied by "a pond of large dimensions" [43] (now Lake Shawnee) in 1818. This body of water existed as early as 1769, as it is shown on the Faden map, but may well have been expanded by impoundment when the forge was built.

CHAPTER 7

Pioneer Industries and Villages

As significant numbers of agriculturists settled in the Musconetcong drainage system it became possible for entrepreneurs to erect industrial establishments to serve their needs. The most significant of these industries, in both their appearance on the landscape and their impact on the local economy, were those that used the power inherent in the fast-flowing river. In some cases, those industries serving mainly agrarian needs shared power sites with ironworks; in other cases they stood alone, perhaps at a site bypassed by the iron interests. The value of waterpower was well appreciated by early speculators, and promising sites were acquired well in advance of the tide of settlement.

The earliest and most important application of waterpower in a pioneer agrarian community for local needs involved the grinding of grain. In the period before gristmills were established locally for this purpose, settlers had the choice of an inordinately long trip over difficult trails to a distant mill, or of having the grain ground at home by hand. The latter was often the choice first made in remote settlements.

In northwestern New Jersey, the home grinding of grain depended on the utilization of either of two implements. Many women, adhering to Old World precedent, preferred the rotary quern, which consisted of two specially ground and fitted circular stones, perhaps eighteen inches in diameter, the upper of which revolved upon the lower and, in so doing, ground the grain that lay between. Other settlers, who had been more influenced by aboriginal example, used mortars and pestles. The pestle was often of stone, and the mortar of wood. In some cases, the settlers used a section of a hardwood tree for the mortar and a wooden pestle, which was fastened to a bent sapling, thus lessening the work involved. Such devices were termed "plumping mills." [1]

The establishment of grain mills activated by waterpower caused the

117

discontinuance of home-grinding. Settlers traveled long distances, their grain in long bags draped over the backs of several horses, and often spent several days in travel to spare their wives the arduous work involved in hand-grinding wheat to a flour fine enough for baking purposes. At the time of first agricultural settlement in the Musconetcong Valley, John Bowlby, owner of an extensive property in the vicinity of Hampton, made use of mill facilities at Pittstown, a little less than ten miles to the south. His route was by way of an Indian path and often, upon arrival at the mill, he found that he had to wait his turn. Upon occasion, this meant a stay of two or three days away from home.[2]

The role of gristmills in the early settlement of many areas has not been properly examined. It was obviously of benefit to the pioneer to have a mill located relatively nearby and thus save on the inordinate amount of time spent on travel to and from the mill. For example, as early as 1737, a property on the banks of the Musconetcong was advertised as being only "6 Miles from the Place where a new Grist-Mill is going to be erected by Samuel Green."[3]

Unfortunately, there is little information extant on the type or morphology of the early gristmills of northwestern New Jersey. Even those scholars whose interests have included mills have not been concerned with this problem, and the early mills themselves have all vanished. Of log, frame, or a combination of these two building materials, early mills were subject to cannibalization when superseded by more advanced structures or, in many cases, were destroyed by fire.

The best description of an early mill near the Musconetcong Valley and generally in northwestern New Jersey, is contained in Casper Schaeffer's reminiscences of his grandfather, a German pioneer who settled at Stillwater on the Paulinskill, approximately thirteen miles north of Hackettstown, in 1741 or 1742. Within the first few years of his settlement, Schaeffer's grandfather built a simple mill, which served the surrounding farming community for many years. His grandson described the structure and its capacity as follows:[4]

> To create a water power, he threw a low dam of cobbled stones, filled in with gravel, across the stream. He then proceeded to drive in the ground, at the west end of the dam, piles, over which he erected his log mill superstructure; it was now ready for business. Its dimensions being small, its execution was on a corresponding scale, from three to five bushels being the ordinary quantity it would grind in a day.

It can be seen that the small capacity of this mill may have caused many to wait their turn just as John Bowlby did at Pittstown.

Although the description of the original Schaeffer mill, compiled through both the author's memory of the remains of the mill in his youth and by conversations with his grandfather, is slight, available evidence indicates that it was probably a tub mill. Tub mills were the simplest and most inexpensive mills that the pioneers could build. They were activated by a horizontal waterwheel approximately eight feet in diameter or less, with oblique paddles. Water was channeled in to strike the upper part of the wheel in the direction of a tangent with its circumference. Buckets were set in the wheel obliquely so that the water struck them at right angles. The wheel, the vertical shaft to which it was attached, and the upper millstone, revolved as one unit. The term "tub mill" was applied because the wheel had a tub or hoop around it that confined the water until its motive force was extracted. All parts of the early tub mills, save the millstones, could easily be made of wood, saving the pioneer miller great trouble and expense. Tub mills were certainly present in early settlements in Hunterdon County, and tradition indicates that they were almost universal among the early German settlers of that county.[5]

The rapid increase in population throughout northwestern New Jersey, especially during the seventh decade of the eighteenth century, heightened the demand for local milling services in the region. On the Musconetcong, as well as on neighboring streams, gristmills were erected to service this demand. Gristmills were built as early as 1758 at Bloomsbury, before 1761 at present Warren Glen, and before 1763 near Hackettstown. A map published in 1776 shows only the place name "Salmons Mill" at what was then the settlement of Bloomsbury. Gristmills which may have been built at least as early were in operation between Changewater and Penwell in 1765, at Squire's Point in 1769, and at Waterloo in 1770, and at the outlet of Lake Hopatcong in 1773. Mills which were known to have been in operation before the Revolution were located at Beattystown, Asbury, and on the Barker property northeast of Finesville. Mill construction was adversely affected by the economic dislocations resulting from the Revolution and probably ceased for the duration.[6]

In 1784, two gristmills were being operated in Asbury, and another was built near Penwell, perhaps as early as 1785. In the next decade a gristmill was built on the north bank of the stream at Finesville in 1791; on the north bank at Riegelsville before 1793; on the south bank in the same vicinity in 1796; and on a small brook entering the Musconetcong at Anderson in 1798. In 1800 a gristmill was built on the south bank of the Musconetcong at New Hampton, and about the same time the "Point Mills," were constructed at Squire's Point.[7]

With the probable exception of the gristmills constructed on brooks

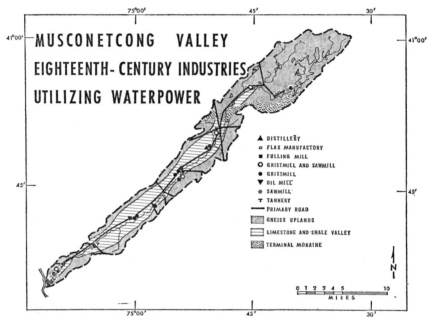

MUSCONETCONG VALLEY
EIGHTEENTH-CENTURY INDUSTRIES
UTILIZING WATERPOWER

▲ DISTILLERY
▫ FLAX MANUFACTORY
■ FULLING MILL
◉ GRISTMILL AND SAWMILL
● GRISTMILL
▼ OIL MILL
✳ SAWMILL
т TANNERY
— PRIMARY ROAD
▨ GNEISS UPLANDS
▤ LIMESTONE AND SHALE VALLEY
▧ TERMINAL MORAINE

N

0 1 2 3 4 5   10
MILES

Compiled from various sources.

tributary to the main stream, the mills established on the Musconetcong proper were probably not simple tub mills. They were designed to make use of a larger quantity of water than tub mills required, and also to satisfy a demand greater than could be met by smaller-scale operations. Also, at least half of the mills were established at the iron forges, where a more advanced technological knowledge than that possessed by simple farmers was available. Unfortunately, again data are limited; little has been published on the early mills, and fires and cannibalization have taken their toll.

The best account of the establishment of a gristmill during the later phase of pioneer settlement in northwestern New Jersey is again that of Casper Schaeffer's grandson. Fortunately, the younger Schaeffer was himself a miller for part of his life, and was familiar with the second structure erected by his grandfather, which was located on a site near that of the first mill.[8]

> About the year 1764 the second mill was built . . . having a head race about a quarter of a mile long, and twenty-five or thirty-feet wide by which a greater fall and water power were obtained. This mill, though not large, was a great advance on the former one, containing two runs of

stones, with bolts and other appurtenances, rendering it much more efficient. . . . Connected with this establishment there was also a sawmill
and an oil-mill.

Apparently this mill was of wood construction, as it burned to the
ground in the early part of the nineteenth century. The mill was a
three-story affair with outside stairs, which the miller used to carry the
grain in to be ground, and later, out to the waiting horse or wagon of
the farmer. The later nineteenth-century mill, built after the destruction
of its predecessor by fire, was described as having been able to "perform
three times as much work as the old mill" with the use of the same
amount of waterpower.

Another gristmill of the day, located on the Musconetcong at Hackettstown, was advertised for sale in 1777. It was described as being "a large
frame mill with two pair of stones, the one pair sopes, the other cullen,
one pair for merchant and the other for country work, with four boult-
ing cloths, all in good order. . . ." [9]

Although most of the early mills served a local market, grinding
wheat, rye, buckwheat, oats, and maize for farmers who came as often as
twice a week for this service, later mills also engaged in merchant work.
Merchant mills bought grain from the farmers, manufactured it into
flour, and then sent it to a larger market. The mill located at Hackettstown, and its associated property, was leased by a miller named William
Allen in 1778 from Garret Rapalje, the owner, for six hundred bushels
of wheat per year.[10] Payment in kind indicates that Allen probably
received a toll from the farmers rather than hard cash in payment for
his services. This was a common practice in the eighteenth and nineteenth centuries.[11]

Mills in use on the Musconetcong, and elsewhere in the northwestern
part of the state during the greater part of the eighteenth century, were
for the most part powered through the use of undershot waterwheels.
This type of wheel was placed in running water in such a way that the
paddles on its lower side would be struck by the flowing water and thus
rotate the wheel. The undershot waterwheels in use usually consisted
of two large wooden wheels on the same shaft, often being from
twenty-five to thirty feet in diameter and having paddles one to two feet
wide. These wheels turned in shallow water and did not require the
construction of dams as did the later overshot wheels. On occasion,
simple dams were built, at first probably much like Casper Schaeffer's
grandfather's first dam. The mill at Hackettstown may have lain below
such a dam. In such a case, water was probably conveyed to the waterwheel by means of a small canal or race dug from just above the dam to
the mill site. This was a practice well known in northwestern Europe

as early as medieval times, and was of relatively easy execution.[12] At the Squire's Point Forge in 1769, the gristmill joined "one end of the forge dam. . . ." [13]

In the case of the later Schaeffer mill, no dam is mentioned, and it is possible that many of the early undershot mills were not associated with dams. The Schaeffer mill had an extraordinarily long and wide raceway, implying that an undershot wheel, activated by the force of the current, rather than an overshot wheel, activated by the weight of the falling water, was in use. Other evidence for the presence of undershot rather than overshot mill wheels includes Schaeffer's statement that a still later mill, built in the nineteenth century, was three times as effective, with the same power source, as the mill built in 1764. This may well reflect a switch to an overshot wheel in the later mill. John Smeaton's experiments in England, beginning in the 1750's, indicated that whereas an undershot wheel could have an efficiency of twenty-two per cent, an overshot wheel could transfer up to sixty-three per cent of the force of falling water to a mill shaft. Also, Johann Schoepf, traveling through the Middle States after the Revolution, thought of overshot wheels as being "a sort rare in America," [14] and a committee report, published in 1769, stated that the use of the overshot wheel in the iron industry of New Jersey was "new in America." [15] Since at least half of the mills in use on the Musconetcong at that time were erected by iron interests, it is unlikely that more sophisticated devices would be utilized to power mills, which were a secondary interest, than were used to power the forges.

The foregoing is not to disclaim the use of overshot wheels early in the eighteenth century. Indeed, Charles Hoff of Kingwood, approximately six miles south of the Musconetcong, possessed "One over-shot Stone Grist-mill," [16] in 1755. On the Musconetcong, however, it is most likely that the eighteenth-century mills were undershot.

Another quite necessary pioneer industry that depended on water-power in the eighteenth century was sawmilling. At some sites sawmilling preceded the milling of grain. This occurred at Coe's Forge at the outlet of Lake Hopatcong in 1764, where a gristmill did not appear until perhaps 1773, and also at present Bloomsbury, where a sawmill seems to have preceded the establishment of a gristmill in 1758. At Changewater Forge, a sawmill was established as early as 1756, and at Chelsea Forge as early as 1763. In both cases, gristmills do not seem to have been established until a much later date.[17]

In 1770 a survey mentions that one Doctor Ogden had lately built a sawmill on "the Main Branch of Musquenetung Pond [Lake Hopatcong] about 2 Miles and ½ up sd. Branch from sd. Pond." [18] The report also stated that "the water Stands ponded for a considerable distance," indicating that a dam had been built. This sawmill was apparently an uneconomic investment, for a survey sixteen years later in the same vicinity mentions "an old Frame of a Sawmill built by Doctor Ogden. . . ." [19] Sparcity of settlement in this rugged glaciated region probably generated at best a low demand for lumber products.

Other sawmills were associated with gristmills. In many eighteenth-century advertisements, the term "Grist and Saw-Mill" or "Grist-mill and Saw-mill," is used, indicating that one structure served to house both activities. Such, apparently, was the case at Greenwich Forge in 1761, at Squire's Point Forge in 1765, and at Andover Forge in 1770. A sawmill was also attached to Helm's Mill, built near Hackettstown before 1763. The property advertised by Mark Thompson in 1777, which lay in Hackettstown, included a gristmill and also "a saw mill joining to the other mills. . . ." In 1796, William, John, and Edward Hunt erected a sawmill on the north bank of the river in Greenwich Township. This apparently was an operation independent of grain milling and may have in part depended on the timber being rafted down the Delaware at the time.[20]

The early sawmills, which were apparently mostly of wood construction, met the needs of the settlers for home construction. There was a preference among many pioneers for construction in frame instead of log or stone. Before the construction of sawmills in the region, lumber went through a laborious process of being squared with a broadaxe, raised on a scaffold six or seven feet high, and then being sawed by two men, one above and one below, operating a pitsaw. One hundred feet per day was a good output for two men working hard. This was much too slow a process to provide the lumber needed for the wave of settlers that engulfed northwestern New Jersey in the 1760's, and the establishment of water-driven sawmills was much encouraged by the increased demand for lumber.

Sawmills, like gristmills, were probably activated by undershot wheels. The waterwheel activated a crank, which powered a sash saw. This consisted of a saw sliding up and down in a frame like the mechanism of a modern window sash.[21]

It is instructive to note that a will probated in 1749 included the estimated value of a gristmill and a sawmill on the Union Furnace property in Hunterdon County. The gristmill was valued at one hundred pounds sterling and the sawmill at but thirty. This probably reflects the basic difference in value between these two structures in eighteenth-century New Jersey.[22]

Another need of the pioneer farmer was clothing. In early days, and

even well into the nineteenth century, much cloth was woven in the
home. Homespun, especially woolens, was not suitable for wear until
it had been further processed. Fulling was especially necessary. This
involved beating the cloth vigorously with paddles and compressing it
in water. This process caused it to shrink to a greatly reduced length
and width. Also, the fibers became so entangled that the pattern of
the weave was less noticeable, and the fabric became smoother, thicker,
and firmer. Such cloth lasted much longer than ordinary homespun.
Fulling was at first a home industry but there is little evidence as to
how it was done in New Jersey. The task, however, was probably
onerous, and the application of waterpower for the purpose was wel-
comed.[23]

In 1773 "a fulling mill with a new dam, new shaft, and all necessary
implements in good repair," [24] was in operation near Hackettstown.
John Crooks was apparently the fuller at that time. The mill was still
in operation in 1778, being run by one Peter Caskey.[25]

Another use of waterpower was for the crushing of flaxseed for linseed oil. Oil mills were rare in the eighteenth century and little is
known of them. In some cases a waterwheel activated pestles, which
crushed the seed, and in smaller operations the seed was crushed by
being passed through rollers.[26] An oil mill is said to have been located
at Halls Mills (Asbury) in 1784.[27]

In 1790 John Smith, who had been a boss collier at Andover,
leased the land associated with the forge. He and his brothers farmed the
denuded tract and carried on linen manufacturing in the old mill
building associated with the forge. This enterprise met an early end
because of the burning of the mill. The mill presently on the site is of
stone, indicating that its origin is probably later.[28]

Another household occupation that later became a local industry
was tanning. In the days of first settlement, each family did its own
tanning and currying. These operations were carried out mostly in the
fall. Skins were soaked in lye to loosen the hair, which was later
scraped off. The hides were then soaked in a strong solution of tannin,
which was derived from oak and hemlock bark. The tanning solution
was contained in a large wooden vat or trough sunk into the ground.

As more hides became available it became profitable for individuals
to engage in tanning on a commercial scale. Commercial tanning was
generally done on a share basis, with the farmer paying for the
tanner's services in kind. The tanner could then sell his skins elsewhere for cash.

The typical commercial tannery of the eighteenth century in New
Jersey was located along the banks of a stream and consisted of sev-

eral sheds containing vats and a tan mill. The vats or troughs were of two types. One type was oblong, of wood, and sunk into the ground near a stream with the upper portion protruding slightly above ground level. These were open at the top and closed at the bottom. The other type of trough was of similar construction but was located entirely above ground level. Those above ground level acted as "limes," in which lime water would remove hair from the hide. The pits or vats below ground level had several functions. Some held fermented infusions of dog or chicken manure, which removed the lime and softened the fibers of the hide. Others held tan liquor produced by steeping oak or hemlock bark in water. The hides were worked in these vats after being removed from the infusion of fermented manure. The need for relatively large quantities of water served to limit tanneries to streamside sites.

Tan mills were integral parts of commercial tanneries and were generally housed in open sheds. Horses were used to turn alternate wooden and stone wheels in a trough about fifteen feet in diameter in order to crush the bark from which tannin was extracted.[29]

In the Musconetcong Valley, where the vicinity known as "Hacket's" had early prominence as a source of supply for skins, there were at least two and probably three early tanneries. The earliest of these, possibly established before 1764, was at Hackettstown. John Buckley, of English descent, was the tanner and apparently his business prospered. Another early tannery, probably relying on the Musconetcong for its water supply, was the "tan mill" located on Sir Robert Barker's tract in Alexandria Township. Reference to this operation is contained in an advertisement of the Barker tract for auction by James Parker, probably dating immediately after the Revolution. At any rate, a "Tan Yard" was listed on the tax records of Alexandria Township in 1785 as belonging to one Alexander Lock. In 1805, Thomas Elder of Bloomsbury offered a "tanyard to let" on the banks of the "Musconitkong" River near the village of Bloomsbury.[30] In this tanyard the vats were filled by spouts from the forebay of the mill, indicating that waterpower was used to crush the bark.

Elder's tanyard was said to have access to quantities of bark on reasonable terms. It is probable that the continuing use of surviving woodlands for the burning of charcoal made large quantities of bark available for the tanning industry. This was probably an additional factor that had encouraged tanners to locate in the valley.

Another industry of some local importance, which arose as large quantities of grain and apples became available, was distilling. In 1811, Francis Asbury lamented that his namesake village would be a pleasant place if it were not for "the brewing and drinking of miserable whisky. . . ."[31] Stills were common on large farms in the state in the late eighteenth century. In 1792, Thomas Bowlby paid ten shillings "for brick to set the still" on a property in Bethlehem Township. Joseph Anderson built a still at Anderson in the early years of the nineteenth century, and Ziba Osmun constructed an apple-brandy distillery in Beattystown before the end of the eighteenth century.[32]

Stills depended upon grain and apples as raw materials, both of which were available in large amounts toward the end of the eighteenth century. Another consideration was the presence of a small, cool rivulet or spring, the waters of which could be used in condensing the evaporated spirits.

Stills were commonly made by coppersmiths, and consisted of three main parts: (1) a large bulbous vessel, which varied in capacity, to which was attached a tube through which non-volatile material was drawn off; (2) a smaller bulbous vessel fitted into the top of the larger vessel and which in turn fed into a tapering tube which was attached to (3) the condenser, which consisted of a "worm" or coil of copper tubing immersed in cool water. The whole was set in a brickwork stove, and a wood fire was used to evaporate the alcohol.

The structures enclosing stills were often of a temporary nature but some were built of stone. Surviving structures are narrow in relation to length, possess gable roofs, and have their entrances located on the long side. Quite often, distilleries were set into the sides of hills, evidently to make use of springs.[33]

The lists of county tax ratables extant indicate the numbers of mills, stills, and tanyards in existence in particular townships for certain years. In the Musconetcong drainage system and environs, such lists, including the number of taxpayers, are available for Greenwich Township in 1774, Alexandria Township in 1785, Bethlehem Township in 1785, Lebanon Township in 1785, and Roxbury Township in 1788.

The earliest records, those of Greenwich Township, indicate that nine gristmills, three sawmills, and one fulling mill were located there in 1774. The number of taxpayers is set at 204. In Alexandria Township, eleven years later, there were four gristmills, one sawmill, and one tanyard, and 273 taxpayers. At the same time, in Bethlehem Township, four gristmills, four sawmills, one still, and 239 taxpayers existed. In Lebanon Township, also in 1785, there were eleven gristmills, five sawmills, three stills, one fulling mill, and 299 taxpayers. In Roxbury Township, three years later, there existed eight gristmills, eleven sawmills, one fulling mill, two tanyards, three stills and 713 taxpayers.

Unfortunately, enough dates are not available to indicate whether or not the above ratios are truly representative of the relative numbers of population and service industries in the region during the eighteenth century. If they are, it would indicate that the approximate ratio of families to gristmills would be 48:1, to sawmills 72:1; to stills 247:1; and to fulling mills and tanyards 576:1.

There are frequent references in the wills of residents of the townships lying partially in or contiguous to the Musconetcong Valley of industries that were conducted in the household but were largely commercial in nature. There are many references to weavers and their tools and also to blacksmiths, who also seem to have worked at home. Other occupations included that of "cupper," "wheel wright," "tailor," and "cordwainer." [34]

Dispersed settlement was the rule in most of northwestern New Jersey during the eighteenth century. Settlers thought of themselves as living in certain "towns," and their mail was so addressed, but the nature of these towns was far different from those of the present day. Johann Schoepf, in describing Maidenhead, six miles southwest of Princeton, as consisting of but five or six houses in 1783, was speaking of a situation common in New Jersey at that time: [35]

> There are in America a number of such places called towns, where one must look for the houses, either not built or scattered a good distance apart, that is to say, certain districts are set off as Townships, (market or town districts), the residents of which live apart on their farms, a particular spot being called the town, where the church and tavern stand and the smiths have their shops—because in one or the other of these community buildings the neighbors are accustomed to meet. And when later professional men, shop-keepers, and other people who are not farmers come to settle, their dwellings group themselves about the church and the shops.

This was the situation that obtained in the Musconetcong Valley at the same time. Settlement was not planned. The mixed ethnic origins of the settlers allowed hamlets to evolve in haphazard fashion.

The location of agglomerated settlements in the Musconetcong Valley seems to have been the result of several factors. The river, in nearly every case, as a supplier of waterpower, acted as a focal point, but other considerations as well influenced community locations. Accessibility was a major factor. The more successful villages in terms of later growth were located on major thoroughfares and often in crossroads locations. Most of these routeways were of aboriginal origin. In addition, in the case of ironworking communities, supplies of wood and ore were important locational factors, as was access to pig iron and markets. On the other hand, pioneer service centers depended on a fairly numerous nearby agricultural population and this, in turn, depended on fairly level, fertile limestone soils.

The first nuclei of later agglomerated settlements to become established were the ironworking communities. As has been seen, at an early date most of these were already performing the functions of service communities for the surrounding agricultural population. Sawmills, gristmills, general stores, and smithies, which were patronized by the surrounding farmers, encouraged many iron communities to remain in existence after the manufacture of iron was no longer a major activity. Especially durable were those communities that had access to important roads and large agricultural populations.

The first settlement in the Musconetcong Valley to warrant cartographic recognition was Changewater, which appeared on the Lotter map of *ca.* 1748.[36] Only the nearby furnaces at Durham, Oxford, and Union appeared as place-names at that time, indicating the preeminence of iron communities as population concentrations. Ten years later, a map of similar scale [37] again showed only the place-name Changewater in the Musconetcong Valley. The most accurate and

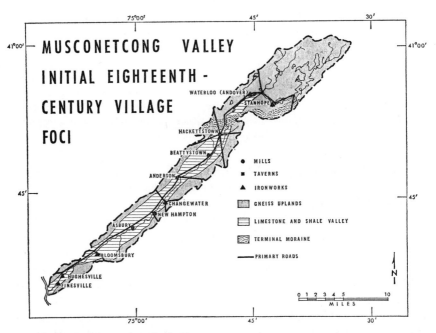

Compiled from various sources.

complete listing of place-names in the Musconetcong Valley appears on the Faden map, the data for which was gathered in 1769 (Appendix I). The Faden map locates nine communities in the valley, of which all but one (Hackettstown) were ironworking communities.

A later forge community, Stanhope, which also acted as an agricultural service center, arose at the intersection of the improved Minisink Path with the Musconetcong, probably shortly before 1800. Waterpower, the presence of excellent overland transport for the day, a ready supply of wood, and a prosperous agricultural population encouraged the establishment of "two iron forges, a gristmill, two sawmills, a blacksmith shop, and about a dozen dwelling houses," but with "no hotel, church, schoolhouse, or store in the place. . . ." [38]

Of the iron communities established in the eighteenth century, only two declined to mere mill sites in the nineteenth century. These were Squire's Point and Brookland forges. Both were in narrow portions of the valley where good agricultural land was limited, and both were far from the sites of important crossroads.

The appearance of communities that served primarily the needs of the agricultural population followed the establishment of commercial agriculture and dense agricultural settlement. The first of the service centers that arose to serve local needs was Hackettstown, a focal point for the roads of the day, and a site of some importance to the former aboriginal inhabitants of the area. As late as 1773, Hackettstown consisted of but five or six structures, one of which was an inn. The settlement coalesced around a mill and a Presbyterian meeting house, both of which were built in the early 1760's. In later years gristmills, sawmills, and fulling mills were added to the village as was the inn and a store. [39]

Beattystown was first known as "Beatty's Mills" after the gristmill, which was erected before 1776. There was also a tavern at that time, which was of some importance locally. Before 1800 the village was quite a thriving one and was apparently more of a business center than Hackettstown, being the chief market in that part of the state for grain and other produce. This was perhaps due to the vigor of local capitalists. One of the few general stores in the Musconetcong Valley was located there in 1800. [40]

Asbury also antedated the Revolution in its origin. At the time of the war it consisted of only two buildings, a gristmill on the north bank of the river, and a dwelling on the south bank. By 1807, there were "about forty houses in or near this village, of all descriptions," indicating the rapid period of growth that occurred generally in agglomerated settlements in the late eighteenth and early nineteenth centuries.[41]

Two other villages in the Musconetcong Valley, Anderson and New Hampton, coalesced about the establishment of important inns or taverns. Mills were erected somewhat later to meet the local demand. Anderson was established by Joseph Anderson, who settled about 1787 and built a hotel shortly thereafter. He was a large landholder and encouraged others to settle near him. In 1800 the hamlet boasted a physician, a blacksmith, and a gristmill.[42]

New Hampton owed its existence to the location of several taverns, which served the needs of travelers passing through the area. The first tavern was established before 1763. A gristmill was built in 1800.[43]

The naming of communities in the Musconetcong Valley during the eighteenth century followed no set procedure. All settlement place-names, however, seem to fall within three of Stewart's [44] proposed classes: possessive, commemorative, and descriptive. The greater number of settlements in the valley during the eighteenth century were named after actual family names and thus can be labeled as having possessive toponyms. "Hughes," the forge community which is shown on the Faden map (Appendix I), became Hughesville in the nineteenth century. The name is derived from the Hughes family, who owned Greenwich Forge and who were long resident in the area. The "Bloomsburg" of Faden was a mistake in orthography and was actually Bloomsbury, a forge community named after the Bloom family who resided in the area. Faden's "Squire's Point" became "Squier's Point" in later maps but the forge community itself evaporated. Squier may be a family name, although this is uncertain. The "Point" most likely refers to a local promontory. Hackettstown, which Faden also misspells as "Halketstown," was named after Samuel Hackett, an influential landowner who was one of the first settlers. The place-name was originally Helms' Mills in 1763 but by 1768 was named after Hackett, as a will dated in that year listed Edward Dunlop of "Hackettstown" as executor.

Later and less important settlements were also named after local settlers and entrepreneurs. "Beatty's Mills" became Beattystown after the mill owner, and "Anderson" or "Andersontown" was named after Joseph Anderson, the founder of the village. Hall's Mills, named after the owner of the local gristmills, became Asbury, after Bishop Francis Asbury laid the cornerstone of the small Methodist church erected in that community in 1800. Thus, Asbury now possesses a commemorative place-name.

There is great doubt as to the origin of the place-name Stanhope.

It is possible that "the English people first resident there christened it after the somewhat noted Stanhopes of England." If such is the case, this would also be a commemorative name.

The commemorative place-names of some settlements were inspired by localities far removed. Andover, for example, which became Waterloo in the nineteenth century, was named after Andover, in Hampshire, England, the birthplace of one of the owners of the ironworks established there. The community of New Hampton was probably named after a "Hampton" elsewhere, but exactly where is not certain. New Hampton preceded the establishment of Hampton, formerly known as Hampton Junction, by many years. The place-name New Hampton is at least as early as 1809, since Jacob Swayze's estate in that year included "wheat in the ground at New Hampton."

The smallest number of community place-names seem to have been those that were essentially descriptive. Changewater, the earliest agglomerated settlement, was originally "Change Water." A lame explanation for this designation is that it was so called "because of the separation and conducting of the waters from the upper and lower banks of the Musconetcong into two counties, Warren and Hunterdon, by the mill race of the 'Old Forge.' "

Brookland, the forge community located at the outlet of Lake Hopatcong, also may have owed its name to a description by the locals. Brookland is the name given the forge in every early account. It is only after 1810, when a tax assessor listed the property as "Brooklyn Forge," that the latter name came into use. Later writers have stated that a former owner of the forge named it after his birthplace, Brooklyn, New York, but this is unlikely, considering the universal use of the name Brookland by eighteenth-century writers. It is, however, also of interest to note that a "Brookland" existed on western Long Island in the middle of the eighteenth century (Appendix I) and that settlers from that area settled much of Morris County.[45]

CHAPTER 8

Markets and Transport

Essential to the ultimate success of agricultural settlement was a market for the products of the pioneers. As early as the latter part of the seventeenth century this need was recognized by the duly constituted authorities of the settled areas. In 1681 a market was opened at Burlington in West Jersey, and in 1686 one was established at Perth Amboy in East Jersey.[1] Undoubtedly, during the days of earliest settlement, the pioneer farmers of the Musconetcong Valley drove their livestock south by way of the existing network of Indian paths to these weekly markets.

Although the Burlington and Perth Amboy markets may have sufficed in early times, when the settlement of the northwestern portion of New Jersey was relatively sparse, as settlement progressed there was much desire on the part of agriculturists to have nearer outlets for their livestock and produce. In 1746, the authorities of Trenton felt that the demand was strong enough to establish another official outlet for the pioneer farmers.[2]

> These are to give Notice, that on Wednesday the 16th Day of April next, at the Borough Town of Trenton, in the County of Hunterdon, in the Province of New Jersey, will be held and kept a FAIR for selling and buying of all Manner of Horses, Mares, Colts, Cows, Calves, Steers, Hogs, Sheep, and all other Cattle, Goods, Wares, and Merchandizes whatsoever: Which said FAIR will be held and kept the same Day abovementioned, and two Days next following pursuant to a Clause in a Charter of Privileges lately granted to the said Borough Town of Trenton, for that Purpose.

Twenty-two years later, the town of Newark initiated a three-day fair in the third week of October, which was to be a yearly occurrence. The fair was established because of the fact that at that time "many

132

Inconveniencies frequently attended the Sale of Horses, Horn Cattle, Sheep and Swine, for want of some publick convenient stated Market or Fair, where Sellers and Buyers may meet for that purpose." [3] The emphasis on livestock probably indicates that traffic was expected to come from a distance, and quite possibly northwestern New Jersey was included in the hinterland of the Newark Fair.

Although markets and fairs retained some importance in New Jersey during the eighteenth century, port cities such as New Brunswick, New York, and Philadelphia soon became the immediate or ultimate destination of most agricultural products. An observer in 1783 noted the primacy of New York and Philadelphia in this regard.[4]

> New York on the one side and Philadelphia on the other long since drew to themselves the trade of Jersey, and without great exertions and the capital assistance of rich merchants this established course of trade is not to be altered. The produce of Jersey is the same as that of both adjoining provinces, and the Jerseymen find a better market and longer credit in those two cities than in their own.

In northwestern New Jersey, Philadelphia was the market most often used by farmers and iron interests. Grain and bar iron were conveyed to Philadelphia by way of the Delaware in the spring, and livestock was driven overland to Newark and New York.

Locations too far from the Delaware to make profitable use of conveyance by water sent their produce overland to New Brunswick, and to a port a short distance up the Raritan from that city, Raritan Landing. The reason for the popularity of these two markets in the mid-eighteenth century was the fact that cash transactions were the rule, whereas in Newark and Philadelphia barter was often the method of exchange. Also, goods were regularly transshipped from Raritan Landing and New Brunswick by sloop to New York, where prices were higher than in Philadelphia. Pehr Kalm, the Swedish traveler, noted that in 1749 it was a regular practice to transport produce by wagon from the Trenton area to New Brunswick, whence it would be conveyed by sloop to New York, and sold there.

New Brunswick was also nearer northwestern New Jersey in terms of linear distance and in terms of actual travel over the poor roads of the day. In 1777 a property in Hackettstown was advertised as being "35 miles from Brunswick Landing and 50 from New York, but the passage to the latter is not very clear at present." [5] Traffic to New Brunswick from northwestern New Jersey came by way of the Amwell road by wagon. New Brunswick drew produce from as far west as Bloomsbury in the Musconetcong Valley, less than ten miles from the

Delaware, during the late eighteenth century. From New Brunswick, produce was taken by sloop to New York where Pehr Kalm saw "vessels from New Brunswick, laden with wheat which lay loose on board, with flour packed up in barrels, and also with great quantities of linseed. . . ." [6] New Brunswick's trade during the eighteenth century covered a wide area, extending all the way from the West Indies to the Atlantic seaboard to the north. Grain, pork, and leather were the major exports at this time.[7] Iron also reached the seaboard by way of the Raritan Valley. Cornelius Low of Raritan Landing offered, among other goods, the "best refined and bloomery Iron" [8] for sale in 1761.

Transition from a pioneer agricultural economy dependent upon subsistence agriculture and the casual raising of livestock for market, to one of commercial grain farming, greatly depended upon improvements in the transportation network. Needless to say, the prosperity of the iron industry and the various pioneer industries serving the agricultural population also required improvement in communications.

Earliest contact and travel between older communities and those on the fringe of pioneer settlement had been by means of the dense network of Indian trails already in existence at the time of first European contact. These, however, being footpaths, limited traffic to travel on foot or horseback, and imposed a serious obstacle to increased trade. In order to facilitate faster and more voluminous travel and trade, the early settlers soon set to work to widen and level the Indian paths, which then provided the basis for widened trade and faster travel. It is of interest to note that many of the most important roads to and from the Musconetcong drainage system as depicted on a map compiled from data gathered in 1769, followed the original aboriginal alignment. (See Appendix I.)

Despite the ease with which the system of Indian paths could be used, from the time of earliest settlement the system proved inadequate for the needs of Europeans. European traffic often emanated from points not served by the footpaths of the Indians, which ran primarily between village and garden sites to hunting grounds and the sea, and not to locations of great interest to Europeans, such as power sites. From the first, the Lords Proprietor of New Jersey had realized the inadequacy of the Indian footpaths, and had encouraged the establishment of true roads. The General Assembly later also provided for road construction, unfortunately at the option of locally elected officials, and by means of haphazard labor levies on the local inhabitants, who were at best unwilling workers.

An act of the Assembly which greatly influenced road construction throughout the state was first promulgated in 1716 and remained in force until 1760, by which time many of the major arteries in northern New Jersey had been completed. The act required that roads be four rods in width, laid out for the convenience of the inhabitants, and cause as little disadvantage as possible for the property holders. Although the width of public roads was set by this act, the wording was rather vague as to the proper course they should take. As early surveys had most often been laid out by the metes-and-bounds system, and as each deed included "an allowance for high ways," roads were most often constructed along the periphery of property lines, so as best to accommodate the owners. Also, as many property boundaries were laid along former Indian paths, road construction was eased. The result of this legislated influence on road construction was, then, a network of roads which was, considering the nature of the terrain, often far more sinuous than necessary.[9]

In later days, private interests also improved or constructed roads to serve their own needs. Forges in the Musconetcong Valley during the latter portion of the eighteenth century supplied rum "for the use of the working on the Roads."[10] In 1794, James Parker wrote to John Cooley "I have not done with the road intended to be laid out in the Valley [the Musconetcong Valley near Riegelsville] where I shall be next Thursday for that purpose. . . ."[11]

Narrow private farm roads were also being laid out in the area during the latter part of the eighteenth century. In 1789 Joseph Lewis recorded going to "Adam Winegardens on Schooly's Mountain to lay a drift way for him across a field in possession of W. Searle. . . ." On the same day, Lewis also "went to lay a road from David Sovereens corner by the road leading to Hackettstown thro' by Henry Sovereen's Fred Sovereens and so on to the main road by Will Allpock's about 3¼ miles, which we laid."[12]

Throughout the eighteenth century most of the roads in New Jersey were poor, and those in the more sparsely settled areas were doubly so. Tree stumps often remained in the right-of-way and many roads were ungraded, causing great difficulties for travelers both on horseback and in vehicles. Poorly drained areas were corduroyed or filled in with broken stone, causing an extremely rough transit. Washouts occurred after nearly every heavy rain. In common with the roads of the rest of the state, those of the Musconetcong Valley remained poor throughout the eighteenth century. In 1768, the Reverend William Frazer reported that his congregation near Changewater[13]

> does not seem calculated to be joined with Amwell and Kingwood as they
> are separated by a ridge of high mountains which the frost and snow in

winter render quite impassable and even in good weather I find it very troublesome from the distance which is 25 miles and the roughness of the roads—to attend once in three weeks.

In February of 1780, Samuel Williams of Greenwich Forge wrote Richard Backhouse at Durham Furnace that he had to send a lighter wagon to transport charcoal since "the Roads is So bad I was afraid to Send the Coal Waggon. . . ." [14] James Parker complained in December of 1789 that he had to get an employee to "Geer up his Waggon and drive me to Jno Sherrard the road so Ruff and Mountainous that there is no possibility of going in my sulky. . . ." [15] Road conditions did not improve much before the advent of the turnpike era. In the spring of 1807, Francis Asbury complained that "rough roads, damp weather, and daily preaching, has brought me low." [16] In addition to being in poor condition, roads in the area were inadequately marked, and strangers often lost their way. Thomas Anburey, who traveled through Hackettstown in 1778, noted that the "inhabitants only compute the distance [by road] at a guess." [17] He compared New Jersey unfavorably to Pennsylvania, where there were at least milestones.

Another problem for eighteenth-century traffic in northern New Jersey was the crossing of the many swift streams of the Highlands. Local officials were responsible for initiating and carrying through bridge construction, as they were for the roads. In many localities bridge construction lagged. The first bridge built over the Musconetcong by Sussex County was in 1770.[18] Although the location of this structure is not given, it probably did not lie near the stream's mouth, since on April 25th, 1789, James Parker recorded in his diary that he had tried to cross the lower portion of the river "but the waters were so high I could not cross . . . at any of the fording places." Twenty-one years before, the Reverend Frazer, probably residing near Changewater, described the Musconetcong as "a River which the heavy rains and snow in the winter time render almost impassable. . . ."

Bridges built in New Jersey during colonial days were almost all built of wood. Timbers spanned the river, and planks were laid as flooring. In 1774 an act of the Assembly provided that bridges were to have well-fitted flooring. Bridges spanning the Musconetcong in the latter days of the eighteenth century were probably built in this way.

Crossing the Delaware was a problem of greater magnitude, but was essential to the well-being of iron forges receiving pig iron from Durham Furnace. The early agricultural pioneers who preceded the iron interests into the area probably crossed by means of canoes, as John Reading had in 1715. Later traffic could not be accommodated by such frail craft, and ferry service soon was established to meet the greater demands of the iron interests and commercial agriculture. The first ferry that crossed the Delaware in the vicinity of the Musconetcong Valley came into existence after 1742, in response, especially, to the establishment of forges in the valley. It was known as Stillwell's, Brink's, or the Durham Cave Ferry, and served to link Holland Township, Hunterdon County, with the riverbank immediately in front of Durham Cave on the Pennsylvania side and, ultimately, with the Durham Furnace.

Shortly after 1774, the Durham Cave Ferry was superseded by a ferry established by Benjamin Shenk, which connected the site of present Riegelsville, Pennsylvania, with the river frontage on the Delaware immediately north of the Musconetcong in present Riegelsville, New Jersey. Shenks or "Shanks" Ferry remained an important link between the forges on the Musconetcong and Durham Furnace throughout the eighteenth century.[19]

Ferries in use on the Delaware during the eighteenth century were described by Thomas Anburey in 1778 as being "flat bottom boats, large enough to contain a waggon and horses; they are a safe conveyance; and . . . they are rowed with oars. . . ."[20] In times of high water, ferries had difficulty in crossing. During the 1780's, a request was sent to the manager of Durham Furnace, urging that he "send Piggs to the River as fast as Convenient, as there may be a Difficulty in getting them over for sometime to come. . . ."[21]

The earliest cartographic representation of the road network of northwestern New Jersey insofar as it affected the Musconetcong Valley is depicted on Thomas Jefferys' map of the state for 1758 (Appendix VII). Only one road is shown crossing the Musconetcong. This major route of the day ran from Easton–Phillipsburg southward, crossing the river in the vicinity of Bloomsbury and continued on toward Trenton. Since iron forges having intercourse with Oxford and Durham furnaces were well established by this time, it can be assumed that at least secondary wagon trails had been established, probably insofar as possible making use of the existing network of Indian trails. The main road through Bloomsbury was itself an improvement on the Malayelick Path of Indian days.

Another major road shown on the Jefferys map, although not passing through the Musconetcong Valley, facilitated travel to New Brunswick by intersecting with the Trenton–Phillipsburg road at "Hofs" (present Pittstown). From its intersection with the Trenton–

Phillipsburg road, the road to New Brunswick continued on to the vicinity of Milford, on the Delaware. Thus, at least as early as 1758, main roads were open to move products of forge and farm to markets located to the south and southeast.

Finest in detail of the eighteenth-century maps dealing with New Jersey as a whole is the Faden map (Appendix I), which was published in London in 1777, but which relied upon data gathered in 1769. The Faden map depicts a well-developed road system linking all portions of the Musconetcong Valley with the major population agglomerations and markets to the south. The only major omission on the Faden map appears to be that of the "New Road," a much-traveled route of the first settlers, which ran from Easton–Phillipsburg through Asbury to New Hampton.[22]

The great density of the road pattern depicted on the Faden map in relation to that shown on the Jefferys map does not suggest a flurry of road-building activity in the eleven-year period between the date of publication of the latter and the period of data gathering for the former. Most likely, the road system depicted by Faden was largely in existence in 1758, but was imperfectly known to the cartographers of the day.

Several new roads were laid out after the Revolution and before the turnpike-building period. A main road was opened from Hackettstown southwest to Pittstown. This road is plainly shown on the Lewis map of 1796 (Appendix VIII), and was termed the "public or great road leading from the Union forge to Hacketts town," when it was altered in 1798.[23]

Another main road, perhaps in existence before the Revolution, but not shown on maps of that day, was a route running north from Long (German) Valley to Andrew Miller's tavern on the Musconetcong at Penwell, and then to Phillipsburg–Easton via Washington. Theophile Cazenove traveled over this road in 1794, and mentioned that it was a major route for the "pioneers who go from the East to Pittsburg, Kentucky, etc. . . ." This route was shorter than the one through Hackettstown. Cazenove described it as being "the upper road which is the shorter but not so good. . . ." Most traffic went via Hackettstown, and the "upper road" offered little in the way of accommodations for travelers. According to Cazenove "the innkeepers . . . [were] chiefly farmers, who [ran] hotels as a side line." [24]

With the slight changes mentioned, which were probably accomplished mainly by widening and improving the existing system of secondary roads, the road network of 1769, as depicted by the Faden map, remained to furnish a relative ease of overland contact between the Musconetcong Valley and other areas in the state throughout the eighteenth and early nineteenth centuries.

The means of overland conveyance for both men and goods led progressively from pack- and riding-horses, carts and sleds, to wagons and coaches as the road system gradually improved during the nineteenth century. Where adequate roads were lacking, riding-, pack-, or sled-drawing horses were the major means of transport. Horses were used to bring produce and grain to market or mill, and also to transport iron ore to furnace and bloomery, and finished bar iron to market.[25] Horses remained important for travel long after the roads had improved enough to permit the use of wheeled vehicles. Johann Schoepf, a German traveler, while en route between New York and Philadelphia remarked that [26]

> The whole way . . . not a foot-passenger met us. Few passengers met us at all, but in every case riding or driving. To go a-foot is an abomination to the American, no matter how poor or friendless, and at times he hits upon a means—he steals a nag from the pasture or borrows one without asking.

The horse as an important means of conveyance and as a prestige symbol maintained its position throughout northwestern New Jersey in pioneer days. Casper Schaeffer recalled that during the 1790's horseback riding was universal, and that even "the ladies, both young and old, were very expert at this exercise." [27]

One of the means of conveyance for both men and goods in early days of settlement was the sled. These were of rude construction, being entirely of wood at first. Runners were made of split hickory saplings and were fastened to the body by means of wooden pins. Sleds were drawn by two horses and were used both in summer and winter. During the summer they acted as vehicles for general use on and about the farm, and in winter were used to transport produce to market. During the 1780's, wagons were practically unknown in much of Sussex County (then including Warren County), and sleds were the primary means of conveying grain to market.[28] In 1794, Theophile Cazenove spoke of Easton as a great center of trade, and noted that the farmers of the area, which included northwestern New Jersey, "bring here the produce of the neighborhood, especially in winter, when there is snow. . . ." [29] This occurred most often during January and February. Frequent references to the use of sleds in other portions of the northwestern part of New Jersey indicate that the practice was almost universal.

As roads improved, carts and wagons gradually replaced horses and sleds in the conveyance of produce and goods. Ox carts made their appearance at an early date. The sale of "one yoke of oxen and the cart with chain and other tackling belonging thereto," [30] in 1754 by Robert Schooley, residing just a few miles north of the Musconetcong Valley, indicates that such conveyances were certainly known before that time. Ox carts were of crude construction, consisting of wheels made from the bases of tree trunks, preferably white oak, and a simple wooden frame.[31]

As roads improved, heavy ox carts gave way to the lighter, horse-drawn Jersey wagon. This vehicle was derived from earlier crude uncovered wagons in use on the farm. It consisted of a long flat-bottomed chassis resting on enormous wheels, with a white or black canvas roof supported by large hoops of which the front and rear were largest in circumference. Four to six horses were required to draw the Jersey wagon, and it was widely used in the latter part of the eighteenth century for both freight and passengers.[32] The wagons used in the Musconetcong Valley during the 1780's were probably of this type.

The iron industry also turned to wagons for the purpose of transport when road conditions ameliorated. Wagons in use by iron interests were apparently of two types: a "Body Waggon" for the hauling of finished iron, and a "Coal Wagon" for transporting charcoal. The coal wagon was a huge wagon lined with iron sheeting, having a rectangular, flat-bottomed chassis, and four spoked wheels of which the rear pair was the larger. Body wagons had a capacity of at least two tons and brought bar iron from the Musconetcong Valley to points as far away as Philadelphia. The body wagon was often substituted for the coal wagon in carrying charcoal during the winter. The greater weight of the coal wagon made travel more difficult when the roads were in poor condition.[33]

At the end of the eighteenth century, the Conestoga wagon began to replace the Jersey wagon for freighting in northwestern New Jersey. The Conestoga wagon was probably developed in the vicinity of Conestoga Creek in eastern Pennsylvania and first came into prominence in 1755. These were huge wagons, with chassis curved like the bottom of a boat, ends slanted outward; and were covered with canvas stretched over hoops. The rear wheels were somewhat larger than the front wheels, five or six feet in diameter and shod with tires six inches wide. The wagon itself was over twenty feet in length, required a six-horse team, and could carry six tons.[34]

An indication of the increasing economic importance of the Musconetcong Valley and its environs was the extension of a stage line to Hackettstown from Morristown in 1775. The proposed route of travel was by way of Flanders, Black River, and Mendem (Mendham) the first day, with an overnight stop in Morristown. From that point carriage was by way of Newark and Powles Hook Ferry (Jersey City), where a connection could be made with New York City. A one-way trip from Hackettstown to Powles Hook encompassed two days.[35]

Travel by stage was perhaps less pleasant than on horseback. Passengers were expected to push the wagon when it got stuck, as it often did. The stage wagon itself was merely an adaptation of the long-bodied Jersey wagon, without doors, windows, or panels. Passengers entered over the front wheels to the three or four benches of the interior. There were no springs, and since only clumsy linchpins held the wheels, they had a tendency to slip and let the axle down, to the great discomfiture of the passengers. Heavy-springed English mail coaches were not introduced until the nineteenth century.[36]

The appearance of the stage coach served to break the comparative isolation of the Musconetcong Valley, and newspapers, private letters, and light freight had an ease of access that had been denied them before.

In the southwestern portion of the Musconetcong Valley, and in much of western New Jersey, where overland traffic to New York or New Brunswick was difficult or impossible in early days, the major outlet became the Delaware River and the major market the port of Philadelphia. Goods were carried down the Delaware by means of the Durham boat, a craft developed during the fourth decade of the eighteenth century at Durham Furnace, for the carriage of pig and bar iron to Philadelphia. One reliable source described the Durham boats in the mid-eighteenth century as being [37]

> made like troughs, square above the heads and sterns, sloping a little fore and aft; generally 40 or 50 feet long, 6 or seven feet wide, and 2 feet 9 inches, or 3 feet deep, and draw 20 or 22 inches water when loaden.

These craft were able to carry five or six hundred bushels of wheat per trip, or as much as twenty tons of iron. Later Durham boats were increased in size to a length of sixty feet, a width of eight feet and a depth of forty-two inches. Durham boats ordinarily moved down the river with freshets, of which there were generally three a year, each of which lasted from two or three weeks to three months. Before improvements in river navigation were completed in the 1790's, the boats took approximately two days to reach Philadelphia from Durham and roughly five days to make the return journey against the current. Propulsion downstream was assured by the current, and on occasion long oars or a sail attached to a movable mast were used. The boats were poled and, where possible, sailed upstream.[38]

Trade between the Musconetcong Valley and Philadelphia by way of the Delaware probably began as early as the development of the Durham boat. Several letters still extant indicate some of the scope and nature of the trade. In November of 1767, one John Sherrard of Alexandria Township wrote Thomas Riche, a merchant in Philadelphia: "I am using my utmost Endeavours to get my Beef and Pork down to you which I hope shall do very soon." Three years later, in January, Sherrard wrote Riche again. "I have sent you 20 Bush Rye 14 D° Buckwheat. This Fresh came so sudden that I could not get any oats for you." [39]

In the 1780's, forges also were availing themselves of the services of Durham boats. John Stotesbury, at Greenwich Forge, noted sending "pr Walter Fields Boat Sixty five Barrs Iron to be delivered to Mess Miles & Morgan, Merchants Philada. . . ." [40]

Trade by way of the Delaware increased greatly after 1770. In that year the inhabitants of Sussex County, incensed because of the failure of many New York merchants to accede to the Non-Importation Agreement of the American colonists on British goods, publicly declared: [41]

> altho' our Connections with them, have hitherto led us to their Markets, by a long and tedious LAND-Carriage, we will now turn out Trade of Wheat, Iron &c., by the more natural and easy Water Carriage down the River Delaware, to our Friends at Trenton and Philadelphia. . . .

After the Revolution, traffic on the Delaware fell off for a few years. Business conditions were poor and several rapids in the river often made navigation a hazardous undertaking. In 1789, the Pennsylvania Assembly, realizing the importance of rapid, inexpensive transport on the river, made an appropriation for the improvement of navigation. In 1791 a contract was let to clear some of the rapids, and despite great difficulties, this was accomplished in the same year.[42] Three years later, when Theophile Cazenove passed through Easton, he found that a Durham boat took only twenty-four to thirty hours to reach Philadelphia and three days to return, a great improvement. One of the more prominent merchants of the town was Mordecay Peirsol, who bought grain from nearby farmers during December, January, and February and sent it down the river to Philadelphia in April or March.[43] Much of his business was probably conducted with grain from farms in the Musconetcong Valley.

CHAPTER 9

Summary and Conclusions: The Evolution of the Cultural Landscape

Aboriginal occupation of the Musconetcong drainage system occurred when men of the Paleo-Indian cultural tradition entered the region, perhaps as early as ten thousand or more years ago. Extensive burning may have been engaged in by these hunters in order to drive the typical fauna of the day to strategic points where they could be dispatched with ease. This burning would most certainly have altered the composition of the local flora.

Little is known of the prehistoric folk who succeeded the Paleo-Indians and preceded the Indians known historically. Since no sites are known for these people in the Highlands, data were used concerning the famed Abbott site, near Trenton. The cultural sequence at the Abbott site indicates that a hunting, fishing, and gathering economy succeeded that of the Paleo-Indians. Later, shellfish from the Atlantic coast were gathered, and agriculture, apparently at first concerned with the cultivation of tobacco, became a minor activity *ca.* A.D. 900. Forest clearing by these people was probably minimal, although it is not known whether or not fire had a role in their procurement of game.

Much direct evidence exists concerning the historic aborigines, who began to be encountered in large numbers by Europeans during the early seventeenth century. In New Jersey, these aborigines were for the most part known as the Lenape, who became consolidated as a result of the European advance to the interior in the early years of the eighteenth century. The environs of the Musconetcong Valley were occupied by the Munsi subdivision of the Lenape, who may have numbered as many as three hundred persons in that locality. Indian settlements clustered in locations where an adequate supply of potable water was readily available, and where a southern exposure could be found. Of almost sixty sites known, only six are located northeast of the terminal moraine, and but twelve are more than a few yards from the Musconetcong itself. Further, the great majority of sites are associated with remnants of the outwash of the Wisconsin terminal moraine, and few are located on the gneiss or slaty-shale uplands. This indicates the important place of agriculture in the economy of the historic aboriginal occupants of the Musconetcong Valley. Sandy gravels were much more amenable to being worked with the primitive implements at hand than were the soils generally found on upland surfaces or generally northeast of the terminal moraine. Lake Hopatcong was an exception to this rule. Prior to the impoundment of the lower pond by a charcoal iron interest, abundant stretches of sandy gravel allowed cultivation. Also, the locale was favored insofar as both forest and lacustrine faunas were concerned.

Agriculture played a major role in the aboriginal economy. Hoe gardening, chiefly concerned with the cultivation of the maize-bean-squash complex, served to modify the natural landscape by the establishment of small garden plots, which were cleared by girdling the trees in the area to be cultivated, causing them to defoliate.

Ancillary to agriculture, but still of great importance to the economy, was gathering. Gathering involved the collection of a large inventory of plant foods. At least a few of the species that were collected may have been either favored or discouraged by this activity. Among the species favored may have been the potato-bean, which seems to have been favored by the loosening of the soil that occurred during the gathering process; and the hazelnut, which often surrounded village sites. Some species were affected adversely, but little is known of this. Certain tubers, which were prized by aborigine and European alike in the early eighteenth century, were later decimated by the semidomesticated hogs of both groups.

Hunting provided the major sources of protein for the aboriginal diet. Deer, bear, and elk were especially prized. These species were adversely affected during the time of first European contact by the fact that they were overhunted by Indians because of trade with the whites. The elk and the giant beaver may have been rendered extinct by aboriginal hunters in the prehistoric period.

A major effect on the flora of the region occurred through the use of fire to drive game. Wide spaces were devoid of forest vegetation at the time of first white contact. These were subsequently reforested by natural means after aboriginal burning ceased and, at least in one case, a forest almost entirely of chestnut resulted.

A major influence of the aborigines on the Europeans involved the early settlement by the latter group. Europeans desired cleared land for use as pasture, and Indian old fields were often favored sites for the efforts of the early surveyors. Also, the Indian network of footpaths served as the prime routes of penetration into the Highlands by the early European settlers. These, only slightly altered in many cases, became the foundation for the present-day road network.

Settlement in the Musconetcong drainage system by European pioneers occurred within the first two decades of the eighteenth century. Settlement by Europeans occurred largely after surveyors had penetrated the area and had surveyed the most valuable parcels of land—those with power sites, those with obviously valuable deposits of minerals, and those with fertile-seeming soils that had been denuded of forest by Indian burning or clearing. The metes-and-bounds system of surveying was in use, and often led to difficulties when later, more accurate surveys could be made.

The surveying of lands in the van of pioneer settlement in both East and West Jersey during the eighteenth century, was for the benefit of the proprietors of both divisions of the state, who in fact owned the land. Because of the reluctance on the part of the proprietors to subdivide and sell outright small freeholds, the earliest agricultural settlement in the Musconetcong Valley was, in many cases, by squatting. This led to much difficulty for the holders of large parcels of land and also to a ruinous exploitation of the land they occupied by the squatters. Later, when effective law enforcement was extended to the frontier, many former squatters were forced to come under lease. Smaller tracts, obviously intended for freeholders, became available only in the 1760's when the main influx of population into the region occurred.

Earliest of the ethnic groups to settle in the Musconetcong Valley were the English. This is clearly reflected in the toponymy of the region. English settlers were derived in large part from the older settlements in southwestern New Jersey and from New Englanders who penetrated from the New England settlements in what was then East Jersey. Next of the ethnic groups on the scene seem to have been the Dutch, who largely were derived from the Dutch settlers of the Raritan watershed, although some also had come overland from the older

Dutch settlements in northeastern New Jersey and southern New York. Scotch-Irish settlers, who began to arrive in large numbers at the port of Philadelphia between 1710 and 1720, arrived in the Musconetcong Valley by 1739. German settlers inundated the earlier settlements in the southwestern portion of the valley mostly after 1760, coming largely from the older German settlements in Pennsylvania

In the last decade of the eighteenth century, settlers began to desert the more marginal agricultural lands of the valley and move to the agricultural frontier in Ohio and New York. By this time, the entire Musconetcong drainage system was quite mixed as to ethnic stock. The largest unacculturated group was probably that of the Pennsylvania-Germans, who were continuing to move into the area at the end of the century. It is probable that the southwestern portion of the valley remained as the most densely settled area in the drainage system.

Even in the glaciated region northeast of the Wisconsin terminal moraine, pioneer agricultural land use preceded the charcoal iron industry into the Musconetcong Valley. Initial crops were for subsistence and included chiefly buckwheat and flax. Livestock were of greater importance than crops in terms of what could be economically transported to market. Cattle, hogs, and horses were of primary importance in the days of earliest settlement, and were allowed to wander about freely in the woods. Pioneers burnt the woods in order to keep them free of undergrowth and free the native grasses for immediate growth in the spring.

Improvements in the transportation network allowed a shift from the subsistence agriculture and emphasis on livestock of the days of earliest settlement, to the production of commercial grain crops, chiefly wheat and rye. The establishment of many charcoal iron industries in the valley immediately after its first settlement by subsistence farmers also served to encourage commercial agriculture by providing a good local market for agricultural produce.

Deforestation by the iron interests was a major influence in the establishment of agriculture in many localities. Wide deforestation contributed to the decline of the iron industry, and the deforested land was then occupied by pioneer agriculturists. This occupation was permanent on the excellent limestone soils southwest of the Wisconsin terminal moraine, and temporary on the boulder-strewn, glaciated soils northeast of the terminal moraine.

In general, agricultural practices were quite poor among the pioneer settlers. There does not seem to be any correlation between land use and any particular ethnic group. Land was easily obtained, labor was dear. Squatters, especially, cultivated ruinously, and often illegally cut the woods for sale to the local charcoal iron interests. Freeholders were more concerned with maintaining their woodlands, and tenants were forced to do so, but both were not particularly sophisticated agriculturists.

It is instructive to note that land values and crop yields were higher in the German districts of Pennsylvania than they were in the Musconetcong Valley at the end of the eighteenth century. This encouraged the migration of Pennsylvania-Germans into the valley to take advantage of the excellent limestone soils and low land prices.

One of the major imprints of the agriculturists on the landscape of the Musconetcong Valley was that of fencing, which at first was used to keep wandering stock out of the enclosed crops. The snake, or worm fence, became the type most widely used, especially to separate field from field.

Permanent deforestation of the rich limestone soils located south of the terminal moraine in the Musconetcong Valley was the chief areal alteration of the landscape by the eighteenth-century agriculturists. Although agriculture was carried on sporadically in the days of earliest settlement northeast of the Wisconsin terminal moraine, most marginal locations were allowed to come back into woodland in later days. Woodlots were clear-cut, which allowed the sprout hardwoods to become the dominant flora. Among these, the chestnut, an especially vigorous sprouter and rapid-growing tree, was favored.

Occupation of the Musconetcong Valley by pioneers of European descent was first expressed in their habitations. These were erected near a ready source of water. Outbuildings and barns were built later, after agricultural clearing had taken place. Both habitations and outbuildings of the days of earliest settlement were largely of log construction, although frame structures were also known at an early date.

Eighteenth-century newspaper advertisements very clearly indicate that log structures entered the Highlands from the south and perhaps the west as well. The favored type of log dwelling appears to have been of one-and-one-half stories, and was perhaps of Pennsylvania-German provenance. Details of the construction of similar structures that have been catalogued by the Historic American Buildings Survey show many Swedish traits, however. Thus, acculturation is indicated.

After the pioneer agriculturists had completed the initial phases of developing their farms, many turned to the improvement of their habitations, and substituted structures of frame or stone for those of logs.

New Englanders built either the one-room-deep or two-room-deep

East Jersey cottage, which had evolved in the northeastern portion of the state through Flemish influence on a house type of New England origin. Both variations of the type can be easily traced from the east into the Musconetcong Valley.

The house type that dominates the valley today, especially southwest of the terminal moraine, is the "I" house. This type is largely of English origin and entered the Highlands along with the stream of pioneers from southwestern New Jersey and southeastern Pennsylvania.

Structures auxiliary to habitations arose soon after housing had been constructed. Outside kitchens were built largely in those areas outside the New England sphere of influence. Stone springhouses are similarly located on the landscape today, and are probably in the main a German contribution.

Little information is available on the first structures used to protect livestock during the winter season. At first, abandoned log habitations may have been used. One solution was the erection of the barrack, the only important Dutch contribution to the farmstead. These were often built before barns appeared, and were widely adopted by all ethnic groups. When formal barns were erected, they seem to have been of two major types: (1) the English barn, and (2) the bank barn. The English barn seems to have been introduced largely by settlers of New England origin, as its present distribution in the Musconetcong Valley suggests. The bank barn, or as it is often known in the western part of New Jersey, the "overshot" barn, seems to have arrived at the end of the pioneer period, probably through the agency of later German emigrants from Pennsylvania.

Dutch barns, which had their entrance at the gable end, in contrast to both the English and bank barns, probably did enter the Musconetcong Valley along with Dutch pioneers, but as with most Dutch material culture traits other than the barrack, were not widely accepted by other ethnic groups.

The charcoal iron industry entered the Highlands at the beginning of the eighteenth century and exerted the leading economic influence in many locations for much of the century. In the Musconetcong drainage system, however, the industry entered the region after initial pioneer agricultural occupance had been established. This was true even in the area that had felt the effects of the Wisconsin glacial advance.

Iron interests, in their location, depended on the ready availability of three major resources. These were: (1) iron ore; (2) dense woodlands that could be processed into charcoal; and (3) immediately accessible waterpower. With the deforestation of the Musconetcong Valley by both iron interests and agriculturists, the loss of the English market in the post-Revolutionary era, and successful foreign competition, the charcoal iron industry waned, and was almost entirely eclipsed southwest of the Wisconsin terminal moraine during the latter years of the eighteenth century. Only in the locations that were not conducive to agricultural pursuits was the cutover forest allowed to regenerate itself, and thus support a rather marginal iron industry.

The most important change in the landscape engendered by the activities of the iron interests was deforestation. Wide areas owned by the iron interests were clear-cut, without any thought as to regeneration, and forge interests also prevailed upon squatter and tenant alike to provide wood they did not own for processing into the charcoal required for forge operation. Clear-cutting favored the rapid sprouters, and the composition of the regenerated woodlands, which could be found on steep slopes and in areas generally unfit for agriculture, changed to favor trees such as the chestnut.

Pioneer service industries were soon established in the valley in response to local demand. Most important of the service industries were those which utilized waterpower. Many of these were established in conjunction with the charcoal iron industry. Early German pioneers seem to have introduced the tub mill, a simple water-driven device for grinding grain. Later, grain and other mills seem to have been powered mainly by undershot waterwheels, which did not demand the impoundment of water. Gristmills were of primary importance to agriculturist and forge worker alike, but were concentrated in the fertile limestone belt. Sawmills were often constructed in conjunction with gristmills, but were generally later in time. Sawmills were constructed both northeast and southwest of the terminal moraine. Their value was generally far less than that of a gristmill.

Early mill structures appear to have been mostly of frame construction, although there are references to log structures. Unfortunately, the early wooden structures have all disappeared because of fire and cannibalization.

Additional industries depending at least in part on waterpower included fulling, oil milling, flax manufacture, and the crushing of tanbark. All of these were found in the Musconetcong Valley during the eighteenth century. Distilling was also of some local importance, and depended on a local supply of apples or grain, and on a source of cool water to cause condensation of the spirits.

Settlement in the Musconetcong Valley during the early pioneer days was not of the agglomerated type. The isolated farmstead pre-

vailed, as it did for the most part in the Middle Colonies. Settlement
was not planned, nor did intact groups take up blocks of land. Villages arose for several reasons. The earliest village nuclei were around
the ironworking centers, which were also important service centers for
the local agriculturists. As the iron industry declined, many of these
settlements remained to use the waterpower for service industries.
Other settlements also had as their chief locational factor the presence
of waterpower, but in addition were near rapid routes of communication, and a dense agricultural population. This tended to concentrate
villages on the fertile limestone soils southwest of the Wisconsin
terminal moraine.

Essential to the ultimate success of pioneer settlement was a market
for agricultural products. This was also true for the products of the
forges and furnaces. The establishment of various markets early in
the eighteenth century made possible the sale of livestock by the subsistence farmer. As the population grew more dense, the road system
was improved and extended, the roads most often taking a rather
sinuous course, following the old Indian trails and the property lines
laid out by the metes-and-bounds system of survey.

Transportation overland was effected largely by the use of the Jersey
wagon, and later by the introduction of the Conestoga wagon from
Pennsylvania, with the destination of both iron and agricultural products being New Brunswick and New York to the east, and Philadelphia to the west. In the western part of the valley, much trade moved
down the Delaware to Philadelphia in Durham boats, which had been
first developed at nearby Durham, Pennsylvania.

The Musconetcong Valley has been occupied by man for perhaps
ten thousand years. During this long period of time the most obvious
effect of the physical environment has been that of the last glacial
advance in limiting the sites of human occupance. Known locations
of aboriginal settlement are generally in much greater abundance in
the limestone valley south of the Wisconsin terminal moraine than
they are in either the limestone valley or the gneiss uplands north
of the terminal moraine. This is also true of the early farmsteads and
later agglomerated settlements of the descendants of European pioneers. The affects of other aspects of the physical environment are
more difficult to assess, and are actually mostly of importance in that
they were *perceived* quite differently by people of varying cultural
backgrounds. For example: aborigines relied on maize as their staple
crop; European pioneers thought it difficult or impossible to raise in
the Highlands at first, and instead relied on wheat and rye. Today
maize is thought of as a much more suitable crop in the area than

wheat or rye. The climate has not changed, perception and economy have.

The principal of initial occupance is well illustrated in the Musconetcong Valley today. The cultural landscape reflects a continuity from the eighteenth-century pioneer period to the present. Houses and barns, as well as many auxiliary structures, still reflect types established in the area during the eighteenth century. This is true despite the relatively recent arrival of many present owners of rural property.

The dominant assemblage of rural structures south of the terminal moraine today ("I" house, bank barn, springhouse), reflects the importance of the Delaware Valley as the main routeway of men and ideas into the southern Highlands. This situation has existed since the initial settlement of the region, as is indicated by the distribution of log structures in the eighteenth century. The "I" house and the springhouse are of undoubted eighteenth-century provenance in the Highlands, while the bank barn may be in large part a function of the later arrival of Pennsylvania-Germans seeking reasonably priced lime-rich farmland in the late eighteenth and early nineteenth centuries. In this connection, there does appear to be a definite orientation of all three of the structures involved in the Delaware Valley assemblage to the limestone valley southwest of the terminal moraine.

A more poorly defined but distinct eighteenth-century imprint on the cultural landscape also has been left by the apparently less vigorous diffusion of New England culture traits into the region. The New England assemblage in the region includes the English barn and variations of the East Jersey cottage. These structures are far fewer in total numbers in the region than are their counterparts from the Delaware Valley. The new England assemblage is far more likely to occur north of the terminal moraine or on the gneiss uplands than is the Delaware Valley assemblage.

Dutch influence on the cultural landscape seems to have vanished almost completely. Although the barrack rapidly diffused via the Raritan Valley and became a part of both the Delaware Valley and the New England assemblages in the state, the distinctive Dutch barn met with little acceptance by those whose cultural traditions were not Dutch. The lack of Dutch barns in the Musconetcong Valley today may also indicate a hitherto unrecognized sparcity of Dutch settlers in the area. Perhaps the same is true of New Englanders in relation to the large numbers penetrating the region via the Delaware Valley. The general lack of Dutch barns and barracks appearing in advertisements of farms in the extreme northwestern portion of the state certainly suggests a lack of significant numbers of Dutch pioneers entering the region by way of the Old Mine Road. The outside kitchen, so often associated with Dutch barns in eighteenth-century advertisements of property, is also associated with the Delaware Valley stream of diffusion of culture traits, and thus is not suitable evidence for determining cultural influences.

The continuity of aspects of the eighteenth-century landscape to the present can also be seen in the region's road network, settlement pattern, and property lines. The late eighteenth-century road pattern as shown by an early nineteenth-century map (Appendix II), agrees most closely with the present road pattern appearing on an aerial photo of the southwestern portion of the Musconetcong Valley taken in 1964 (photo section). Dispersed farmsteads, probably largely of eighteenth-century origin, can also be discerned on this photo, as can the agglomerated settlement of Finesville, which owes its location to the establishment of Chelsea Forge on the site *ca.* 1751. A crossroads situation and the presence of fertile limestone soils also have helped the village to maintain itself to the present day. The metes-and-bounds system of survey can still be seen in the present field patterns. Some of the present field divisions at least in part hark back to the original early eighteenth-century property lines. (See Appendix V and photo section). One boundary is especially noteworthy. The line surveyed to bound Elizabeth Backon's property with that of John Bray and Andrew Heath, almost due north of Finesville, has remained intact for two hundred and fifty years!

Appendixes

Appendix I

Appendix I. Northern New Jersey in 1769. Scale approximately 1:1,101,000. Source: William Faden, *The Province of New Jersey Divided into East and West, Commonly Called the Jerseys* (Charing Cross, London: William Faden, 1777). From the original in the Rutgers University Library (much reduced).

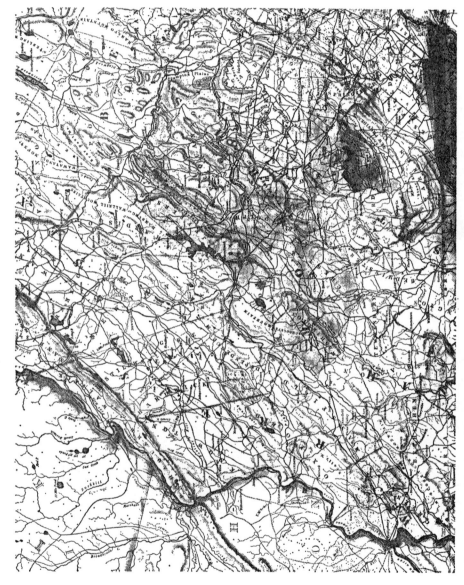

Appendix II. The Musconetcong Valley in 1828. Scale approximately 1:575,000. Source: Thomas F. Gordon, *A Map of the State of New Jersey* (Philadelphia: H. S. Tanner, 1828). From the original in the New Jersey Historical Society (much reduced).

Appendix III *

TEMPERATURE AND PRECIPITATION DATA FOR THREE WEATHER STATIONS NEAR THE MUSCONETCONG VALLEY AVERAGES OF MONTHLY MEANS

1931–1955

STATION	MONTHLY MEANS												ANNUAL TOTALS
	Jan.	Feb.	Mar.	April	May	June	July	Aug.	Sept.	Oct.	Nov.	Dec.	
Flemington													
Temperature	31.9	32.3	40.8	51.1	62.1	70.8	75.7	73.6	66.8	56.1	44.4	33.5	53.3
Precipitation	3.36	2.63	4.13	3.65	4.34	3.92	4.38	5.33	3.49	3.18	3.76	3.35	45.52
Newton													
Temperature	27.9	28.1	36.9	48.2	59.4	67.5	72.5	70.2	63.1	52.9	41.1	29.9	49.8
Precipitation	3.10	2.51	3.58	3.60	4.24	4.47	4.68	4.66	3.86	3.43	3.74	3.13	45.0
Phillipsburg													
Temperature	30.4	30.9	39.3	50.2	61.4	69.8	74.4	72.3	65.2	52.2	42.9	32.5	53.2
Precipitation	3.87	3.00	4.24	3.90	4.30	4.39	5.64	5.31	4.02	3.49	3.76	3.57	48.64

* U. S. Department of Commerce, Weather Bureau, *Climatology of the United States; Climates of the States: New Jersey,* Bulletin No. 60-28 (December, 1959), 6.

Appendix IV

COMMON AND SCIENTIFIC NAMES OF NATIVE NORTH
AMERICAN FLORA MENTIONED IN THE TEXT

Common Name	Scientific Name
American chestnut	*Castanea dentata*
American licorice	*Falcata comosa*
American lotus	*Nelumbo lutea*
blackberries	*Rubus* sp.
black oak	*Quercus velutina*
black walnut	*Juglans nigra*
bottle gourd	*Lagenaria siceraria*
butternut	*Juglans cinerea*
cat-tail flag	*Typha latifolia*
crab apple	*Malus coronaria*
cranberry	*Vaccinium macrocarpon*
elm	*Ulmus americana*
ginseng	*Aralia quinquefolia*
grapes	*Vitis* sp.
hazelnut	*Corylus americana*
hemlock	*Tsuga canadensis*
hickories	*Carya* sp.
jack-in-the-pulpit	*Arisaema attorubus*
Jerusalem artichoke	*Helianthus tuberosus*
kidney bean	*Phaseolus vulgaris*
lima bean	*Phaseolus lunatus*
maize or Indian corn	*Zea mays*
morning glory	*Ipomoea pandurata*
oaks	*Quercus* sp.
pepper root	*Dentaria diphylla*
persimmon	*Diospyros virginiana*
plum	*Prunus americana*
*potato-bean or hopniss	*Glycine apios*
pumpkin	*Cucurbita pepo*
sassafras	*Sassafras varifolium*
slippery elm	*Ulmus fulva*
strawberries	*Fragaria virginiana*
sugar maple	*Acer saccharum*
sunflower	*Helianthus annuus*
*swamp potato or katniss	*Sagittaria longirotra*
sweet flag	*Acornus calamus*

* W. L. McAtee, "Names of American Plants in Books on Kalm's Travels,"
Torreya XLI (1941), 151–160.

Appendix IV continued

Common Name	Scientific Name
sycamore	*Platanus occidentalis*
*taw-ho	*Peltandra virginica*
tobacco	*Nicotiana rustica*
tulip-poplar	*Liriodendron tulipifera*
white cedar	*Chamaecyparis thyoides*
wild ginger	*Asarum canadense*
wild hemp	*Apocynum cannabinum*
yellow birch	*Betula lutea*
yellow pond lilly	*Nymphaea advena*

Appendix V. Southwestern Musconetcong Valley, eighteenth-century property divisions. Scale approximately 1:35,200. Source: D. Stanton Hammond, "Sheet C, Hunterdon County, New Jersey," *Map Series #4* (n.p.: Genealogical Society of New Jersey, 1965).

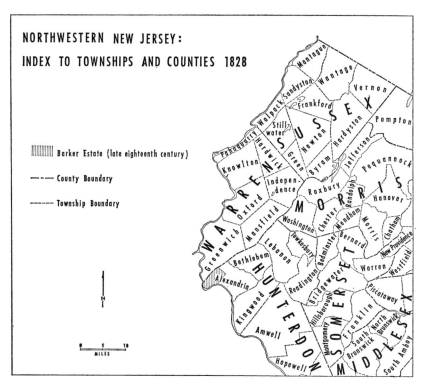

NORTHWESTERN NEW JERSEY:
INDEX TO TOWNSHIPS AND COUNTIES 1828

|||||||| Barker Estate (late eighteenth century)

—·— County Boundary

—————— Township Boundary

MILES

Appendix VI. Compiled from various sources.

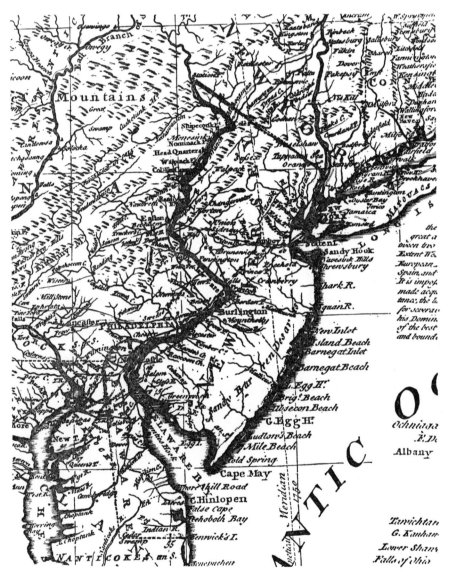

Appendix VII. *A General Map of the Middle British Colonies in America,*
by Thomas Jefferys. Published in Philadelphia by Lewis Evans, 1758.
From the original in the New Jersey Historical Society.

Appendix VIII. The Musconetcong Valley in 1795. Scale approximately
1:655,800. Source: Samuel Lewis, "The State of New Jersey Compiled
from the Most Authentic Information," *Carey's American Edition of
Guthries Geography Improved*, anon. (Philadelphia: M. Carey, 1795).
From the original in the Rutgers University Library.

Notes

Preface

1. Several alternate approaches, depending upon the availability of data, and the focus of interest, are set forth in Harry Roy Merrens, "Historical Geography and Early American History," *William and Mary Quarterly*, 22 (1965), 529–548.

2. Carl O. Sauer, "The Morphology of Landscape," *University of California Publications In Geography*, II (1925), p. 47.

3. *Visitor's Guide: Places of Note and Beauty on Schooley's Mountain and Vicinage*, p. 5.

4. Fred Kniffen, "Folk Housing: Key to Diffusion," *Annals of the Association of American Geographers*, LV (1965), 551.

5. Elmer T. Clark (ed.), *The Journal and Letters of Francis Asbury*, II, 537.

Chapter 1

1. The foregoing statistics may be found in Cornelius Clarkson Vermeule, *Report on Water-Supply, Water-Power, the Flow of Streams and Attendant Phenomena*.

2. Fenneman has classified the rugged plateau-like surface of the Highlands as comprising the Reading Prong of the New England Upland, and traces it from the Taconic Mountains in Connecticut to its terminus at Reading, Pennsylvania. See Nevin N. Fenneman, *Physiography of Eastern United States*, p. 368.

3. Peneplanation has been suggested as the cause of this accordance by many writers, and Schooley's Mountain is often cited as the type location of a peneplain. See Carl O. Dunbar, *Historical Geology*, pp. 359–360.

4. William Morris Davis, "The Rivers of Northern New Jersey, with Notes on the Classification of Rivers in General," *Geographical Essays*, p. 494.

5. Rollin D. Salisbury, *et al.*, *The Glacial Geology of New Jersey*, Geological Survey of New Jersey, Final Report of the State Geologist, V, 253.

6. William Morris Davis and J. W. Wood, "The Geographic Development of Northern New Jersey," *Proceedings of the Boston Society of Natural History*, XXIV (1890), 397.

7. Other invaluable sources that touch upon the geology and geomorphology of the Musconetcong Valley include Douglas Johnson, *Geomorphology of the Central Appalachians;* and *Stream Sculpture on the Atlantic Slope: A Study in the Evolution of Appalachian Rivers;* J. Volney Lewis, *The Geology of*

New Jersey; J. Volney Lewis *et al., Geologic Map of New Jersey;* and Kemble Widmer, *The Geology and Geography of New Jersey.*

8. Nineteenth-century data are available in Vermeule, *Report on Water-Supply* . . . , p. 144. For twentieth-century data see J. V. B. Wells, *Surface Water Supply of the United States, Part 1-B; North Atlantic Slope Basins, New York to York River.* Geological Survey Water Supply Paper No. 1622, pp. 227–228.

9. See E. Lucy Braun, *Deciduous Forests of Eastern North America,* p. 428; John E. Cantlon, "Vegetation and Microclimates on North and South Slopes of Cushetunk Mountain, New Jersey," *Ecological Monographs,* XXIII (July, 1953), 242; and C. F. Korstian and Paul W. Stickel, "The Natural Replacement of Blight-Killed Chestnut in the Hardwood Forests of the Northeast," *Journal of Agricultural Research,* XXXIV (April, 1927), 647. A suggestion of man's impact through time on the American chestnut can be found in Peter O. Wacker, "Man and the American Chestnut" (Abstract), *Annals of the Association of American Geographers,* LIV (1964), 440–441.

10. There are numerous sources, including James Alexander Papers, New York Historical Society Library, New York. (Manuscripts in the collection of this society are cited hereafter as *NYHS.*) See also John Reading, "Copy of Journal of _____ Reading, While Surveying Lands in the Northern Part of New Jersey, April 17th to June 10th, 1715," *Proceedings of the New Jersey Historical Society,* X (January, July, and October, 1915), 35–46, 128–133; and James P. Snell (ed.), *History of Sussex and Warren Counties,* pp. 43–44. The latter contains John Lawrence's notes of 1743.

11. Much confusion is involved in the study of soils maps of Northern New Jersey. The entire drainage system of the Musconetcong has been mapped, and portions are included on the *Sussex Area Sheet* of 1911, the *Belvidere Area Sheet* of 1917, and the *Bernardsville Sheet* of 1919 and, most recently, twenty-eight sheets published by the Soil Conservation Service in 1953 cover the soil series and land-use-capability classes of Warren County, New Jersey. Unfortunately, the identification of, and the criteria used in the identification of soil series vary widely from map to map, as do the areas occupied by the soil series. For example—in placing the *Bernardsville Sheet* on the southern boundary of the *Sussex Area Sheet* it becomes readily apparent that what has been mapped as "Rough stony land" on the *Sussex Area Sheet* is described, with different boundaries, as the "stony phase" of "Gloucester loam" on the *Bernardsville Sheet,* this despite the fact that "Gloucester stony loam" has been located elsewhere on the *Sussex Area Sheet.* The stony phase of the Gloucester loam which appears in some portions of Warren County included in the *Belvidere Area Sheet* becomes the "Chatfield and Oquaga extremely rocky loams" on *Sheet No. 12* of the Soil Conservation soil map of Warren County. Such confusion is found throughout the areas not included by recent soil maps. Unfortunately, only Warren County has been remapped with the more recent criteria for identifying soil series, so that meaningful soil maps covering the greater part of the Musconetcong

drainage system simply do not exist. See J. C. F. Tedrow *et al., Warren County Soils: Their Nature, Conservation, and Use* [pamphlet]; United States Department of Agriculture, Bureau of Soils, *Soil Map: New Jersey; Belvidere Sheet* and *Sussex Area Sheet;* United States Department of Agriculture, Bureau of Soils in cooperation with the Department of Conservation and Development of New Jersey, *Soil Map: New Jersey; Bernardsville Sheet;* and United States Department of Agriculture, Soil Conservation Service and the New Jersey Agricultural Experiment Station, *New Jersey: Warren County Soil Conservation District, Warren County, Physical Land Conditions.*

Chapter 2

1. A good general reference work on the Indians of North America is Harold E. Driver, *Indians of North America.* The distribution of surface finds of Clovis points in the Delaware Valley may be found in Ronald J. Mason, "Indications of Paleo-Indian Occupation in the Delaware Valley," *Pennsylvania Archaeologist,* XXIX (1959), 1, 6.

2. The *possibility* of man's appearance in southern New York State by 10,500 B.C. in accordance with recent geological and ecological data along with associated radiocarbon dates, is stated in William A. Ritchie, *The Archaeology of New York State,* p. 12. For the northeastern United States as a whole, Ritchie more conservatively places the advent of Paleo-Indian at before 7,000 B.C. *Ibid.,* pp. 1–30. New Jersey's state archaeologist, in an earlier publication, dated the Paleo-Indian period in New Jersey as beginning *ca.* 8,000 B.C. and lasting until *ca.* 3,000 B.C. Dorothy Cross, *Archaeology of New Jersey,* II, 169.

3. The sole radiocarbon date may be found in W. S. Broecker and J. L. Kulp, "Lamont Natural Radiocarbon Measurements, IV," *Science,* CXXVI (December 20, 1957), 1328. Oliver P. Hay indicates the numerous finds of Pleistocene fauna in New Jersey in *The Pleistocene of North America and its Vertebrated Animals from the States East of the Mississippi River and from the Canadian Provinces East of Longitude 95°,* pp, 63–68; 132–133; 149; 226–227; 237; 246; 248; 267.

4. Carl O. Sauer, "Geographic Sketch of Early Man in America," *Geographical Review,* XXXIV (October, 1944), 543–552.

5. J. E. Potzger, "What Can Be Inferred from Pollen Profiles of Bogs in the New Jersey Barrens," *Bartonia,* XXVI (1952), 22.

6. Unless indicated, the entire discussion of the Abbott Farm site is from Cross *et al., Archaeology of New Jersey,* II, 1–10, 192–197.

7. Indiana Historical Society, *Walam Olum or Red Score: The Migration Legend of the Lenni Lenape or Delaware Indians,* p. 318.

8. An excellent general work on the Delawares is William W. Newcomb, "The Culture and Acculturation of the Delaware Indians," *Anthropological Papers,* Museum of Anthropology, University of Michigan, X (1956).

9. Population numbers for the aboriginal inhabitants of North America are contained in James Mooney, "The Aboriginal Population of America North of Mexico," ed. J. R. Swanton, *Smithsonian Miscellaneous Collections* LXXX (1928). Stephen Shaffer estimated the number of aborigines resident at Lake Hopatcong in the eighteenth century by counting the number of fire pits still in evidence in the early nineteenth century. "Indian Village or Pipe Water Town," Shaffer Papers, Morristown Public Library. (Manuscripts in the collection of this library are cited hereafter as MPL.)

10. Data on Lenni Lenape settlement patterns in New Jersey are available in the following: Dorothy Cross, "The Indians of New Jersey," *Proceedings of the New Jersey Historical Society*, LXX (January, 1952), 5; W. H. Hayes, *Indian Life in New Jersey*, pp. 1, 31–32; Alanson Skinner, *The Indians of Newark Before the White Men Came* [pamphlet], p. 7; and Alanson Skinner and Max Schrabisch (comps.), *A Preliminary Report of the Archaeological Survey of the State of New Jersey*, p. 35.

11. Dorothy Cross, "Houses of the Lenni Lenape," *The Archaeological Society of New Jersey News Letter*, I (October, 1940), 11–12.

12. Gabriel Thomas, *An Account of Pennsylvania and West New Jersey*, p. 53.

13. Richard Blome, *The Present State of His Majesty's Isles and Territories in America*, p. 98; cited by William Nelson, *Indians of New Jersey*, p. 27.

14. Samuel Smith, *The History of the Colony of New Jersey*, 2d ed., p. 142.

15. Max Schrabisch, *Archaeology of Warren and Hunterdon Counties*, p. 26.

16. The best single source on the Indian sites investigated to date is Cross, *et al.*, *Archaeology of New Jersey*, I. Appendix A, "Map of the State of New Jersey Showing Indian Sites," is especially useful. On the Indians in the vicinity of Lake Hopatcong, see also Charles A. Philhower, "The Indians About Lake Hopatcong," *Archaeological Society of New Jersey Bulletin*, XIII (1957).

17. Snell, *History of Sussex and Warren Counties . . .* , p. 468.

18. Adolph B. Benson (ed. & trans.), *Peter Kalm's Travels in North America: The English Version of 1770*, I, 268.

19. George Henry Loskiel, *History of the Mission of the United Brethren Among the Indians in North America*, p. 68.

20. Abraham Luckenbach, "The Moravian Indian Mission on White River; Diaries and Letters, May 5, 1799, to November 12, 1806," ed. L. H. Gipson, *Indiana Historical Collections*, XXIII (1938), 598–599.

21. Isaack de Rasieres, "Letter of Isaack de Rasieres to Samuel Blommaert, 1628," *Narratives of New Netherland*, ed. J. F. Jameson, p. 10.

22. Charles A. Philhower, "Agriculture and the Foods of the Indians of New Jersey," *Proceedings of the New Jersey Historical Society*, LVIII (April, 1940), 99. Unless indicated otherwise, the entire discussion of aboriginal plant foods and the gathering of shellfish and mollusks is based upon this article and upon Cross, *Proceedings of the New Jersey Historical Society*, LXX.

23. Cross, *et al.*, *Archaeology of New Jersey*, I, 147.

24. Peter Lindestrom, *Geographia Americae With an Account of the Dela-*

ware Indians, Based on Surveys and Notes Made in 1654–1656, ed. Amandus Johnson, pp. 213–214.

25. For a discussion of aboriginal fishing, see Cross, *Proceedings of the New Jersey Historical Society,* LXX, 3; and Nelson, p. 42.

26. John W. Lequear, *Traditions of Hunterdon,* p. 104.

27. Thomas Budd, *Good Order Established in Pennsylvania and New Jersey in America,* ed. Edward Armstrong, p. 9.

28. Alanson A. Haines, *Hardyston Memorial: A History of the Township and the North Presbyterian Church, Hardyston, Sussex County, New Jersey,* p. 12.

29. Benson, p. 119; Benjamin B. Edsall and J. F. Tuttle, *The First Sussex Centenary,* pp. 25–26; Haines, p. 12; E. D. Halsey (ed.), *History of Morris County, New Jersey,* p. 18.

30. T. F. Chambers, *The Early Germans of New Jersey,* p. 178.

31. Johann David Schoepf, *Travels in the Confederation: 1783–1784,* I, pp. 164–165.

32. John Heckewelder, *History, Manners, and Customs of the Indian Nations Who Once Inhabited Pennsylvania and the Neighboring States,* 2d ed. rev., pp. 158–159.

33. Smith, pp. 112–113.

34. Warren Fretz, "Old Methods of Taking Fish," *Papers of the Bucks County Historical Society,* V (1926), 362–372; Thaddeus S. Kenderdine, "Hunting, Traping [*sic*] and Fishing in Bucks County," *Papers of the Bucks County Historical Society,* V (1926), 739.

35. Cornelius C. Vermeule, "Early Transport in and About New Jersey," *Proceedings of the New Jersey Historical Society,* IX (April, 1924), 107.

36. Charles A. Philhower, "The Indians of the Morris County Area," *Proceedings of the New Jersey Historical Society,* LIV (October, 1936), 264–265.

37. C. D. Deshler, "The Early Roads in New Jersey." Paper read before the New-Brunswick Historical Club, on Wednesday Evening, May 26, 1880, p. 1, Special Collections Division, Rutgers University Library. (Manuscripts in the collection of this library are cited hereafter as RUL.)

38. Francis W. Halsey (ed.), *A Tour of Four Great Rivers, the Hudson, Mohawk, Susquehanna and Delaware in 1769; Being the Journal of Richard Smith of Burlington, New Jersey,* pp. 70–71.

39. A discussion of the Indian paths of northern New Jersey along with their significance may be found in the following additional sources: Chambers, p. 178; Amelia S. Decker, *That Ancient Trail,* pp. 6–7; Ralph Ege, *Pioneers of Old Hopewell, with Sketches of Her Revolutionary Heroes,* pp. 195–196; Halsey, *History of Morris County . . .* pp. 20, 373; Wheaton J. Lane, *From Indian Trail to Iron Horse; Travel and Transportation in New Jersey, 1620–1860,* p. 17; George S. Mott, "The First Century of Hunterdon County, State of New Jersey," *Proceedings of the New Jersey Historical Society,* V (January, 1878), 67; Charles A. Philhower, "The Minisink Indian Trail," *Proceedings of the New Jersey Historical Society,* VIII (July, 1923); Philhower, "The Abo-

rigines of Hunterdon County, New Jersey," *Proceedings of the New Jersey Historical Society*, XI (October, 1926), 516–517; Philhower, *Proceedings of the New Jersey Historical Society*, LIV, 262–265; P. W. Schaefer, *et. al.*, "An Historical Map of Pennsylvania"; Schrabisch, p. 42; James P. Snell (ed.), *History of Hunterdon and Somerset Counties, New Jersey*, p. 106; Oscar M. Voorhees, *The Exterior and Interior Bounds of Hunterdon County, New Jersey* [pamphlet], p. 15.

40. Daniel G. Brinton and Albert S. Anthony, *A Lenape-English Dictionary*, pp. 50, 149.

41. William C. Reichel, *Names Which the Lenni Lenape or Delaware Indians Gave to Rivers, Streams, and Localities Within the States of Pennsylvania, New Jersey, Maryland and Virginia*, p. 29.

42. D. X. Junkin, *A Discourse Delivered on the Centenary of the First Presbyterian Church, Greenwich, New Jersey* [pamphlet], p. 27; Henry Race, "Rev. William Frazer's Three Parishes: St. Thomas's, St. Andrew's, and Musconetcong, New Jersey; 1768–1770," *The Pennsylvania Magazine of History and Biography*, XII (1888), 214.

43. The following sources may be consulted with regard to aboriginal toponyms appearing in the Musconetcong Valley: Matthew S. Henry, "Indian Names of Rivers, Creeks &c in the State of New Jersey," 1856, p. 83, New Jersey Historical Society. (Manuscripts in the collection of this society are cited hereafter as NJHS.) Philhower, *Archaelogical Society of New Jersey Bulletin*, XIII, 14–15; Hubert G. Schmidt, *Some Hunterdon Place Names*, pp. 22–23; Writers Program of the Works Projects Administration in the State of New Jersey, *The Origin of New Jersey Place Names*, pp. 24–25.

44. Budd, p. 36.

45. Smith, p. 179.

46. William Roome, *The Early Days and Early Surveys of New Jersey*, p. 25.

47. John W. Barber and Henry Howe, *Historical Collections of the State of New Jersey*, p. 244.

48. Smith, p. 183.

49. Snell, *History of Somerset and Hunterdon . . .* , p. 431.

50. Alfred Philip Muntz, "The Changing Geography of the New Jersey Woodlands, 1600–1900" (unpublished Ph.D. dissertation, Department of Geography, University of Wisconsin, 1959), p. 40.

51. John Pearse, *A Concise History of the Iron Manufacture of the American Colonies*, p. 69.

52. See, for example, Cross, *et al.*, *Archaeology of New Jersey*, I, 147–148; and Hay, pp. 237, 308–311.

Chapter 3

1. E. D. Halsey, *History of Morris County . . .* , p. 40.

2. Lequear, p. 85. This legend probably preserves the spirit of such occurrences if not the actual facts in this case. The year of the Coxe and Bowlby

surveys has been put at 1740. Col. Daniel Coxe, however, died in 1737 (N.J.A. 1st Ser. X. 225–227). Properties resurveyed from previous owners to Bowlby in the vicinity of the supposed competition with Coxe have been dated at 1763, and 1765. (D. Stanton Hammond, "Hunterdon County, New Jersey Provincial Patents," April, 1963.)

3. Garret Rapalje to James Parker, June 12, 1771, James Alexander Papers, NYHS.

4. William Coxe to John Emley, April 13, 1762, John Emley Papers, Hunterdon County Historical Society, Flemington, New Jersey. (Manuscripts in the collection of this society are cited hereafter as HCHS.)

5. Edsall and Tuttle, p. 25.

6. Charles S. Boyer, *Early Forges and Furnaces in New Jersey*, pp. 233–236.

7. Edsall and Tuttle, p. 25.

8. Lequear, p. 86.

9. William A. Whitehead, *et al.* (eds.), *Archives of the State of New Jersey: Documents Relating to the Colonial, Revolutionary, and Post Revolutionary History of the State of New Jersey*, First Series, 42 vols.; and William S. Stryker, *et al.* (eds.), *Archives of the State of New Jersey: Documents Relating to the Revolutionary History of the State of New Jersey*, Second Series, 5 vols. (These volumes will be cited hereafter as N.J.A., 1st Ser., and N.J.A., 2nd Ser.)

10. James Parker, "Abstracts of W. McAdams Proceedings on Sir Robert Barkers Tract," 1765, James Parker Papers, RUL.

11. For lands becoming available during the Revolution, see N.J.A., 2nd Ser., III, 112–113, 532–533, 535–536; and IV, 278. For unused land see Rayner W. Kelsey (ed. & trans.), *Cazenove Journal, 1794: A Record of the Journey of Theophile Cazenove Through New Jersey and Pennsylvania*, p. 14.

12. John Rutherfurd, "Notes on the State of New Jersey," *Proceedings of the New Jersey Historical Society*, I (1867), 88.

13. Snell, *History of Hunterdon and Somerset* . . . , p. 189.

14. Snell, *History of Warren and Sussex* . . . , p. 594.

15. John Lowrey, "A History of the First Presbyterian Church of Hackettstown, New Jersey, 1886," p. 5, RUL. John Harold Nunn, *The Story of Hackettstown, New Jersey, 1754–1955*, p. 7.

16. Snell, *History of Hunterdon and Somerset* . . . , pp. 414–415.

17. See Decker, 18–19; Charles Gilbert Hine, *History and Legend, Fact, Fancy and Romance of the Old Mine Road, Kingston, New York to the Mine Holes of Pahaquarry*, p. 13; and Reading, p. 95.

18. N.J.A., 1st Ser., XXIII, 219.

19. Snell, *History of Hunterdon and Somerset* . . . , pp. 183–186.

20. Benson, I., p. 117.

21. Hubert G. Schmidt, *Rural Hunterdon: An Agricultural History*, p. 30; Snell, *History of Hunterdon and Somerset* . . . , pp. 186–187.

22. Lequear, p. 106; Mott, p. 65; Snell, *History of Hunterdon and Somerset* . . . , pp. 189, 431.

23. Snell, *History of Sussex and Warren* . . . , p. 592.

24. The settlements of some ethnic groups can be most accurately dated and located by the establishment of their churches. Two especially valuable general sources in this connection for New Jersey are Edwin S. Gaustad, *Historical Atlas of Religion in America;* and Frederick L. Weis, *The Colonial Churches and the Colonial Clergy of the Middle and Southern Colonies, 1607–1776.*

25. Race, p. 214.

26. John Cooley, "List of Tennants in Alexandria who are deficient in paying Their Rents either in whole or in part," 1789, John Cooley Papers, HCHS; B. F. Fackenthal, Jr., "Copies of Early American Iron Industries Relating Specially to Durham Iron Works and the Forges Connected Therewith Being Mostly Copies of Original Papers, Documents and Extracts From the Account Books of the Durham Iron Works Now in the Library of the Bucks County Historical Society, Doylestown, Pennsylvania together With Some Historical Notes," [1942?]; and "Greenwich and Chelsea Forges," (Looseleaf typed notebook, consisting of over one hundred pages of deeds, maps, etc., often unnumbered), [1942?], B. F. Fackenthal, Jr. Collection, Bucks County Historical Society, Doylestown, Pennsylvania. (Manuscripts in the collection of this society are cited hereafter as BCHS.) Honeyman, p. 868; James Parker, "Miscellaneous Memoranda," James Parker Papers, RUL.

27. Cornelius C. Vermeule, "Raritan Valley, Its Discovery And Settlement," *Proceedings of the New Jersey Historical Society*, XIII (July, 1928), 287.

28. John C. Honeyman, "Zion, St. Paul and Other Early Lutheran Churches in Central New Jersey," *Proceedings of the New Jersey Historical Society*, X (October, 1925), 408; and XI, 191.

29. Chambers, pp. 201–204.

30. Snell, *History of Sussex and Warren . . .* , p. 43.

31. Daniell Cooper, "Survey for Josiah Lindsley," April, 1759, James Alexander Papers, NYHS.

32. Stephen Shaffer, "Names of Settlers Living on Lake [Hopatcong] Shore Prior to Year 1800," Stephen Shaffer Papers, MPL.

33. John Ford, "Freedholders List, Morris County, New Jersey, August 31, 1752," Department of Education, Division of State Library, Archives and History Microfilm and Records Unit, Trenton, New Jersey. (Manuscripts in the collection of this department are cited hereafter as NJSL.)

34. [Phinehas Fitz Randolph?], "Brookland Pond [Lake Hopatcong] Record Book, 1788–1791," NJHS.

35. Sources on the Dutch movement up the Raritan Valley include Lequear, pp. 91–92; Mott, p. 66; Snell, *History of Hunterdon and Somerset . . .* ; and Vermeule, *Proceedings of the New Jersey Historical Society*, IX and XIII.

36. See [Fitz Randolph?], *passim;* Roome, p. 75; and Tuttle, p. 47.

37. For Dutch movements into northwestern New Jersey by way of the Old Mine Road, see Decker, p. 1; A. Van Doren Honeyman (ed.), *Northwestern New Jersey: A History of Somerset, Morris, Hunterdon, Warren and Sussex Counties*, II, 603; and Snell, *History of Sussex and Warren . . .* , pp. 26, 44.

By 1790 the "Dutch" population of Sussex County was estimated to number approximately 3,250, or a little more than 17 per cent of the county's total. See Marcus L. Hansen, "The Minor Stocks in the American Population of 1790," *Annual Report of the American Historical Association for the Year 1931*, pp. 396–397. It is not known how large a percentage of these people may have come via the Old Mine Road.

38. George W. Cummins, *History of Warren County*, p. 72.

39. Junkin, p. 27.

40. Snell, *History of Sussex and Warren* . . . , p. 30.

41. Race, p. 213.

42. Cummins, p. 73.

43. John C. Honeyman, *Proceedings of the New Jersey Historical Society*, IX, 270.

44. Other sources including information on Scotch-Irish settlements in this portion of New Jersey include Charles A. Hanna, *The Scotch-Irish; or the Scot in North Britain, North Ireland, and North America*, II, 118–119; Carrie J. Hoffman, "Bloomsbury: Brief Historical Sketch," 1948, p. 2, RUL; A. Van Doren Honeyman, *Northwestern New Jersey* . . . , II, 674, 687–689, 693, 807; John C. Honeyman, *Proceedings of the New Jersey Historical Society*, XI, 194; Hubert G. Schmidt (ed.), *Lesser Crossroads*, pp. 66–67; Snell, *History of Sussex and Warren* . . . , pp. 581–582.

45. Benson, I, 121.

46. N.J.A., 1st Ser., XIX, 571.

47. Parker, "Miscellaneous Memoranda. . . ."

48. Sources on the movement of Germans into northwestern New Jersey in the eighteenth century include Chambers, p. 36; Albert B. Faust, *The German Element in the United States with Special Reference to its Political, Moral, Social, and Educational Influence*, I, 149–150; A. Van Doren Honeyman, *Northwestern New Jersey* . . . , II, 688; John C. Honeyman, *Proceedings of the New Jersey Historical Society*, IX, 256–270, 348–363; X, 294–306, 406–407; XI, 191, 541; XII, 331; Walter A. Knittle, *Early Eighteenth Century Palatine Emigration*, p. 31, 189; Lequear, pp. 94–95; Hubert G. Schmidt, "Germans in Colonial New Jersey," *The American German Review* (June–July, 1958), 4–9; Schmidt, *Lesser Crossroads*, pp. 38–39; and Snell, *History of Sussex and Warren* . . . , pp. 32, 704, 729.

49. Smith, p. 500. The statement on the rapidity of settlement is found in Edsall and Tuttle, p. 45.

50. E. D. Halsey, *History of Morris County* . . . , p. 22.

51. Thomas Anburey, *Travels Through the Interior Parts of America*, II, 157.

52. Scattered census data covering counties are available in *Compendium of Censuses 1726–1850*, p. 41. Scattered data on relative population densities in northwestern New Jersey are included within "County Tax Ratables, 1778–1822," Department of Education, Division of State Library, Archives and History Microfilm and Records Unit, Trenton, New Jersey. Unfortunately,

the data pertaining to the townships in existence in the Musconetcong Valley during the period are too scattered to allow accurate mapping of the population distribution.

53. James Parker to John Cooley, September 28, 1792, James Parker Papers, RUL.

54. Joshua Gilpin, "Journey to Bethlehem," *The Pennsylvania Magazine of History and Biography*, XLVI (1922), 25.

55. Scattered references to continued movement into the region in the late eighteenth century include Chambers, p. 176; Cummins, p. 241; Snell, *History of Hunterdon and Somerset . . .* , pp. 418, 430; and Snell, *History of Sussex and Warren . . .* , pp. 595–596, 729.

56. Richard P. McCormick, *Experiment in Independence*, p. 189; and Mott, p. 106.

57. "Returns of Surveys," James Alexander Papers, NYHS.

58. Cornelius C. Vermeule, "Some Early New Jersey Place Names," *Proceedings of the New Jersey Historical Society*, X (July, 1925), 248.

59. Selected generic toponyms in the northeastern United States are dealt with by Wilbur Zelinsky in his landmark article "Some Problems in the Distribution of Generic Terms in the Place-Names of the Northeastern United States," *Annals of the Association of American Geographers*, XLV (1955). See especially pages 327–329. Local surveyors' accounts of place-names may be found in Reading, pp. 35–46, 128–133; and James Van Kirk, "Field Book, 1813–1815," NJHS.

Chapter 4

1. Thomas F. Gordon, *A Gazetteer of the State of New Jersey*, p. 185; Muntz, p. 318.

2. Cooper, "Survey for Josiah Lindsley."

3. N.J.A., 1st Ser., XXIV, 95.

4. The practice of clearing by burning was also widely practiced in upland locations in western Europe during and before the eighteenth century. See, for example, E. Estyn Evans, "The Ecology of Peasant Life in Western Europe," *Man's Role in Changing the Face of the Earth*, ed. William L. Thomas, Jr., *et al.*, p. 229. Swedes and Finns on the Delaware used their traditional methods of clearing and manuring by burning at the time of their arrival in the seventeenth century. See Amandus Johnson, *The Swedish Settlements on the Delaware; Their History and Relation to the Indians, Dutch and English, 1638–1664*, II, 527–529; and John H. Wuorinen, *The Finns on the Delaware, 1638–1655*, p. 100.

5. William M. Johnson (comp.), *Memoirs and Reminiscences together with Sketches of the Early History of Sussex County, New Jersey, by Casper Schaeffer*, p. 65.

6. N.J.A., 1st Ser., XXIV, 145.

7. Ege, p. 191.

8. "Account Book, Greenwich Forge, New Jersey, June 9, 1783—April 3, 1784," "Durham Furnace & Greenwich Forge, New Jersey, Ledger, April 1, 1780—July 1, 1782," and "Parts of Old Journals, Chelsea Forge, New Jersey, 1783–1789," *passim,* Fackenthal Collection, BCHS; Benson, I, 183–184, II 634; Percy W. Bidwell and John I. Falconer, *History of Agriculture in the Northern United States 1620–1860,* p. 8, 97; Rutherfurd, p. 87; Carl R. Woodward, "Agriculture in New Jersey," reprinted from *New Jersey: A History,* Vol. I, ed. Irving S. Kull, p. 28.

9. Bidwell and Falconer, pp. 14, 96–97. The view that Germans grew more rye than farmers of other ethnic stocks has been challenged in James Thomas Lemon, "A Rural Geography of Southeastern Pennsylvania in the Eighteenth Century: The Contributions of Cultural Inheritance, Social Structure, Economic Conditions and Physical Resources" (unpublished Ph.D. dissertation, University of Wisconsin, 1964), pp. 244–247.

10. "Account Book, Greenwich Forge . . . ," "Parts of Old Journals . . . ," *passim,* Fackenthal Collections, BCHS; James Parker to Robert Barker, November 3, 1788, Parker Papers, RUL; Schmidt, *Lesser Crossroads,* p. 113.

11. Bidwell and Falconer, p. 45; Rutherfurd, p. 87; Schoepf, p. 44; Smith, p. 499.

12. Parker, "Miscellaneous Memoranda. . . ."

13. Benson, I, 89.

14. Bidwell and Falconer, p. 79; Edsall and Tuttle, p. 71; Ege, p. 191; and Hubert G. Schmidt, *Rural Hunterdon, An Agricultural History,* p. 99.

15. N.J.A., 2nd Ser., III, 169.

16. "Durham Furnace and Greenwich Forge . . . ," p. 64.

17. *Ibid.,* p. 77.

18. References on flax and flax culture in New Jersey include Helen E. D. Acton, "Charles Kirk's Review of a Century," *Papers of the Bucks County Historical Society,* VII (1937), 96; Bidwell and Falconer, p. 134; Ege, p. 191; George H. Larison, "The Mode of Life in Our Early Settlements," *Papers of the Bucks County Historical Society,* I (1887), 464; Uzal Ogden to the Society for the Propagation of the Gospel in Foreign Parts, July 8, 1771, Nelson Burr Papers, RUL; Grier Scheetz, "Flax and Its Culture," *Papers of the Bucks County Historical Society,* III (1909), 483–484; Hubert Schmidt, *Flax Culture in Hunterdon County,* New Jersey, p. 5; and Harry B. Weiss and Grace M. Weiss, *Forgotten Mills of Early New Jersey,* p. 7.

19. "Indenture between James Parker and Ishmael Lane, March 25, 1793," Parker Papers, RUL.

20. Benson, II, 616–617.

21. Kelsey, p. 10. Agreements as to land use on the Barker tract may be found in "Leases re Sir Robert Barker's Tracts of Land in East [West] Jersey 1760–1793," Parker Papers, RUL. Other references to the popularity of apple trees in the area may be found in Thomas Capner to John, Samuel, and Row-

land Coltman, November 17, 1787, Capner Papers, HCHS; and William Johnson, *Memoirs and Reminiscences* . . . , p. 31.

22. Kelsey, pp. 10–12; Schmidt, *Lesser Crossroads,* pp. 382–383; and Woodward, pp. 18–21.

23. Rutherfurd, p. 85.

24. Schmidt, *Lesser Crossroads,* p. 117; and Woodward, pp. 17–18.

25. N.J.A., 1st Ser., XXV, 188.

26. Benson, I, 279.

27. N.J.A., 1st Ser., XXVI, 143.

28. Benson, I, 236, 266; Budd, p. 36; Larison, p. 461; N.J.A., 1st Ser., XI, 280; and Smith, p. 187.

29. N.J.A., 1st Ser., XXVIII, 424.

30. E. D. Halsey, *History of Morris County* . . . , p. 238.

31. Bethlehem Township records appear in Snell, *History of Hunterdon and Somerset* . . . , p. 458.

32. "Greenwich and Chelsea Forges . . . ," p. 242.

33. William Johnson, *Memoirs and Reminiscences* . . . , p. 78; and Woodward, pp. 22–23.

34. Rutherfurd, p. 81.

35. Ogden to the S.P.G.F.P., July 8, 1771.

36. Kelsey, p. 15.

37. Lequear, p. 177.

38. Rutherfurd, p. 87.

39. Haines, p. 33; Larison, p. 461; Ogden to the S.P.G.F.P., July 8, 1771; and Woodward, pp. 26–27.

40. Rutherfurd, p. 87.

41. *Loc. cit.*

42. Ogden to the S.P.G.F.P., July 8, 1771.

43. Larison, p. 461; Woodward, p. 25.

44. N.J.A., 2nd Ser., I. 13.

45. Anburey, p. 163; Benson, I, 111, 122–123; William Johnson, *Memoirs and Reminiscences* . . . , pp. 68, 83, 86; Woodward, p. 25.

46. *Phleum pratense* and *Trifolium pratense.* See Benson, I, 180, 266; Budd, pp. 36, 38; N.J.A., 1st Ser., XXIX, 117; Schmidt, *Rural Hunterdon* . . . , p. 119; and Smith, pp. 169, 174.

47. Benson, I, p. 308.

48. Parker, "Abstracts of W. McAdams Proceedings . . . ." Unless it is indicated otherwise, all quotations referring to the Barker tract are from this source. The relationship between landlord and tenant in northwestern New Jersey during the latter half of the eighteenth century is best set forth in Richard P. McCormick, "The West Jersey Estate of Sir Robert Barker," *Proceedings of the New Jersey Historical Society,* LXIV (July, 1946), 118–155.

49. Snell, *History of Hunterdon and Somerset* . . . , p. 415.

50. Indenture between James Parker and John Houghton, March 25, 1790, Parker Papers, RUL.

51. Parker, "Diary," December 15, 1789, RUL. See also Roome, pp. 52–53.

52. N.J.A., 1st Ser., XXIX, 22.

53. Rutherfurd, p. 81; and Woodward, p. 29.

54. Kelsey, pp. 14, 28–29.

55. Gilpin, p. 24.

56. For a contrasting view regarding the aptitude of eighteenth-century Pennsylvania-Germans for agriculture, see James T. Lemon, "The Agricultural Practices of National Groups in Eighteenth-Century Southeastern Pennsylvania," *The Geographical Review*, LVI (1966), 467–496.

57. The list of tenants on the Barker tract is found in Lequear, p. 173. Farm acreages in East and West Jersey are compared in Woodward, p. 13.

58. Edsall and Tuttle, p. 17; Schmidt, *Rural Hunterdon . . .* , p. 98.

59. References to stump fences and to worm fences include Benson, I, 50, 238–239; Henry W. Gross, "Old Fences in Bucks County," *Papers of the Bucks County Historical Society*, V (1926), 429–430; Schmidt, *Rural Hunterdon . . .* , pp. 95, 279; Frank S. Swain, "Passing Events," *Papers of the Bucks County Historical Society*, V (1926), 322; and Woodward, p. 30. The appearance of the stake-and-rider fence in New Jersey before 1780 is indicated in N.J.A., 2nd Ser., IV, 529. The reference to the worm fence in the Tirol is found in Henry C. Mercer, *Ancient Carpenter's Tools*, 2nd ed., p. 20.

60. Benson, I, 115.

61. Benson, I, 50, 239; Gross, pp. 430–432; Schmidt, *Rural Hunterdon . . .* , p. 187; Swain, pp. 332–333.

62. Gross, pp. 430–432; E. B. O'Callaghan (ed.), *Documents Relative to the Colonial History of the State of New York*, I, 367; and Schmidt, *Rural Hunterdon . . .* , p. 187.

63. John Emley, "Memorandum Book Barker Lands Hunterdon & Sussex, 1792," John Emley Papers, HCHS.

64. Wilbur Zelinsky, "Walls and Fences," *Landscape*, VIII (Spring, 1959), 20.

65. Arthur Cecil Bining, *Pennsylvania Iron Manufacture in the Eighteenth Century* ("Publications of Pennsylvania Historical Commission," Vol. IV), pp. 30–31.

66. These descriptive quotes may all be found in advertisements reprinted in the *New Jersey Archives*. The sources, in order of appearance, are: 1st Ser., XX, 637–638; XXIV, 122; XXVII, 272; and XXIX, 403. 2nd Ser., I, 380; and II, 94.

67. N.J.A., 2nd Ser., III, 287.

68. Gordon, p. 185.

69. N.J.A., 1st Ser., XXIX, 507.

70. Snell, *History of Sussex and Warren . . .* , p. 467.

71. See, for example, N.J.A., 1st Ser., XLII, 8, 43, 90.

72. Barber and Howe, p. 244.

73. N.J.A., 1st Ser., XXXIX, 443.

74. Snell, *History of Sussex and Warren . . .* , p. 467.

Chapter 5

1. Lequear, p. 85.

2. Snell, *History of Sussex and Warren* . . . , pp. 743–744.

3. Peter McGuire (contrib.), "Journal of a Journey to the Westward," *The American Historical Review*, XXXVII (October, 1931), 69.

4. Fred Kniffen and Henry Glassie, "Building in Wood in the Eastern United States: A Time-Place Perspective," *The Geographical Review*, LVI (January, 1966) 58–59; and Harold R. Shurtleff, *The Log Cabin Myth: A Study of the Early Dwellings of the English Colonists in North America*, p. 4.

5. Seymour Williams, *et al.*, "New Jersey Historic American Buildings Survey: Outline of the Development of Early American Architecture Compiled by the Historic American Buildings Survey," 1939, NJHS, pp. 51–53.

6. Benson, I, 272; II, 726.

7. *Ibid.*, II, 728.

8. Thomas T. Waterman, *The Dwellings of Colonial America*, p. 119.

9. G. H. Larison, "Last Primitive Houses near Howell's Ferry," quoted in Schmidt, *Rural Hunterdon* . . . , p. 91.

10. Sigurd Erixon, "The North-European Technique of Corner Timbering," *Folkliv*, I (1937), Fig. 25.

11. Larison, *Papers of the Bucks County Historical Society*, I, 462.

12. Joseph F. Folsom, "General Daniel Morgan's Birthplace and Life," *Proceedings of the New Jersey Historical Society*, XIV (July, 1929), 290.

13. R. M. Acton, "A Short History of the Glass Manufacture in Salem County, New Jersey," *The Pennsylvania Magazine*, IX (1885), 343–344.

14. Benson, II, 727.

15. Waterman, p. 123; and Shurtleff, p. 174. For a reference to corner fireplaces in single-story log houses in Bucks County, see Larison, *Papers of the Bucks County Historical Society*, I, 462. The "long groove," or V joint can be seen in Erixon, Fig. 25.

16. Lequear, p. 176.

17. John C. Honeyman, *Proceedings of the New Jersey Historical Society*, XI, 68.

18. Schmidt, *Lesser Crossroads* . . . , p. 54.

19. Peter Stryker, "Journal of a Trip from Belleville, N. J. as a Reformed Church Minister, to Preach in Vacant Congregations Westward and Southwestward, 1815–1816," RUL.

20. Harry M. Tinkcom, Margaret B. Tinkcom, and Grant M. Simon, *Historic Germantown from the Founding to the Early Part of the Nineteenth Century* ("Memoirs of the American Philosophical Society," 1955), p. 27.

21. I am indebted to students in my Historical Geography of Anglo-America course at Rutgers for extracting this as well as other material from the *New Jersey Archives*. This was done in the fall semester of 1965. An analysis of data concerning log houses in the *New Jersey Archives* also appears in Peter O. Wacker, "The Log House in New Jersey" (unpublished paper prepared

for the Open Session in Cultural Geography, Association of American Geographers Annual Convention, Toronto, Canada, 1966).

22. Lequear, p. 85.

23. For background information on this log house see "Presentation of a Log House by the Citizens of Doylestown to the Bucks County Historical Society," *Papers of the Bucks County Historical Society,* IV (1917), 198. The Pennsylvania-German V notch is not to be confused with the technique called the "V joint" in the W.P.A. survey. See Kniffen and Glassie, p. 59.

24. Historic American Buildings Survey, National Park Service, *Historic American Buildings Survey: Catalog of the Measured Drawings and Photographs of the Survey in the Library of Congress, March 1, 1941,* pp. 216–251; and *Historic American Buildings Survey: Supplement, Catalog of the Measured Drawings and Photographs of the Survey in the Library of Congress, Comprising Additions Since March 1, 1941,* alphabetical sequence, 11 pp. Measured drawings referred to in the text are also in the possession of the Division of Archives, State Library, Trenton, New Jersey. These will be cited hereafter as HABS, N. J.; Kniffen, *Annals of the Association of American Geographers,* LV, 549–577; and Thomas J. Wertenbaker, *The Founding of American Civilization: The Middle Colonies.*

25. N.J.A., 1st Ser., XXIV, 232.

26. *Ibid.,* 2nd Ser., IV, 286–287.

27. The "I" house was first identified as such in Fred B. Kniffen, "Louisiana House Types," *Annals of the Association of American Geographers,* XXVI (December, 1936), 185. This house type is also dealt with in Kniffen, *Annals of the Association of American Geographers,* LV, 555. The alteration of roof lines in order to meet the preference for the "I" type can be seen in HABS, N. J., Measured Drawings, Cooper and Lawrence House, Burlington (*ca.* 1690); Grant House, Salem (1721); Rogers House, Springside vicinity (1718); Wildes House, Arneytown (1720); Woolston House, Evansville vicinity (1715); *et passim.*

28. Personal communication from Fred B. Kniffen, Professor, Department of Geography and Anthropology, Baton Rouge, Louisiana, October 14, 1965.

29. The presence of this house type in the Delaware Valley in the early eighteenth century may be seen in HABS, N. J., Measured Drawings, Blue Anchor Tavern, Blue Anchor (1740); French House, Fellowship Vicinity (1729); Gill Homestead, Tavistock (1742); *et passim.* A similar house type of New England origin, which is based on Georgian lines, may be seen in Kniffen, *Annals of the Association of American Geographers,* LV, 558–559; Wertenbaker, p. 155.

30. Wertenbaker, p. 153.

31. HABS, N. J., Measured Drawings, Oakford House, Alloway (1736); Revell House, Burlington (1685); Stille House, Swedesboro (1753); *et passim.*

32. Schmidt, *Rural Hunterdon . . . ,* p. 93.

33. The sources of the advertisements cited, in order of appearance, are N.J.A., 1st Ser., XXV, 295; *Ibid.,* 2nd Ser., I, 298; *Ibid.,* 1st Ser., II, 502;

Ibid., 1st Ser., XXVI, 389; 2nd Ser., II, 349, 454–455, 473; IV, 295; *Ibid.*, 1st Ser., XXXI, 46. For the Middlebush kitchen see Ralph Voorhees, "The Raritan and its Early Holland Settlers," *Our Home*, I (1873), 495.

34. A. Haller Gross, "The Old Spring Houses of Bucks County," *Papers of the Bucks County Historical Society*, IV (1917), 396.

35. Benson, I, 161.

36. An advertisement mentioning a springhouse at Greenwich Forge appears in N.J.A., 1st Ser., XXIX, 409. The early appearance of springhouses in Bucks County is cited in A. Haller Gross, p. 396. The use of springhouses by Pennsylvania-Germans is mentioned in I. Daniel Rupp (ed.), *An Account of the Manners of the German Inhabitants of Pennsylvania, Written 1789, by Benjamin Rush*, p. 12.

37. These quotations, in order, are from the following sources: Schmidt, *Rural Hunterdon . . .* , p. 93; N.J.A., 1st Ser., XIX, 474; Schmidt, *Lesser Crossroads . . .* , pp. 123–124; and N.J.A., 1st Ser., XIX, 474.

38. Schmidt, *Rural Hunterdon . . .* , p. 94.

39. Tax records describing barns in Bucks and Northampton counties have been reprinted in Alfred L. Shoemaker, "The Barns of 1798," *The Pennsylvania Barn* ed. Alfred L. Shoemaker, pp. 91, 95. The quotation is from Henry J. Kauffman, "The Log Barn," *The Pennsylvania Barn*, p. 29.

40. Race, p. 214.

41. McGuire, p. 69. The advertisement of William Gammon's farm appears in N.J.A., 1st Ser., 52. Other advertisements indicating association of log houses and frame barns in the Highlands include *Ibid.*, XXV, 303–304; 2nd Ser., I, 552; and III, 168–169.

42. N.J.A., 2nd Ser., III, 3.

43. Benson, I, 235.

44. *Ibid.*, 117

45. Anburey, p. 162. An advertisement of a Dutch barn indicating typical dimensions is found in N.J.A., 1st Ser., XII, 103. Another source for eighteenth-century Dutch barn dimensions is found in Voorhees, p. 495. The probable origin of the Dutch barn is set forth in Wertenbaker, pp. 58–64.

46. N.J.A., 1st Ser., XXVI, 389.

47. The best source on the bank barn is Shoemaker, "The Pennsylvania Barn," *The Pennsylvania Barn*, pp. 6–8. The possible Old World origin of this barn type is set forth in Wertenbaker, pp. 321–324. The first known bank barn in northwestern New Jersey is mentioned in William M. Johnson, *Memoirs and Reminiscences . . .* , p. 68.

48. Schmidt, *Rural Hunterdon . . .* , p. 95.

49. N.J.A., 1st Ser., XX, 644.

50. McGuire, p. 69.

51. Wertenbaker, p. 64.

Chapter 6

1. Gordon, p. 185.

2. Boyer, 1; and E. D. Halsey, *History of Morris County . . .* , p. 40.

3. See, for example, Bining, pp. 152–157; Boyer, pp. 8–9; E. D. Halsey, *History of Morris County* . . . , p. 41; and N.J.A., 1st Ser., XXVI, vii.

4. N.J.A., 1st Ser., XXVII, 231.

5. Boyer, p. 10; Victor S. Clark, *History of Manufactures in the United States: 1607–1860*, p. 219; Fackenthal, "Early American Iron Industries . . . ," pp. 195, 201; B. F. Fackenthal, Jr., "Thomas Wright of Dyerstown, Pennsylvania," *Papers of the Bucks County Historical Society*, IV (1917), 662; and Snell, *History of Sussex and Warren* . . . , p. 78.

6. Fackenthal, "Early American Iron Industries . . . ," p. 201.

7. Victor S. Clark, *History of Manufactures* . . . , p. 221; Alfred Philip Muntz, "Forests and Iron: The Charcoal Iron Industry of the New Jersey Highlands," *Geografiska Annaler*, XLII (1960), 322; and Rutherfurd, p. 86.

8. Charles Laubach, "The Durham Iron Works," *Papers of the Bucks County Historical Society*, I (1883), 242.

9. Sources on eighteenth-century charcoal iron furnaces include Bining, pp. 30, 77–82; J. Leander Bishop, *A History of American Manufactures from 1608 to 1860*, I, 480; Boyer, p. 5; Victor S. Clark, *History of Manufactures* . . . , p. 20; Laubach, p. 235; H. R. Schubert, *History of the British Iron and Steel Industry from c. 450 B.C. to A.D. 1775*, p. 157, *et passim;* and "Extraction and Production of Metals: Iron and Steel," *A History of Technology*, edited by Charles Singer *et al.*, IV, 105.

10. The sources for these dates are, in order, as follows: Laubach, p. 235; Snell, *History of Sussex and Warren* . . . , p. 582; Boyer, pp. 234, 147, 103–104, 26; and N.J.A., 1st Ser., XXIX, 403.

11. Fackenthal, "Early American Iron Industries . . . ," p. 218.

12. Sources on the technology of eighteenth-century charcoal iron forges include Bining, pp. 83–90; Bishop, p. 480; Boyer, pp. 10–13; and Schubert, *History of the British Iron and Steel Industry*, pp. 157–160.

13. N.J.A., 1st Ser., XXVIII, 253.

14. The examples quoted are from N.J.A., 2nd Ser., IV, 286; and *Ibid.*, 1st Ser., XXVI, 302.

15. Fackenthal, "Early American Iron Industries . . . ," p. 179.

16. N.J.A., 2nd Ser., I, 380.

17. "Durham Furnace and Greenwich Forge . . . ," p. 10, *et passim.*

18. See Fackenthal, "Early American Iron Industries . . . ," pp. 175, 201, 203, 207, 209, 221; and "Day Book of Aaron Musgrave & Company," June 10, 1783, BCHS.

19. N.J.A., 1st Ser., XXVI, 319.

20. *Ibid.*, XXVII, 272.

21. Jacob L. Bunnell (ed.), *Sussex County Sesquicentennial*, p. 29.

22. The sources for these dates are, in order, as follows: Boyer, p. 52; "Greenwich and Chelsea Forges . . . ," pp. 239–239a; Boyer, p. 55; Thomas Bartow to William Alexander, August 20, 1761, Alexander Papers, NYHS; Boyer, p. 217; *Ibid.*, p. 30; and Hoffman, p. 2.

23. Sources on the technology of eighteenth-century bloomeries include Bining, p. 76; Boyer, pp. 3–4; E. D. Halsey, *History of Morris County* . . . , p. 235; and Rutherfurd, p. 86.

24. Muntz, *Geografiska Annaler*, XLII, 319.

25. The sources for these dates are, in order, as follows: Edsall and Tuttle, p. 30; Moses Bigelow, "Stanhope Forges And Furnaces, Sussex County," *Proceedings of the New Jersey Historical Society*, LVIII (1940), 266–268; Halsey, *History of Morris County* . . . , p. 235; and Edward A. Webb (ed.), *The Historical Directory of Sussex County, New Jersey*, p. 70.

26. Schoepf, II, 7.

27. E. D. Halsey, *History of Morris County* . . . , pp. 39, 43; Roome, p. 23; and Schoepf, II, 34.

28. Thomas Millidge to William Alexander, July 12, 1750, Alexander Papers, NYHS.

29. Snell, *History of Hunterdon and Somerset* . . . , p. 461.

30. N.J.A., 1st Ser., XX, 637–638.

31. Webb, p. 70.

32. *Loc. cit.*

33. Frank K. Swain, "Charcoal Burning in Buckingham Township," *Papers of the Bucks County Historical Society*, IV (1917), 467–469; and Henry H. Tryon, "A Portable Charcoal Kiln," *Black Rock Forest Bulletin*, V (1933), 3–5.

34. Schoepf, I, 36–37. See also Schubert, *History of the British Iron and Steel Industry*, pp. 221–222.

35. Fackenthal, "Early American Iron Industries . . . ," p. 242.

36. Parker, "Abstracts of W. McAdams Proceedings . . . ."

37. Parker, "Journey to Barkers Ville from Feb. 29 to March 10, 1785," Parker Papers, RUL.

38. These quotations, in order, are from the following sources: N.J.A., 1st Ser., XXIX, 403; *Ibid.*, 474; and Snell, *History of Warren and Sussex* . . . , p. 467.

39. Parker, "Diary," December 17, 1789.

40. Muntz, *Geografiska Annaler*, XLII, 322.

41. John R. Chapin, "Artist-Life in the Highlands of New Jersey," *Harper's Magazine*, XX (April, 1860), 579–580.

42. Morris Canal and Banking Company, *Souvenir of the Dismantling and Reconstruction Work in Progress along the Morris Canal*, p. 14.

43. E. D. Halsey, *History of Morris County* . . . , p. 231.

Chapter 7

1. Ege, p. 119; Haines, p. 16; Lequear, p. 85; Henry C. Mercer, "Survival of Ancient Corn Mills in the United States," *Papers of the Bucks County Historical Society*, IV (1917), 733–734; Smith, p. 114; and Harry B. Weiss and Robert J. Sim, *The Early Grist and Flouring Mills of New Jersey*, p. 9.

2. Lequear, p. 85.

3. N.J.A., 1st Ser., XI, 494.

4. William M. Johnson, *Memoirs and Reminiscences* . . . , p. 30.

5. Henry S. Engart, "Notes on Gristmills and Milling in Pennsylvania,"

Papers of the Bucks County Historical Society, VII (1937), 114, 118–119; Lequear, pp. 85, 177; Schmidt, *Rural Hunterdon . . .* , p. 444; and Weiss and Sim, p. 39.

6. The sources for the dates of establishment of these mills, in order, are: A. Van Doren Honeyman, *Northwestern New Jersey . . .* , III, 687; Fackenthal, "Early American Iron Industries . . . ," p. 241a; Lowrey, p. 3; Major Holland, *Map of New York, New Jersey, Pennsylvania and Quebec;* N.J.A., 1st Ser., XXIV, 527; *Ibid.,* XXVI, 302; *Ibid.,* XXVII, 272; *Ibid.,* XXIX, 104; Snell, *History of Hunterdon and Somerset . . .* , p. 727; *Ibid.,* p. 461; and Lequear, p. 173.

7. The sources for the dates of establishment of these mills, in order, are: Snell, *History of Sussex and Warren . . .* , p. 708; Snell, *History of Hunterdon and Somerset . . .* , p. 450; Walton Advertising and Printing Company, *Fifty Years of Paper Making: A Brief History of the Origin, Development and Present Status of the Warren Manufacturing Company 1873–1923,* p. 2; Snell, *History of Sussex and Warren . . .* , p. 727; and Snell, *History of Hunterdon and Somerset . . .* , p. 450.

8. William M. Johnson, *Memoirs and Reminiscences,* pp. 31–32.

9. N.J.A., 2nd Ser., I, 298.

10. N.J.A., 2nd Ser., III, 510.

11. Engart, pp. 108–109; and Weiss and Sim, p. 10.

12. A. Stowers, "Watermills, *c* 1500–*c* 1850," *A History of Technology,* ed. Charles Singer *et al.,* IV, 202; and Weiss and Sim, pp. 38–39.

13. N.J.A., 1st Ser., XXVII, 20.

14. Schoepf, I, 191.

15. N.J.A., 1st Ser., XXVIII, 253.

16. *Ibid.,* XXIV, 67.

17. The sources for these dates, in order, are: Boyer, p. 46; N.J.A., 1st Ser., XXIX, 104; Snell, *History of Hunterdon and Somerset . . .* , p. 466; N.J.A., 1st Ser., XX, 2; and *Ibid.,* XXIV, 122.

18. Return of Survey, Thomas Millidge to Thomas Bartow, August 21, 1770, Alexander Papers, NYHS.

19. Return of Survey, Lemuel Cobb to William Alexander, September 17, 1786, Alexander Papers, NYHS.

20. The sources for these dates, in order, are: Fackenthal, "Early American Iron Industries . . . ," p. 242; N.J.A., 1st Ser., XXIV, 527; *Ibid.,* XXVII, 272; Lowrey, p. 3; N.J.A., 2nd Ser., I, 298; and B. F. Fackenthal, Jr., "Improving Navigation on the Delaware River with Some Account of its Ferries, Bridges, Canals, and Floods," *Papers of the Bucks County Historical Society,* VI (1932), 153.

21. Lequear, p. 176; Schmidt, *Rural Hunterdon . . .* , p. 422; Eric Sloane, *American Barns and Covered Bridges,* p. 44; and Weiss and Sim, p. 10.

22. N.J.A., 1st Ser., XXIII, 260.

23. Harry B. Weiss and Grace M. Ziegler, *The Early Fulling Mills of New Jersey,* pp. 7–10; and N.J.A., 1st Ser., XXIV, 677.

24. N.J.A., 1st Ser., XXVIII, 569.

25. A. Van Doren Honeyman, *Northwestern New Jersey* . . . , II, 689.

26. Weiss and Weiss, pp. 7–16.

27. Snell, *History of Sussex and Warren* . . . , p. 708.

28. *Ibid.*, p. 467.

29. Harry B. Weiss and Grace M. Weiss, *Early Tanning and Currying in New Jersey*, pp. 16–19.

30. The sources for these dates, in order, are: Haines, p. 105; James Parker, "To be sold at Publick Auction at the new Coffee house in second Street Philadelphia on Tuesday the sixth day of October at five o' clock in the Evening" [1785–1790?], Parker Papers, RUL; "County Tax Ratables," Book 860, Alexandria Township, July, 1785; and Weiss and Weiss, *Early Tanning* . . . , p. 61.

31. Elmer T. Clark, *The Journal and Letters of Francis Asbury*, II, 672.

32. The sources for these dates, in order, are: N.J.A., 2nd Ser., XXXIV, 28; Snell, *History of Sussex and Warren* . . . , p. 727; and *Ibid.*, p. 730.

33. Harry B. Weiss, *The History of Applejack or Apple Brandy in New Jersey from Colonial Times to the Present*, pp. 63, 67, 72, 143, 147.

34. Abstracts of these wills may be found in N.J.A., 1st Ser., XXIII, XXX, XXXII, XLII, *et passim*.

35. Schoepf, II, 46.

36. Tob. Conr. Lotter, *Pennslyvania Nova Jersey Et Nova York Cum Regionibus Ad Fluvium Delaware In America Sitis.*

37. Thomas Jefferys, *A General Map of the Middle British Colonies in America.*

38. Webb, p. 21.

39. Lowrey, p. 4; Nunn, p. 7; Snell, *History of Sussex and Warren* . . . , p. 582.

40. Snell, *History of Sussex and Warren* . . . , pp. 726–727; Weaver & Kern (compilers), *Warren County History and Directory*, p. 418.

41. Elmer T. Clark, *The Journal and Letters of Francis Asbury*, II, 537.

42. Snell, *History of Sussex and Warren* . . . , p. 727.

43. Charles S. Boyer, *Old Inns and Taverns in West Jersey*, p. 222; Snell, *History of Hunterdon and Somerset* . . . , p. 448.

44. George R. Stewart, "A Classification of Place Names," *Names*, II (1954), 1–13.

45. The sources for the origins in time and place of these toponyms, in order of appearance, are as follows: Snell, *History of Sussex and Warren* . . . , p. 602; A. Van Doren Honeyman, *Northwestern New Jersey* . . . , II, 687; *Ibid.*, p. 787; Snell, *History of Sussex and Warren* . . . , p. 581; N.J.A., 1st Ser., XXIII, 295; Snell, *History of Sussex and Warren* . . . , p. 727; A. Van Doren Honeyman, *Northwestern New Jersey* . . . , II, 725; Snell, *History of Hunterdon and Somerset* . . . , p. 461; Snell, *History of Sussex and Warren* . . . , p. 466; *Ibid.*, p. 442; Schmidt, *Hunterdon County Place Names*, p. 23; N.J.A., 1st Ser., XLI, 370; Fackenthal, "Early American Iron Industries . . . ," pp. 255, 257, 262; Weaver & Kern, p. 467; [Fitzrandolph?],

"Brookland Pond Record Book"; N.J.A., 2nd Ser., III, 510; Charles D. Platt, *Dover History,* p. 511; Boyer, *Early Forges and Furnaces* . . . , p. 47; and N.J.A., 2nd Ser., III, 94.

Chapter 8

1. Woodward, p. 32.
2. N.J.A., 1st Ser., XII, 301.
3. *Ibid.,* XXVI, 250.
4. Schoepf, I, 23.
5. N.J.A., 2nd Ser., I, 298.
6. Benson, I, 135.
7. References to trade emanating from northwestern New Jersey include A. Van Doren Honeyman, *Northwestern New Jersey* . . . , II, 620; Lane, p. 136; Mott, p. 107; and John P. Wall, "The New Brunswick of Over a Century Ago," *Proceedings of the New Jersey Historical Society,* VIII (January, 1922), 36–37.
8. N.J.A., 1st Ser., XX, 565.
9. Lane, pp. 33, 37–41.
10. "Day Book of Aaron Musgrave & Co., . . . ," June 27, 1782, Fackenthal Collection, BCHS.
11. James Parker to John Cooley, August 20, 1794, Parker Papers, RUL.
12. "Diary of Joseph Lewis," *Proceedings of the New Jersey Historical Society,* LXII (July, 1944), 171.
13. Race, p. 215.
14. Fackenthal, "Early American Iron Industries . . . ," p. 199.
15. Parker, "Diary," December 17, 1789.
16. Elmer T. Clark, *The Journal and Letters of Francis Asbury,* II, 537.
17. Anburey, p. 164.
18. A. Van Doren Honeyman, *Northwestern New Jersey* . . . , II, 606.
19. Fackenthal, *Papers of the Bucks County Historical Society,* VI, 149, 153.
20. Anburey, p. 162.
21. Fackenthal, "Early American Iron Industries . . . ," p. 127.
22. Snell, *History of Sussex and Warren* . . . , p. 704.
23. Boyer, p. 240.
24. Kelsey, pp. 14–15.
25. E. D. Halsey, *History of Morris County* . . . , p. 40; Lane, p. 48; Larison, p. 465; and Pearse, p. 55.
26. Schoepf, I, 55.
27. William M. Johnson, *Memoirs and Reminiscences* . . . , p. 64.
28. Edsall and Tuttle, p. 17; Ege, p. 193.
29. Kelsey, p. 18.
30. Fackenthal, "Early American Iron Industries . . . ," p. 242.
31. Edsall and Tuttle, p. 71; Larison, p. 466.
32. Lane, p. 48; Schmidt, *Lesser Crossroads,* p. 110.

33. Fackenthal, "Early American Iron Industries . . . ," pp. 199, 201, 236; Dennis C. Kurjack, *Hopewell Village National Historic Site*, National Park Service Historical Handbook Series No. 8, p. 15.

34. Lane, pp. 134–136.

35. N.J.A., 1st Ser., XXXI, 100–101.

36. Lane, pp. 81–82, 92; Schmidt, *Lesser Crossroads*, p. 110.

37. Smith, p. 486.

38. References to Durham boats and their capacity include Boyer, *Early Forges and Furnaces* . . . , p. 152; A. Van Doren Honeyman, *Northwestern New Jersey* . . . , II, 619; Lane, pp. 68–69; and N.J.A., 1st Ser., XXVII, 253.

39. John Sherrard to Thomas Riche, November 27, 1767, and January 9, 1770, John Emley Papers, HCHS.

40. Fackenthal, "Early American Iron Industries . . . ," p. 225.

41. N.J.A., 1st Ser., XXVII, 252–253.

42. Lane, pp. 77, 119, 138.

43. Kelsey, p. 19.

Selected Bibliography

I. BOOKS

Anburey, Thomas. *Travels Through the Interior Parts of America.* 2 vols. Boston: Houghton Mifflin Company, 1923.

Barber, John W. and Howe, Henry. *Historical Collections of the State of New Jersey.* Newark, New Jersey: Benjamin Olds, 1861.

Benson, Adolph B. (ed. & trans.). *Peter Kalm's Travels in North America: The English Version of 1770.* 2 vols. New York: Wilson-Erickson Inc., 1937.

Bidwell, Percy W. and Falconer, John I. *History of Agriculture in the Northern United States, 1620–1860.* Washington, D. C.: The Carnegie Institution of Washington, 1925.

Bining, Arthur Cecil. *Pennsylvania Iron Manufacture in the Eighteenth Century.* ("Publications of Pennsylvania Historical Commission," Vol. IV.) Harrisburg, Pennsylvania: Pennsylvania Historical Commission, 1938.

Bishop, J. Leander. *A History of American Manufactures from 1608 to 1860.* 2 vols. Philadelphia: Edward Young & Co., 1866.

Blome, Richard. *The Present State of His Majesty's Isles and Territories in America.* London: n.n., 1687.

Boyer, Charles S. *Early Forges and Furnaces in New Jersey.* Philadelphia: University of Pennsylvania Press, 1931.

––––––. *Old Inns and Taverns In West Jersey.* Camden, New Jersey: Camden County Historical Society, 1962.

Braun, E. Lucy. *Deciduous Forests of Eastern North America.* Philadelphia: The Blakiston Company, 1950.

Brinton, Daniel G. and Anthony, Albert S. *A Lenape-English Dictionary.* Philadelphia: The Historical Society of Pennsylvania, 1888.

Budd, Thomas. *Good Order Established in Pennsylvania and New Jersey in America,* ed. Edward Armstrong. New York: William Gowans, 1865.

Bunnell, Jacob L. (ed.). *Sussex County Sesquicentennial.* Newton, New Jersey: The New Jersey Herald Press, 1903.

Chambers, T. F. *The Early Germans of New Jersey.* Dover, New Jersey: Dover Printing Company, 1895.

Clark, Elmer T. (ed.). *The Journal and Letters of Francis Asbury.* 3 vols. Nashville, Tennessee: Abingdon Press, 1958.

Clark, Victor S. *History of Manufactures in the United States: 1607–1860.* Washington, D. C.: Carnegie Institution of Washington, 1916.

Compendium of Censuses 1726–1850. Trenton: State of New Jersey, Department of State, Census Bureau, 1906.

Cross, Dorothy *et al. Archaeology of New Jersey.* 2 vols. Trenton: The Archaeological Society of New Jersey and the New Jersey State Museum, 1941 and 1956.

Cummins, George W. *History of Warren County.* New York: Lewis Historical Publishing Company, 1911.

Davis, William Morris. *Geographical Essays,* ed. Douglas W. Johnson. 2d ed. New York: Dover Publications, Inc., 1954.

Decker, Amelia S. *That Ancient Trail.* Trenton: the Author, 1942.

Driver, Harold E. *Indians of North America.* Chicago: The University of Chicago Press, 1961.

Dunbar, Carl O. *Historical Geology.* 2nd ed. New York: John Wiley and Sons, Inc., 1963.

Edsall, Benjamin B. and Tuttle, J. F. *The First Sussex Centenary.* Newark, New Jersey: The Daily Advertiser, 1853.

Ege, Ralph. *Pioneers of Old Hopewell, with Sketches of Her Revolutionary Heroes.* Hopewell, New Jersey: Race & Savidge, 1908.

Evans, E. Estyn. "The Ecology of Peasant Life in Western Europe," *Man's Role in Changing the Face of the Earth,* ed. William L. Thomas, Jr. et al. Chicago: University of Chicago Press, 1956, pp. 217–239.

Faust, Albert B. *The German Element in the United States with Special Reference to its Political, Moral, Social, and Educational Influence.* 2 vols. Boston: Houghton Mifflin Company, 1909.

Fenneman, Nevin M. *Physiography of Eastern United States.* New York: McGraw-Hill Book Company, Inc., 1938.

Gaustad, Edwin S. *Historical Atlas of Religion in America.* New York: Harper & Row, 1962.

Gordon, Thomas F. *A Gazetteer of the State of New Jersey.* Trenton: Daniel Fenton, 1834.

Haines, Alanson H. *Hardyston Memorial: A History of the Township and the North Presbyterian Church, Hardyston, Sussex County, New Jersey.* Newton, New Jersey: The New Jersey Herald Press, 1888.

Halsey, E. D. (ed.). *History of Morris County, New Jersey.* New York: W. W. Munsell & Co., 1882.

Halsey, Francis W. (ed.). *A Tour of Four Great Rivers, the Hudson, Mohawk, Susquehanna and Delaware in 1769; Being the Journal of Richard Smith of Burlington, New Jersey.* New York: Charles Scribner's Sons, 1906.

Hanna, Charles A. *The Scotch-Irish or the Scot in North Britain, North Ireland, and North America.* 2 vols. New York: G. P. Putnam's Sons, 1902.

Hay, Oliver P. *The Pleistocene of North America and its Vertebrated Animals from the States East of the Mississippi River and from the Canadian Provinces East of Longitude 95°.* Washington, D. C.: The Carnegie Institution of Washington, 1923.

Hayes, W. H. *Indian Life in New Jersey.* East Orange, New Jersey: n.p., 1936.

Heckewelder, John. *History, Manners, and Customs of the Indian Nations Who Once Inhabited Pennsylvania and the Neighboring States.* 2d ed. rev. Philadelphia: The Historical Society of Pennsylvania, 1876.

Hine, Charles Gilbert. *History and Legend, Fact, Fancy and Romance of the*

Old Mine Road, Kingston, New York to the Mine Holes of Pahaquarry. [New York?]: n.n., 1908.

Historic American Buildings Survey, National Park Service. *Historic American Buildings Survey: Catalog of the Measured Drawings and Photographs of the Survey in the Library of Congress, March 1, 1941.* Washington, D.C.: United States Government Printing Office, 1941.

————. *Historic American Buildings Survey: Supplement, Catalog of the Measured Drawings and Photographs of the Survey in the Library of Congress, Comprising Additions Since March 1, 1941.* Washington, D. C.: United States Government Printing Office, 1959.

Honeyman, A. Van Doren (ed.). *Northwestern New Jersey: A History of Somerset, Morris, Hunterdon, Warren and Sussex Counties.* 5 vols. New York: Lewis Historical Publishing Company, 1927.

Indiana Historical Society. *Walam Olum or Red Score: The Migration Legend of the Lenni Lenape or Delaware Indians.* Indianapolis: Indiana Historical Society, 1954.

Jameson, J. F. (ed.). *Narratives of New Netherland.* New York: C. Scribner's Sons, 1909.

Johnson, Amandus. *The Swedish Settlements on the Delaware; Their History and Relation to the Indians, Dutch and English, 1638–1664.* 2 vols. New York: D. Appleton & Company, 1911.

Johnson, Douglas. *Geomorphology of the Central Appalachians.* International Geological Congress, XVI Session, United States, Guidebook 7. Washington, D. C.: United States Government Printing Office, 1933.

————. *Stream Sculpture on the Atlantic Slope: A Study in the Evolution of Appalachian Rivers.* New York: Columbia University Press, 1931.

Johnson, William M. (comp.). *Memoirs and Reminiscences together with Sketches of the Early History of Sussex County, New Jersey, by Casper Schaeffer.* Hackensack, New Jersey: the Compiler, 1907.

Kauffman, Henry J. "The Log Barn," *The Pennsylvania Barn,* ed. Alfred L. Shoemaker. Lancaster, Pennsylvania: The Pennsylvania Dutch Folklore Center, Inc., 1955, pp. 28–34.

Kelsey, Rayner W. (ed. & trans.). *Cazenove Journal, 1794: A Record of the Journey of Theophile Cazenove Through New Jersey and Pennsylvania.* Haverford College Studies, No. 13. Haverford, Pennsylvania: The Pennsylvania History Press, 1922.

Knittle, Walter A. *Early Eighteenth Century Palatine Emigration.* Philadelphia: Dorrance & Company, 1937.

Kull, Irving S. (ed.). *New Jersey, A History.* 6 vols. New York: The American Historical Society, 1930–1932.

Lane, Wheaton J. *From Indian Trail to Iron Horse; Travel and Transportation in New Jersey, 1620–1860.* Princeton, New Jersey: Princeton University Press, 1939.

Lequear, John W. *Traditions of Hunterdon.* Flemington, New Jersey: D. H. Moreau, 1957.

Lewis, J. Volney. *The Geology of New Jersey.* New Jersey Department of

Conservation and Development Geologic Series, Bulletin 50. Trenton: Mac-Crellish and Quigley, 1940.

Lindestrom, Peter. *Geographia Americae With an Account of the Delaware Indians Based on Surveys and Notes Made in 1654–1656*, ed. Amandus Johnson. Philadelphia: Swedish Colonial Society, 1925.

Loskiel, George Henry. *History of the Mission of the United Brethren Among the Indians in North America*. Translated by Christian Ignatius La Trobe. London: Brethren's Society for the Furtherance of the Gospel, 1794.

McCormick, Richard P. *Experiment in Independence*. New Brunswick, New Jersey: Rutgers University Press, 1950.

Morris Canal and Banking Company. *Souvenir of the Dismantling and Reconstruction Work in Progress Along the Morris Canal*. Passaic, New Jersey: Morris Canal and Banking Company, 1925.

Nelson, William. *Indians of New Jersey*. Paterson, New Jersey: The Press Company, 1894.

Nunn, John Harold. *The Story of Hackettstown, New Jersey, 1754–1955*. Hackettstown, New Jersey: Hackettstown National Bank, 1955.

O'Callaghan, E. B. (ed.). *Documents Relative to the Colonial History of the State of New York*. 15 vols. Albany: Weed, Parsons & Co., 1853–1887.

Pearse, John. *A Concise History of the Iron Manufacture of the American Colonies*. Philadelphia: Allen, Lane, and Scott, 1876.

Platt, Charles D. *Dover History*. Dover, New Jersey: M. C. Havens, 1914.

Rasieres, Isaak de. "Letter of Isaak de Rasieres to Samuel Blommaert, 1628," *Narratives of New Netherland*, ed. J. F. Jameson. New York: C. Scribner's Sons, 1909, pp. 107–109.

Reichel, William C. *Names Which the Lenni Lennape or Delaware Indians Gave to Rivers, Streams, and Localities Within the States of Pennsylvania, New Jersey, Maryland and Virginia*. Bethlehem, Pennsylvania: Henry T. Clauder, 1872.

Ritchie, William A. *The Archaeology of New York State*. Garden City, New York: The Natural History Press, 1965.

Rupp, I. Daniel (ed.). *An Account of the Manners of the German Inhabitants of Pennsylvania, Written 1789, by Benjamin Rush*. Philadelphia: Samuel P. Town, 1875.

Salisbury, Rollin D., et al. *The Glacial Geology of New Jersey*. Geological Survey of New Jersey, Final Report of the State Geologist, Vol. V. Trenton: MacCrellish & Quigley, 1902.

Schmidt, Hubert G. (ed.). *Lesser Crossroads*. New Brunswick, New Jersey: Rutgers University Press, 1948.

——. *Rural Hunterdon, An Agricultural History*. New Brunswick, New Jersey: Rutgers University Press, 1945.

——. *Some Hunterdon Place Names*. Flemington, New Jersey: D. H. Moreau, 1959.

Schoepf, Johann David. *Travels in the Confederation; 1783–1784*. 2 vols. Edited and translated by Alfred J. Morrison. Philadelphia: William J. Campbell, 1911.

Schrabisch, Max. *Archaeology of Warren and Hunterdon Counties.* Reports of the New Jersey Department of Conservation and Development, Bulletin 18, 1917.

Schubert, H. R. "Extraction and Production of Metals: Iron and Steel," *A History of Technology,* ed. Charles Singer *et al.* New York: Oxford University Press, IV, 1955, 99–117.

———. *History of the British Iron and Steel Industry from c. 450 B.C. to A.D. 1775.* London: Routledge & Kegan Paul, 1957.

Shoemaker, Alfred L. "The Barns of 1798," *The Pennsylvania Barn,* ed. Alfred L. Shoemaker. Lancaster, Pennsylvania: The Pennsylvania Dutch Folklore Center, Inc., 1955, pp. 91–96.

———. "The Pennsylvania Barn," *The Pennsylvania Barn,* ed. Alfred L. Shoemaker. Lancaster, Pennsylvania: The Pennsylvania Dutch Folklore Center, Inc., 1955, pp. 4–11.

——— (ed.). *The Pennsylvania Barn.* Lancaster, Pennsylvania: The Pennsylvania Dutch Folklore Center, Inc., 1955.

Shurtleff, Harold R. *The Log Cabin Myth: A Study of the Early Dwellings of the English Colonists in North America.* Cambridge, Massachusetts: Harvard University Press, 1939.

Sickler, Joseph S. *The Old Houses of Salem County.* 2nd ed. Salem, New Jersey: Sunbeam Publishing Company, 1949.

Singer, Charles, *et al. A History of Technology.* 5 vols. New York: Oxford University Press, 1958.

Skinner, Alanson and Schrabisch, Max. *A Preliminary Report of the Archaeological Survey of the State of New Jersey.* Geological Survey of New Jersey Bulletin 9. Trenton: MacCrellish & Quigley, 1913.

Sloane, Eric. *American Barns and Covered Bridges.* New York: Wilfred Funk, Inc., 1954.

Smith, Samuel. *The History of the Colony of New Jersey.* 2nd ed. Trenton: Wm. S. Sharp, 1877.

Snell, James P. (ed.). *History of Hunterdon and Somerset Counties, New Jersey.* Philadelphia: Everts & Peck, 1881.

——— (ed.). *History of Sussex and Warren Counties, New Jersey.* Philadelphia: Everts & Peck, 1881.

Stowers, A. "Watermills, *c* 1500–*c* 1850," in *A History of Technology,* ed. Charles Singer *et al.* New York: Oxford University Press, 1958. Vol. IV, pp. 199–213.

Stryker, William S., *et al.* (eds.). *Archives of the State of New Jersey: Documents Relating to the Revolutionary History of the State of New Jersey.* Second Series, 5 vols. Various Places: State of New Jersey, 1901–1917.

Thomas, Gabriel. *An Account of Pennsylvania and West New Jersey.* Cleveland, Ohio: The Burrows Brothers Company, 1903.

Thomas, William L., Jr. *et al.* (eds.). *Man's Role in Changing the Face of the Earth.* Chicago: University of Chicago Press, 1956.

Tinkcom, Harry M., Tinkcom, Margaret B., and Simon, Grant M. *Historic Germantown from the Founding to the Nineteenth Century.* "Memoirs of

the American Philosophical Society," Vol. XXXIX. Philadelphia: American
Philosophical Society, 1955.

Vermeule, Cornelius Clarkson. *Report on Water-Supply, Water-Power, the
Flow of Streams and Attendant Phenomena.* Geological Survey of New
Jersey, Final Report of the State Geologist, Vol. III, Trenton: The John
L. Murphy Publishing Company, 1894.

Walton Advertising and Printing Company. *Fifty Years of Paper Making:
A Brief History of the Origin, Development and Present Status of the
Warren Manufacturing Company 1873–1923.* Boston: Walton Advertising
and Printing Company, 1923.

Waterman, Thomas Tileston. *The Dwellings of Colonial America.* Chapel
Hill, North Carolina: University of North Carolina Press, 1950.

Weaver & Kern (comps.). *Warren County History and Directory.* Washington,
New Jersey: Press of the Review, 1886.

Webb, Edward A. (ed.). *Historical Directory of Sussex County, New Jersey.*
[Andover, New Jersey?]: n.n., 1872.

Weis, Frederick L. *The Colonial Churches and the Colonial Clergy of the
Middle and Southern Colonies, 1607–1776.* Lancaster, Massachusetts: Society
of the Descendants of the Colonial Clergy, 1938.

Weiss, Harry B. *The History of Applejack or Apple Brandy in New Jersey
from Colonial Times to the Present.* Trenton: New Jersey Agricultural
Society, 1954.

Weiss, Harry B. and Sim, Robert J. *The Early Grist and Flouring Mills of
New Jersey.* Trenton: New Jersey Agricultural Society, 1956.

Weiss, Harry B. and Weiss, Grace M. *Early Tanning and Currying in New
Jersey.* Trenton: New Jersey Agricultural Society, 1959.

————. *Forgotten Mills of Early New Jersey.* Trenton: New Jersey Agricultural
Society, 1960.

Weiss, Harry B. and Ziegler, Grace M. *The Early Fulling Mills of New Jersey.*
Trenton: New Jersey Agricultural Society, 1957.

Wells, J. V. B. *Surface Water Supply of the United States, Part 1-B; North
Atlantic Slope Basins, New York to York River.* Geological Survey Water
Supply Paper No. 1622. Washington, D. C.: United States Government
Printing Office, 1959.

Wertenbaker, Thomas J. *The Founding of American Civilization: The Middle
Colonies.* New York: Charles Scribner's Sons, 1938.

Whitehead, William A. *et al.* (eds.). *Archives of the State of New Jersey:
Documents Relating to the Colonial, Revolutionary, and Post Revolutionary
History of the State of New Jersey.* First Series, 42 vols. Various Places:
State of New Jersey, 1880–1949.

Widmer, Kemble. *The Geology and Geography of New Jersey.* Vol. XIX,
The New Jersey Historical Series. Princeton, New Jersey: D. Van Nostrand
Company, Inc., 1964.

Wuorinen, John H. *The Finns on the Delaware, 1638–1655.* New York:
Columbia University Press, 1938.

II. Pamphlets

Junkin, D. X. *A Discourse Delivered on the Centenary of the First Presbyterian Church, Greenwich, New Jersey.* Easton, Pennsylvania: Geo. W. West, Book and Job Printer, 1875.

Kurjack, Dennis C. *Hopewell Village National Historic Site.* National Park Service Historical Handbook Series No. 8. Washington, D. C.: United States Government Printing Office, 1954.

Mercer, Henry C. *Ancient Carpenter's Tools.* 2nd ed. Doylestown, Pennsylvania: Bucks County Historical Society, 1951.

Roome, William. *The Early Days and Early Surveys of New Jersey.* Morristown, New Jersey: Jerseyman Press, 1883.

Schmidt, Hubert. *Flax Culture in Hunterdon County, New Jersey.* Flemington, New Jersey: Hunterdon County Historical Society, 1939.

Skinner, Alanson. *The Indians of Newark Before the White Men Came.* Newark, New Jersey: Newark Museum Association, 1915.

Tedrow, J. C. F. *et al. Warren County Soils: Their Nature, Conservation, and Use.* New Brunswick, New Jersey: New Jersey Agricultural Experiment Station, 1953.

Visitor's Guide: Places of Note and Beauty on Schooley's Mountain and Vicinage. n.p.:n.n., [*ca.* 1860?].

Voorhees, Oscar M. *The Exterior and Interior Bounds of Hunterdon County, New Jersey.* Flemington, New Jersey: Hiram E. Deats, 1929.

Woodward, Carl R. "Agriculture in New Jersey," reprinted from *New Jersey: A History,* Vol. I, ed. Irving S. Kull. New York: American Historical Society, Inc., 1930.

Writer's Program of the Works Projects Administration in the State of New Jersey. *The Origin of New Jersey Place Names.* Trenton: New Jersey State Library Commission, 1938.

III. Atlases and Maps

Evans, Lewis. *A Map of Pennsilvania, New-Jersey, New York And the Three Delaware Counties.* London: Lewis Evans, 1749.

Faden, William. *The Province of New Jersey, Divided into East and West, Commonly Called the Jerseys.* Charing Cross, London: William Faden, 1777.

Gordon, Thomas F. *A Map of the State of New Jersey.* Philadelphia: H. S. Tanner, 1828.

Hammond, D. Stanton. "Sheet C, Hunterdon County, New Jersey," *Map Series #4,* n.p.: Genealogical Society of New Jersey, 1965.

Holland, Major. *Map of New York, New Jersey, Pennsylvania and Quebec.* London: Robert Sayer and John Bennett, 1776.

Jefferys, Thomas. *A General Map of the Middle British Colonies in America.* Philadelphia: Lewis Evans, 1758.

Lewis, J. Volney, *et al. Geologic Map of New Jersey.* State of New Jersey, Department of Conservation and Economic Development, Division of Planning and Development Atlas Sheet No. 40, 1950.

Lewis, Samuel. "The State of New Jersey Compiled from the Most Authentic Information," *Carey's American Edition of Guthries Geography Improved,* anon. Philadelphia: M. Carey, 1795.

Lotter, Tob. Conr. *Pennsylvania Nova Jersey Et Nova York Cum Regionibus Ad Fluvium Delaware in America Sitis* (Augsburg: n.n., *ca.* 1748).

Schaefer, P. W., *et al. An Historical Map of Pennsylvania.* Philadelphia: Historical Society of Pennsylvania, 1875.

United States Department of Agriculture, Bureau of Soils. *Soil Map: New Jersey; Belvidere Sheet.* Baltimore: A. Hoen & Co. Lith., 1917.

————. *Soil Map: New Jersey; Sussex Area Sheet.* New York: Julius Bien Co., 1911.

———— in cooperation with the Department of Conservation and Development of New Jersey. *Soil Map: New Jersey; Bernardsville Sheet.* n.p.:n.n., 1919.

United States Department of Agriculture, Soil Conservation Service and the New Jersey Agricultural Experiment Station. *New Jersey: Warren County Soil Conservation District, Warren County, Physical Land Conditions.* Beltsville, Maryland: AGR-SCS, 1953.

IV. Periodicals

Acton, Helen E. D. "Charles Kirk's Review of a Century," *Papers of the Bucks County Historical Society,* VII (1937), 95–103.

Acton, R. M. "A Short History of the Glass Manufacture in Salem County, New Jersey," *The Pennsylvania Magazine,* IX (1885), 343–346.

Bigelow, Moses. "Stanhope Forges And Furnaces, Sussex County," *Proceedings of the New Jersey Historical Society,* LVIII (1940), 266–268.

Broecker, W. S. and Kulp, J. L. "Lamont Natural Radiocarbon Measurements, IV," *Science,* CXXVI (December 20, 1957), 1324–1334.

Cantlon, John E. "Vegetation and Microclimates on North and South Slopes of Cushetunk Mountain, New Jersey," *Ecological Monographs,* XXIII (July, 1953), 241–270.

Chapin, John R. "Artist-Life in the Highlands of New Jersey," *Harper's Magazine,* XX (April, 1860), 577–598.

Cross, Dorothy. "Houses of the Lenni Lenape," *The Archaeological Society of New Jersey News Letter,* I (October, 1940), 11–12.

————. "The Indians of New Jersey," *Proceedings of the New Jersey Historical Society,* LXX (January, 1952), 1–16.

Davis, William Morris and Wood, J. W. "The Geographic Development of Northern New Jersey," *Proceedings of the Boston Society of Natural History,* XXIV (1890), 365–423.

"Diary of Joseph Lewis," *Proceedings of the New Jersey Historical Society,* LXII (July, 1944), 167–180.

Engart, Henry S. "Notes on Gristmills and Milling in Pennsylvania," *Papers of the Bucks County Historical Society,* VII (1937), 104–136.

Erixon, Sigurd E. "The North-European Technique of Corner Timbering," *Folkliv,* I (1937), 13–62.

Fackenthal, B. F. Jr. "Improving Navigation on the Delaware with Some Account of its Ferries, Bridges, Canals and Floods," *Papers of the Bucks County Historical Society,* VI (1932), 103–230.

————. "Thomas Wright of Dyerstown, Pennsylvania," *Papers of the Bucks County Historical Society,* IV (1917), 661–670.

Folsom, Joseph F. "General Daniel Morgan's Birthplace and Life," *Proceedings of the New Jersey Historical Society,* XIV (July, 1929), 279–292.

Fretz, Warren. "Old Methods of Taking Fish," *Papers of the Bucks County Historical Society,* V (1926), 360–375.

Gilpin, Joshua. "Journey to Bethlehem," *The Pennsylvania Magazine of History and Biography,* XLVI (1922), 15–38.

Gross, A. Haller. "The Old Spring Houses of Bucks County," *Papers of the Bucks County Historical Society,* IV (1917), 396–397.

Gross, Henry W. "Old Fences in Bucks County," *Papers of the Bucks County Historical Society,* V (1926), 429–432.

Hansen, Marcus L. "The Minor Stocks in the American Population of 1790," *Annual Report of the American Historical Association for the Year 1931,* (1932), pp. 360–397.

Honeyman, John C. "Zion, St. Paul and Other Early Lutheran Churches in Central New Jersey," *Proceedings of the New Jersey Historical Society,* IX (July, 1924), 255–273; IX (October, 1924), 347–370; X (October, 1925), 395–409; XI (January, 1926), 57–70; XI (October, 1926), 532–542; XII (July, 1927), 326–335.

Kenderdine, Thaddeus S. "Hunting, Traping [*sic*], and Fishing in Bucks County," *Papers of the Bucks County Historical Society,* V (1926), 736–740.

Kniffen, Fred. "Folk Housing: Key to Diffusion," *Annals of the Association of American Geographers,* LV (December, 1965), 549–577.

————. "Louisiana House Types," *Annals of the Association of American Geographers,* XXVI (December, 1936), 179–193.

Kniffen, Fred and Glassie, Henry. "Building in Wood in the Eastern United States: A Time-Place Perspective," *The Geographical Review,* LVI (January, 1966), 40–66.

Korstian, C. F. and Stickel, Paul W. "The Natural Replacement of Blight-Killed Chestnut in the Hardwood Forests of the Northeast," *Journal of Agricultural Research,* XXXIV (April, 1927), 631–648.

Larison, George H. "The Mode of Life in Our Early Settlements," *Papers of the Bucks County Historical Society,* I (1887), 459–467.

Laubach, Charles. "The Durham Iron Works," *Papers of the Bucks County Historical Society,* I (1883), 232–249.

Lemon, James T. "The Agricultural Practices of National Groups in Eighteenth-Century Southeastern Pennsylvania," *The Geographical Review*, LVI (1966), 467–496.

Luckenbach, Abraham. "The Moravian Indian Mission on White River; Diaries and Letters, May 5, 1799, to November 12, 1806," ed. L. H. Gipson, *Indiana Historical Collections*, XXIII (1938).

McAtee, W. L. "Names of American Plants in Books on Kalm's Travels," *Torreya* XLI (1941), 151–160.

McCormick, Richard P. "The West Jersey Estate of Sir Robert Barker," *Proceedings of the New Jersey Historical Society*, LXIV (July, 1946), 118–155.

McGuire, Peter (contrib.). "Journal of a Journey to the Westward," *The American Historical Review*, XXXVIII (October, 1931), 65–88.

Mason, Ronald J. "Indications of Paleo-Indian Occupation in the Delaware Valley," *Pennsylvania Archaeologist*, XXIX (1959), 1–17.

Mercer, Henry C. "Survival of Ancient Corn Mills in the United States," *Papers of the Bucks County Historical Society*, IV (1917), 733–734.

Merrens, Harry Roy. "Historical Geography and Early American History," *William and Mary Quarterly*, XXII (1965), 529–548.

Mooney, James. "The Aboriginal Population of America North of Mexico," ed. J. R. Swanton, *Smithsonian Miscellaneous Collections*, LXXX (1928), 1–40.

Mott, George S. "The First Century of Hunterdon County, State of New Jersey," *Proceedings of the New Jersey Historical Society*, V (January, 1878), 60–111.

Muntz, Alfred Philip. "Forests and Iron: The Charcoal Iron Industry of the New Jersey Highlands," *Geografiska Annaler*, XLII (1960), 315–323.

Newcomb, William W. "The Culture and Acculturation of the Delaware Indians," *Anthropological Papers*, Museum of Anthropology, University of Michigan, X (1956).

Philhower, Charles A. "The Aborigines of Hunterdon County, New Jersey," *Proceedings of the New Jersey Historical Society*, XI (October, 1926), 508–525.

———. "Agriculture and the Foods of the Indians of New Jersey," *Proceedings of the New Jersey Historical Society*, LVIII (April, 1940), 93–102.

———. "The Indians About Lake Hopatcong," *Archaeological Society of New Jersey Bulletin*, XIII (May, 1957), 11–20.

———. "The Indians of the Morris County Area," *Proceedings of the New Jersey Historical Society*, LIV (October, 1936), 249–267.

———. "The Minisink Indian Trail," *Proceedings of the New Jersey Historical Society*, VIII (July, 1923), 200–212.

Potzger, J. E. "What Can Be Inferred from Pollen Profiles of Bogs in the New Jersey Barrens," *Bartonia*, XXVI (1952), 20–27.

"Presentation of a Log House by the Citizens of Doylestown to the Bucks County Historical Society," *Papers of the Bucks County Historical Society*, IV (1917), 197–204.

Race, Henry. "Rev. William Frazer's Three Parishes: St. Thomas's, St. Andrew's, and Musconetcong, New Jersey; 1768–1770," *The Pennsylvania Magazine of History and Biography*, XII (1888), 212–232.

[Reading, John.] "Copy of Journal of ———— Reading, While Surveying Lands in the Northern Part of New Jersey, April 17th to June 10th, 1715," *Proceedings of the New Jersey Historical Society*, X (January, July, and October, 1915), 35–46, 128–133.

Rutherfurd, John. "Notes on the State of New Jersey," *Proceedings of the New Jersey Historical Society*, I (1867), 79–89.

Sauer, Carl O. "A Geographic Sketch of Early Man in America," *Geographical Review*, XXXIV (October, 1944), 529–573.

————. "The Morphology of Landscape," *University of California Publications in Geography*, II (October, 1925), 19–53.

Scheetz, Grier. "Flax and Its Culture," *Papers of the Bucks County Historical Society*, III (1909), 482–486.

Stewart, George R. "A Classification of Place Names," *Names*, II (1954), 1–13.

Swain, Frank K. "Charcoal Burning in Buckingham Township," *Papers of the Bucks County Historical Society*, IV (1917), 467–469.

————. "Passing Events," *Papers of the Bucks County Historical Society*, V (1926), 324–339.

Tryon, Henry H. "A Portable Charcoal Kiln," *Black Rock Forest Bulletin*, V (1933).

Tuttle, Joseph. "The Early History of Morris County, New Jersey," *Proceedings of the New Jersey Historical Society*, II (1872), 17–53.

United States Department of Commerce, Weather Bureau. *Climatography of the United States; Climates of the States: New Jersey*, Bulletin No. 60-28 (December, 1959).

Vermeule, Cornelius C. "Early Transport in and About New Jersey," *Proceedings of the New Jersey Historical Society*, IX (April, 1924), 106–124.

————. "Raritan Valley, Its Discovery and Settlement," *Proceedings of the New Jersey Historical Society*, XIII (July, 1928), 282–298.

————. "Some Early New Jersey Place Names," *Proceedings of the New Jersey Historical Society*, X (July, 1925), 241–256.

Voorhees, Ralph. "The Raritan and Its Early Holland Settlers," *Our Home*, I (1873), 490–498.

Wacker, Peter O. "Man and the American Chestnut" (Abstract), *Annals of the Association of American Geographers*, LIV (September, 1964), 440–441.

Wall, John P. "The New Brunswick of Over a Century Ago," *Proceedings of the New Jersey Historical Society*, VIII (January, 1922), 35–40.

Zelinsky, Wilbur. "Some Problems in the Distribution of Generic Terms in the Place-Names of the Northeastern United States," *Annals of the Association of American Geographers*, XLV (1955), 319–349.

————. "Walls and Fences," *Landscape*, VIII (Spring, 1959), 14–20.

V. Manuscripts and Manuscript Collections

Bucks County Historical Society, Doylestown, Pennsylvania.

B. F. Fackenthal, Jr. Collection.

Department of Education, Division of State Library, Archives and History Microfilm and Records Unit, Trenton, New Jersey.

County Tax Ratables, 1788–1822.
Ford, John. Freeholders List, Morris County, New Jersey, August 31, 1752.

Hunterdon County Historical Society, Flemington, New Jersey.

Capner Papers.
John Cooley Papers.
John Emley Papers.

Morristown Public Library, Morristown, New Jersey.

Stephen Shaffer Papers.

New Jersey Historical Society, Newark, New Jersey.

[Fitz Randolph, Phinehas?]. "Brookland Pond Record Book, 1788–1791."
Henry, Matthew S. "Indian Names of Rivers, Creeks, &c in the State of New Jersey, 1856."
Van Kirk, James. "Field Book, 1813–1815."
Williams, Seymour, *et al.* New Jersey Historic American Buildings Survey: Outline of the Development of Early American Architecture Compiled by the Historic American Buildings Survey, 1939.

New York Historical Society, New York, New York.

James Alexander Papers.

Rutgers University Library, New Brunswick, New Jersey.
Collections:

Nelson R. Burr Papers.
James Parker Papers.

Miscellaneous Manuscripts:

Deshler, C. D. "The Early Roads in New Jersey." Paper read before the New-Brunswick Historical Club, on Wednesday Evening, May 26, 1880.
Hoffman, Carrie J. "Bloomsbury: Brief Historical Sketch," 1948.
Lowrey, John. "A History of the First Presbyterian Church of Hacketts-town, New Jersey," 1886.

Stryker, Peter. "Journal of a Trip from Belleville, N. J. as a Reformed Church Minister, to Preach in Vacant Congregations Westward and Southwestward, 1815–1816."

VI. Unpublished Theses

Lemon, James Thomas. "A Rural Geography of Southeastern Pennsylvania in the Eighteenth Century: The Contributions of Cultural Inheritance, Social Structure, Economic Conditions and Physical Resources," unpublished Ph.D. dissertation, Department of Geography, University of Wisconsin, 1964.

Muntz, Alfred Philip. "The Changing Geography of the New Jersey Woodlands, 1600–1900," unpublished Ph.D. dissertation, Department of Geography, University of Wisconsin, 1959.

Index